Foundations in Strategic Management

2nd edition

Jeffrey S. Harrison

University of Central Florida

Caron H. St. John

Clemson University

SOUTH-WESTERN

THOMSON LEARNING

Australia · Canada · Mexico · Singapore · Spain · United Kingdom · United States

Foundations in Strategic Management, 2e
By Jeffrey S. Harrison and Caron H. St. John

Vice President/Publisher: Jack W. Calhoun
Executive Editor: John Szilagyi
Developmental Editor: Jennifer Baker
Marketing Manager: Rob Bloom
Marketing Coordinator: Shannon O'Callaghan
Production Manager: Sharon L. Smith
Production Editor: Starratt E. Alexander
Manufacturing Coordinator: Sandee Milewski
Internal Design: Ann Small, A Small Design Studio, Cincinnati
Cover Design: Rik Moore
Cover Illustration: Digital Stock
Production House and Compositor: Cover to Cover Publishing, Inc.
Printer: Webcom

Printed in Canada
 2 3 4 5 04 03 02 01

For more information contact South-Western College Publishing, 5101 Madison Road, Cincinnati, Ohio, 45227 or find us on the Internet at http://www.swcollege.com

For permission to use material from this text or product, contact us by
• **telephone: 1-800-730-2214**
• **fax: 1-800-730-2215**
• **web: http://www.thomsonrights.com**

Library of Congress Cataloging-in-Publication Data

Harrison, Jeffrey S.
     Foundations in strategic management / Jeffrey S. Harrison, Caron H. St. John.--2nd ed.
          p. cm.
     Includes index.
     ISBN 0-324-07099-3
     1. Strategic planning. I. St. John, Caron H. II. Title.

HD30.28 .H3757 2001
658.4'012--dc21

                                                                        00-066185

PLOT YOUR OWN COURSE

Foundations in Strategic Management treats core topics and current issues in the field directly and concisely without compromising learning. With less than 200 pages and just eight chapters, it flows at a brisk pace. While it is half the size of standard texts, *Foundations* covers all major strategic management topics, including classic and modern theory; draws on the contributions of leading authors in the field; and interlaces all its presentations with current debates, current perspectives, and current examples. *Foundations* gives you strategy at its most essential along with the option to build a course to your own particular specifications: to add your own readings, to run a simulation, to select your own cases, to experiment with exercises—in short, to customize your course to suit your teaching style and goals.

Three theoretical foundations, above all other concerns, influenced the shape of this book:

(1) the traditional strategic management process model, with its emphasis on situation analysis (SWOT), formulation, implementation, and control.
(2) the resource-based model of strategic management, with its emphasis on acquiring and managing resources that develop sustainable competitive advantages.
(3) stakeholder theory, with its emphasis on the organization as the center of a network of contacts with whom it forms mutually beneficial relationships.

Underlying our discussions with these principles kept us on task. In our efforts to deliver content responsive to the very challenging goals you have undoubtedly already set for your students, we searched for a more perceptive way of understanding strategic management and have reason to hope we have found it.

Foundations covers all major strategic management topics, including classic and modern theory; draws on the contributions of leading authors in the field; and interlaces all its presentations with current debates, current perspectives, and current examples. While it is easy to be dismissive of strategic management texts that appear to prefer volume to virtue, we like to think that the value of the insights you are able to offer your students far outweighs the wisdom buried in any book, whatever its size.

CURRENT TOPICS

Issues of current relevance—including resource-based theory, stakeholder management, ethics and enterprise strategy, transactions cost theory, agency theory, restructuring, global competitiveness, and strategic alliances—are treated with depth and sophistication and incorporate cutting-edge research findings. Aided by more traditional discussions of environmental analysis, organizational analysis, joint ventures, mergers and acquisitions, leveraged buyouts (LBOs), manufacturing strategy, and crisis management, the field's newest trends stay linked to our focus on strategic management; that is, on strategies and strategic decisions that seek to create a future for an organization with long-range, or "strategic," planning as a central concern. Issues of e-business and the new economy are reflected throughout the text in examples, concepts, assumptions, and inferences. Examples of strategy formulation and implementation focus on both e-businesses such as Amazon.com or Buy.com, and more traditional companies facing new challenges. Chapter-opening case vignettes feature companies as varied as Cisco Systems, Napster, AOL, Coca-Cola, and Jollibee, demonstrating to students the impact of technology and globalization on business and corporate strategy.

ACADEMICALLY SOLID, GLOBALLY ENGAGED

Foundations pays particular attention to the fundamentals of strategic management and takes a traditional approach to topical organization. Chapter 1 covers the strategic management process. Chapter 2 discusses the external environment, including both the task and the broad environment. Chapter 3 treats the internal environment, internal resources, and strategic direction. Chapter 4 discusses business-level strategy. Corporate-level strategy is tackled in Chapter 5. Chapter 6 focuses on the implementation of functional strategy and organizational structure. Chapter 7 treats strategic control and restructuring. Chapter 8 covers, in more depth, the important topic of global strategy, although international concepts and examples are integrated throughout the text.

Each chapter references global businesses, as well as specific global strategy issues facing all companies in today's ever-changing business environment. In Chapter 8, individual attention is given to implementation issues with respect to global strategy, but these topics also find themselves integrated into the rest of the chapters where applicable, ensuring that the international perspective is more than skin deep. Domestic firms with international ventures and non-U.S.-based organizations are used both as examples of strategic management theory and as meaningful counterweights to domestic-only operations. Many strategy-formulation topics also include global implementation tactics. This mix is especially true in Chapters 2 and 3, where we describe formulation activities together with their implementation.

As we have alluded, instructors of strategic management face significant challenges in fitting all the material they may want to cover into a single capstone course. We are mindful of these challenges and believe we have written a text that is uniquely supportive of them. Perhaps due to frustration, some instructors have altogether dropped use of any published text; but we hope to regain their allegiance with our coordinated yet flexible approach to teaching the strategic management course, combining a concise concepts text with resourceful instructor ancillaries.

For Instructors

Instructor's Manual with Test Bank. The Instructor's Manual with Test Bank (ISBN 0-324-07150-7) includes questions to prompt class discussion, outlines of chapter material, supplementary lecture materials, video recommendations, notes on the chapter-opening case vignettes, and a bank of test questions.

PowerPoint™ Presentation Slides. Over 150 PowerPoint slides, with accompanying summaries in PowerPoint's NotesView, are available to supplement course content. To download now, visit *Foundations'* supporting Web site at http://harrison.swcollege.com.

For Students

Strategize! Experiential Exercises in Strategic Management. Written by Julie I. Siciliano, of Western New England College, and C. Gopinath, of Suffolk University, *Strategize!* (ISBN 0-324-06653-8) provides a series of "Strategy Sessions" through which students can evaluate strategic management theories in incremental and structured ways in advance of applying them to resolve strategic business case problems. Constructed around 17 unique action-oriented Strategy Sessions, *Strategize!* presents a range of experiential exercises and projects for use in class or out. (An accompanying Instructor's Manual is available, ISBN 0-324-07189-2.)

ACKNOWLEDGMENTS

In developing this text, we would like to acknowledge the efforts of the Editorial Staff at South-Western, in particular John R. Szilagyi, Executive Editor; Jennifer Baker, Developmental Editor; and Starratt Alexander, Production Editor. We would also like to gratefully acknowledge the assistance of our colleagues for providing insightful comments and advice on what the current needs of today's instructors are. We appreciate their involvement in this project:

Joseph E. Benson
New Mexico State University

Karen A. Froelich
North Dakota State University

Sidney L. Barton
University of Cincinnati

Roy A. Cook
Fort Lewis College

Rodley C. Pineda
Tennessee University

Dwaine Tallent
St. Cloud State University

Douglas Polley
St. Cloud State University

Walter O. Einstein
University of Massachusetts, Dartmouth

Arthur Goldsmith
University of Massachusetts, Boston

Ernest H. Hall
University of Southern Indiana

Kenneth Aupperle
University of Akron

Lavon Carter
Harding University

Benjamin Oviatt
Georgia State University

Behrouz Aslani
California State Polytechnic University, Pomona

Suzanne Carter
University of Notre Dame

Anthony Chelte
Western New England College

Ronald W. Ferner
Philadelphia College of Bible

Phyllis G. Holland
Valdosta State University

David Marshall Hunt
University of Southern Mississippi

Deborah R. Litvin
Simmons College

Maryanne M. Rouse
University of South Florida

We hope you enjoy this text and find that it accommodates your individual needs.

Jeff Harrison
Caron St. John

A FINAL NOTE TO STUDENTS

Although we recognize that most students of strategic management will not become chief executives of major corporations in the very near future, you should likewise recognize that strategy is not just for those who achieve top-leadership positions. The decision-making tools you develop during this course are extremely relevant to all organizational levels, including many career-entry positions as well as to your own career planning. You won't be long on the job before you discover that the techniques of strategic management, such as those required to pull together an industry or organizational analysis, are highly applicable to all types of organizations, including small entrepreneurial firms and nonprofits. In addition, the material contained in this book will help you understand, appreciate, and think critically about trends of current and future importance to the business community—all formidable skills.

Studying strategic management will help you become better prepared to deal and stay fully engaged with important issues in our increasingly complex, increasingly global business environment, regardless of your position or of the industry in which you work. We strongly encourage you to apply the concepts of strategic management to your own employment and career planning decisions. Many of our students have told us that their understanding of strategic management impressed recruiters and allowed them to ask perceptive questions during interviews. Your understanding of strategic management should not be the artifact of a short stay in a classroom. Don't be tempted to treat it as such.

Dedication:

To Our Parents

BRIEF CONTENTS

CONTENTS

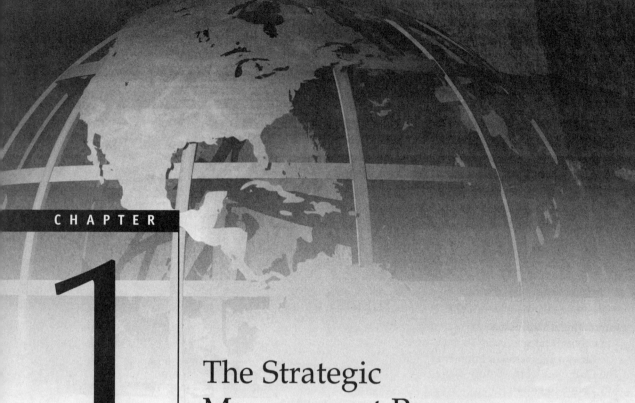

The Strategic Management Process

Cisco Systems

Cisco Systems began selling network routers in 1986. Today it sells over 150 types of networking products, including dial-in access servers, switches, hubs, cable boxes, home modems, and caching engines. On March 27, 2000, Cisco became the most valuable business on earth, with a market capitalization of $531 billion. That title was soon lost to General Electric, but the remarkable thing about Cisco is that it gained the title only 10 years after going public. In those 10 years, the value of Cisco's stock climbed approximately 100,000 percent and the company is still growing by about 30 percent per year. Cisco is now considered one of America's great success stories, along with companies such as Wal-Mart, Intel, and General Electric.

John Chambers, CEO of Cisco and a native of Charleston, West Virginia, considers himself to be "old school." He is very trusting of his executives and partners and prefers a handshake over a written contract. He overcame dyslexia through dogged determination and hard work, eventually completing an MBA at Indiana University. After working for IBM and Wang, Chambers joined Cisco in 1991, becoming CEO in 1995. In his first five years as CEO, Chambers presided over the creation of over $480 billion in stockholder wealth.

With a CEO that simply won't take no for an answer, much of Cisco's growth has come from the acquisition of literally dozens of network product companies. Although most companies experience disappointing results from their acquisitions, Cisco has prospered. Some of these acquisitions, such as the $5.7 billion acquisition of ArrowPoint Communications, are staggering. Cisco acquires not only products from these acquisitions, but knowledge that can be applied across all of its other businesses. Cisco's acquisition strategy is considered one of the most successful in recent history. Cisco is also very active in forming strategic alliances with other companies.

Cisco's success has come in spite of many challenges from its external environment, including probing government regulators and fierce competitors. In 1998, the FTC investigated charges that Cisco had colluded with Lucent and Nortel. Now Cisco General Counsel Dan Scheinman meets with Justice Department officials to explain Cisco's behavior in an effort to preempt government actions. Also, competitors such as Lucent Technologies provide a formidable and ongoing threat to Cisco's dominant industry position. For example, Cisco acquired semiconductor vendor StratumOne followed a few weeks later by Lucent's deal to buy terabit router vendor Nexabit Networks. Both of these acquisitions were expected to enhance router speed.

Looking ahead, Chambers expects voice, data, and video streams to converge. Consequently, Cisco has begun making acquisitions in the telecommunications equipment market.[1]

The most successful organizations are able to acquire and manage resources and capabilities that provide competitive advantages. For example, Cisco has been able to acquire, through acquisitions and strategic alliances, products and skills that have led it to a dominant position in its industry. The resources and capabilities Cisco acquires are carefully fostered and applied to all of its business areas. The processes associated with acquiring and managing organizational resources and relationships with constituencies all fall within the management area generally referred to as Strategic Management.

WHAT IS STRATEGIC MANAGEMENT?

Strategic management is the process through which organizations analyze and learn from their internal and external environments, establish strategic direction, create strategies that are intended to help achieve established goals, and execute those strategies, all in an effort to satisfy key organizational constituencies, which are called stakeholders. A simple model of the strategic management process is illustrated in Exhibit 1.1. The model is not rigid, but simply represents a useful sequence in which to discuss the central topics of strategic management. For example, while the activities may occur in the order specified in the model, especially if a firm is engaging in a formal strategic planning program, they may also be carried out in some other order or simultaneously. Also, the dotted arrows in Exhibit 1.1 indicate that organizations often cycle back to earlier activities during the strategic management process.

Exhibit 1.1   *The Strategic Management Process*

Source: Reprinted with the permission of The Free Press, a Division of Simon & Schuster, Inc., from *Competitive Strategy: Techniques for Analyzing Industries and Competitors* by Michael E. Porter. Copyright © 1980, 1998 by The Free Press.

External and Internal Environmental Analysis

External environmental analysis, discussed in Chapter 2, involves evaluation of the broad and task environments to determine trends, threats, and opportunities and to provide a foundation for strategic direction. The *broad environment* consists of domestic and global environmental forces such as socio-cultural, technological, political, and economic trends. The broad environment forms the context within which the firm and its task environment exist. The *task environment* consists of external stakeholders. *External stakeholders* are groups or individuals outside the organization that are significantly influenced by or have a major impact on the organization.[2] Examples of external stakeholders include customers, suppliers, competitors, government agencies and administrators, and a variety of other external groups that have a stake in the organization. Many of the stakeholders and forces that have the potential to be most important to organizations are shown in Exhibit 1.2. All of the external stakeholders should be analyzed at both the domestic and international levels. In all of the countries in which a company operates, managers must interact with government agencies, competitors, and activist groups, and manage the organization within the countries' socio-cultural, political, economic, and technological context. Thus, Exhibit 1.2 contains both a global and a domestic dimension.

Internal stakeholders, which include managers, employees, and the owners and their representatives (e.g., board of directors), also have a stake in the outcomes of the organization. A fully developed internal analysis also includes a broader evaluation of all of the organization's resources and capabilities to determine strengths, weaknesses, and opportunities for competitive advantage, and to identify organizational vulnerabilities that should be corrected. Internal analysis is the subject of Chapter 2.

As illustrated by the downward pointing arrows in Exhibit 1.1, analysis of the external and internal environments provides an organization with a foundation

---

Exhibit 1.2   *The Organization and Its Environments*

for all of the other tasks of strategic management. For example, an organization's managers should formulate strategies based on internal strengths and weaknesses and in the context of the opportunities and threats found in its external environment. In addition, strategic direction is an outcome of melding the desires of key organizational stakeholders with environmental realities.

Strategic Direction

Strategic direction pertains to the longer-term goals and objectives of the organization. At a more fundamental level, strategic direction defines the purposes for which an organization exists and operates. This direction is often contained in a *mission* statement. Unlike shorter-term goals and strategies, the mission is an enduring part of planning processes within the organization. Often missions describe the areas or industries in which an organization operates. For example, the mission of the New York Stock Exchange is as follows:

> Support the capital-raising and asset-management processes by providing the highest-quality and most cost-effective, self-regulated marketplace for the trading of financial instruments; promote confidence in and understanding of that process; and serve as a forum for discussion of relevant national and international policy issues.[3]

A well-established strategic direction provides guidance to the managers and employees who are largely responsible for carrying it out as well as a greater understanding of the organization for the external stakeholders with whom the organization interacts. Since strategic direction is an important part of the internal organization, it is also discussed in Chapter 3.

Business and Corporate Strategy Formulation

A *strategy* is an organizational plan of action that is intended to move an organization toward the achievement of its shorter-term goals and, ultimately, toward the achievement of its fundamental purposes. Strategy formulation is often divided into three types—corporate, business, and functional, as shown in Exhibit 1.3.

Business strategy formulation, discussed in Chapter 4, pertains to domain direction and navigation, or how businesses compete in the areas they have se-

Exhibit 1.3   *Strategy Formulation in a Multibusiness Organization*

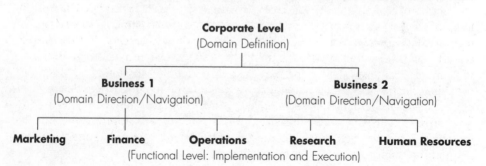

lected. *Corporate strategy formulation*, the subject of Chapter 5, refers primarily to domain definition, or the selection of business areas in which the organization will compete. Although some firms, such as McDonald's, are involved in one basic business, diversified organizations are involved in several different businesses and serve a variety of customer groups. *Functional strategy formulation* contains the details of how the functional areas such as marketing, operations, finance, and research should work together to achieve the business-level strategy. Thus, functional strategy is most closely associated with strategy implementation, the topic of Chapter 6.

Another way to distinguish among the three strategies is to determine the organizational level at which decisions are made. Corporate strategy decisions are typically made at the highest levels of the organization by the CEO and/or board of directors, although these individuals may receive input from managers at other levels. If an organization is only involved in one area of business, then business strategy decisions tend to be made by the same people. In organizations that have diversified into many areas, the different areas may be represented by different operating divisions or lines-of-business. In those situations, business strategy decisions are made by division heads or business unit managers. Functional decisions are made by functional managers, who represent organizational areas such as operations, finance, personnel, accounting, research and development, or information systems.

Strategy Implementation and Control

Strategy formulation results in a plan of action for the organization and its various levels. On the other hand, strategy implementation represents a pattern of decisions and actions that are intended to carry out the plan. *Strategy implementation* (Chapter 6) involves creating the functional strategies, systems, structures, and processes needed by the organization in achieving strategic ends. Functional strategies outline the specific actions that each function must undertake to convert business- and corporate-level strategies into actions. Without a translation of all of the plans into specific actions, nothing will change. Organizational systems are developed to train and compensate employees; assist in planning efforts; reinforce organizational values; and gather, analyze, and convey information. Structures reflect the way people and work are organized, which includes reporting relationships and formation into work groups, teams, and departments. Processes, such as standard operating procedures, are developed to create uniformity across the organization and promote efficiency. Strategy implementation may require changes to any of these factors as the organization pursues new strategies over time.

Good control also is critical to organizational success. *Strategic control*, the topic of Chapter 7, refers to the processes that lead to adjustments in strategic direction, strategies, or the implementation plan when necessary. Managers may collect new information that leads them to re-evaluate their assessment of the environment. They may determine that the organizational mission is no longer appropriate or that the organizational strategies are not leading to the desired outcomes. On the other hand, the strategic control system may tell managers that the environmental assumptions, mission, and strategies are appropriate, but the strategies have not been well executed. In such an instance, adjustments should be made in the implementation process.

As noted earlier, the strategic management process is usually not as sequential or linear as implied by the previous discussion. The activities are usually performed simultaneously, with constant adjustments to assumptions, direction, strategies, and processes as new information is learned and new assessments are made.

Strategic Restructuring

At some point in the life of every organization, growth will slow and some stakeholders will begin to feel dissatisfied. Wal-Mart is an excellent example. After two decades of phenomenal growth in sales, earnings, and stock value, Wal-Mart began to level off in the late '90s. Some assert that Sam Walton's death triggered the decline. Others argued that Wal-Mart was suffering from inevitable market saturation. Regardless of the reason, organizations eventually feel the need to re-evaluate their strategies and the way they are executing them. *Restructuring*, discussed in Chapter 8, typically involves a renewed emphasis on the things an organization does well, combined with a variety of tactics to revitalize the organization and strengthen its competitive position. Currently, popular restructuring tactics include refocusing corporate assets on a more limited set of activities, retrenchment, Chapter XI reorganization, leveraged buyouts, and changes to the organizational structure.

Now that the strategic management process has been described, we will establish a theoretical foundation upon which the rest of the book will be based, followed by a brief discussion of the social responsibilities of modern organizations. Then we will turn our attention to the trends that are moving organizations quickly into a global playing field.

ALTERNATIVE PERSPECTIVES ON STRATEGY DEVELOPMENT

The field of strategic management blends a wide variety of ideas representing many functional areas of business. This diversity may be one reason that scholars and practitioners have not been able to agree on a standard set of theories (i.e., paradigm) to guide the field. Nevertheless, some ideas are more widely adopted than others. The next several sections contain a brief explanation of some of the major theories and ideas upon which our model of the strategic management process is based. These theories are summarized in Exhibit 1.4. Other important theories are woven into the chapters where they are most applicable.

Determinism versus Enactment

The traditional process for developing strategy consists of analyzing the internal and external environments of the organization to arrive at organizational strengths, weaknesses, opportunities, and threats (SWOT). The results from this *"situation analysis,"* as this process is sometimes called, are the basis for developing missions, goals, and strategies.[4] In general, an organization should select strategies that (1) take advantage of organizational strengths and external opportunities or (2) neutralize or overcome internal weaknesses and external threats.

The traditional approach to strategy development is conceptually related to *environmental determinism*. According to this view, good management is associ-

---

Exhibit 1.4 *Ideas and Theories Regarding
the Strategic Management Model*

Situation Analysis
The traditional process for developing strategy, consisting of analyzing the internal and external environments of the organization to arrive at organizational strengths, weaknesses, opportunities, and threats (SWOT). The results form the basis for developing missions, goals, and strategies.

Environmental Determinism
Management's task is to determine which strategy will best fit environmental, technical, and human forces at a particular point in time and then work to carry it out.

Principle of Enactment
Organizations do not have to submit to existing forces in the environment. They can, in part, create their environments through strategic alliances with stakeholders, advertising, political lobbying, and a variety of other activities.

Deliberate Strategy
Managers plan to pursue an intended strategic course. Strategy is deliberate.

Emergent Strategy
Strategy simply emerges from a stream of decisions. Managers learn as they go.

Stakeholder Management
The organization is viewed from the perspective of the internal and external constituencies that have a stake in the organization. Stakeholder analysis is used to guide the strategy process. Stakeholder management is central to the development of mutually beneficial relationships and alliances with external stakeholders.

Resource-Based View
An organization is a bundle of resources. The most important management function is to acquire and manage resources in such a way that the organization achieves sustainable competitive advantages leading to superior performance.

---

ated with determining which strategy will best fit environmental, technical, and human forces at a particular point in time, and then working to carry it out.[5] From this perspective, the most successful organization will be the one that best *adapts* to existing forces. In other words, the environment is the primary determinant of strategy. After a critical review of environmental determinism, a well-known researcher once argued:

> There is a more fundamental conclusion to be drawn from the foregoing analysis: the strategy of a firm cannot be predicted, nor is it predestined; the strategic decisions made by managers cannot be assumed to be the product of deterministic forces in their environments. . . . On the contrary, the very nature of the concept of strategy assumes a human agent who is able to take actions that attempt to distinguish one's firm from the competitors.[6]

The principle of enactment assumes that organizations do not have to submit to existing forces in the environment—they can, in part, create their environments through strategic alliances with stakeholders, advertising, political lobbying, and a variety of other activities.[7] Of course, smaller organizations are somewhat limited in their ability independently to influence some components of their external environments, such as national government agencies and administrators; however, they can typically have more influence on forces in the their local task environments.

It is not necessary to completely reject determinism and the view that organizations should adapt to their environments or the more modern view that organizations can alter their environments through enactment. In reality, the best-run organizations are engaged in both processes simultaneously, enacting those parts of the environment over which the firm can exercise some control and adapting to environmental circumstances that are either uncontrollable or too costly to influence. For instance, Disney altered its environment by buying a major customer of its television programs and movies with the acquisition of Capital Cities/ABC. On the other hand, Disney canceled several large projects, such as an "Americana" themed park and a Rocky Mountain ski resort, in response to pressure from social groups.

Deliberate versus Emergent Strategy Formulation

The traditional school of thought concerning strategy formulation also supports the view that managers respond to the forces discussed thus far by making decisions that are consistent with a preconceived strategy. In other words, strategy is deliberate. *Deliberate strategy* implies that managers *plan* to pursue an *intended* strategic course. On the other hand, in some cases strategy simply emerges from a stream of decisions. Managers learn as they go. An *emergent strategy* is one that was not planned or intended. According to this perspective, managers *learn* what will work through a process of trial and error.[8] Supporters of this view argue that organizations that limit themselves to acting on the basis of what is already known or understood will not be sufficiently innovative to create a sustainable competitive advantage.[9]

The story of the small Honda motorcycle offers support for the concept of emergent strategy. When Honda executives decided to market a small motorcycle, they had no idea it would be so successful. In fact, the prevailing wisdom was that small motorcycles would not sell very well. But Honda executives broke the rules and made the decision to market a small motorcycle. As sales expanded, they increased marketing, and ultimately captured two-thirds of the American motorcycle market. In another example, General Motors had a mini-van on the drawing boards long before Chrysler. On the basis of rational analysis, GM decided that the mini-van would probably not sell.[10] Chrysler's mini-van introduction was extremely successful, and redefined the look of family vehicles. GM's subsequent attempts to enter the market have been largely unsuccessful, although Ford has been successful. In spite of the strength of these examples concerning emergent strategy, it is not a good idea to reject deliberate strategy either. One of the strongest advocates of learning and emergent strategy recently confessed, "we shall get nowhere without emergent learning alongside deliberate planning."[11] Both processes are necessary if an organization is to succeed.

Stakeholder Analysis and Management

The stakeholder view of strategic management considers the organization from the perspective of the internal and external constituencies that have a strong interest in the organization. These stakeholders should be managed in such a way that the organization can achieve its goals and objectives, which are determined by the desires of key stakeholders. One of the common criticisms of the stakeholder approach is that it leads to a situation in which all (or most) stakeholders are equally weighted in the decision-making process. However, this is a misconception. One of the first activities associated with any well-done stakeholder analysis is the establishment of priorities given to each stakeholder. For example, in most organizations owners and customers would have higher management priority than financial intermediaries or special interest groups.

It is helpful to draw a distinction between stakeholder analysis and stakeholder management. *Stakeholder analysis* involves identifying and prioritizing key stakeholders, assessing their needs, collecting ideas from them, and integrating this knowledge into strategic management processes such as the establishment of strategic direction and the formulation and implementation of strategies. Organizations can use the information they collect from stakeholders to develop and modify their strategic direction, strategies, and implementation plans. Organizations can also use information from stakeholders to predict their responses to planned actions, at home and abroad. *Stakeholder management*, on the other hand, includes communicating, negotiating, contracting, and managing relationships with stakeholders, and motivating them to behave in ways that are beneficial to the organization and its other stakeholders. In reality, the processes associated with stakeholder analysis and management overlap. For example, a firm may use a survey both to collect information on customer needs and communicate information about a new service. This book describes many strategies firms are using to manage their stakeholders. A central theme is that many successful organizations have learned that cooperative strategies with external stakeholders can lead to competitive advantages in the global economy.

The Resource-Based View of the Firm

Finally, in recent years another perspective on strategy development has been gaining wider acceptance. It is called the *resource-based view of the firm* and has its roots in the work of the earliest strategic management theorists.[12] According to this view, an organization is a bundle of resources, which fall into the general categories of (1) financial resources, including all of the monetary resources which a firm can draw; (2) physical resources such as plant, equipment, loc and access to raw materials; (3) human resources, which pertains to the background, and training of individuals within the firm; and (4) general zational resources, which includes a variety of factors that are peculiar to organizations. Examples of organizational resources include the formal r structure, management techniques, internal systems for planning and co culture, reputation, and relationships within the organization as well a ships with external stakeholders.[13]

From a resource-based perspective, *strengths* are firm resources ar ties that can lead to a competitive advantage. *Weaknesses* are resource bilities that the firm does not possess but are necessary, res competitive disadvantage. *Opportunities* are conditions in the broad and task environments that allow a firm to take advantage of organizational strengths, overcome organizational weaknesses, and/or neutralize environmental threats. *Threats* are conditions in the broad and task environments that may stand in the way of organizational competitiveness or the achievement of stakeholder satisfaction.

If a resource that a firm possesses allows the firm to take advantage of opportunities or neutralize threats, if only a small number of firms possess it, and if it is costly or impossible to imitate, then it may lead to a sustainable competitive advantage. A *sustainable competitive advantage* is an advantage that is difficult to imitate by competitors and thus leads to higher-than-average organizational performance over a long time period.[14] For example, the success of Marriott is largely attributable to advantages created by resources that have been difficult to duplicate by other companies in the hotel industry. The first is financial controls. Marriott can determine and anticipate construction and operating costs with nearly exact precision. Second, Marriott has developed a distinctive competence in customer service, or "becoming the provider of choice." Looking to the future, Marriott is actively engaged in creating a third organizational capability as the "employer of choice." Marriott executives reason that with fewer people entering the labor force in the 18- to 25-year age group, good workers will become increasingly difficult to attract. Also, good workers are especially important in a service business like hotels because they interact directly with customers.[15]

Many strategy scholars believe that effective development of organizational resources is the most important reason that some organizations are more successful than others. Most of the resources that a firm can acquire or develop are directly linked to an organization's stakeholders. For example, financial resources are closely linked to establishing good working relationships with financial intermediaries. Also, the development of human resources is associated with internal stakeholder management. Finally, organizational resources reflect the organization's understanding of the expectations of society and the linkages it has established with internal and external stakeholders.

The strategic management process model upon which this book is based relies, to some degree, on each of the theories and ideas that have been described in these sections. The sections dealing with analysis of the internal and external environments draw heavily from stakeholder theory, as do the sections dealing with formation of alliances. The entire book is guided by resource-based theory, as even relationships with external stakeholders are viewed as a resource upon which the organization can draw. The other perspectives are also interwoven into the fiber of the book where appropriate. This balanced approach will provide you with a set of tools that will be applicable to a wide variety of organizational circumstances.

All of the popular strategic management perspectives recognize that strategic management entails direction of large amounts of organizational resources—human, physical, financial, and intangible. As organizations conduct their daily business, they influence many stakeholders, including owners, employees, customers, suppliers, and communities. Over time, these stakeholders develop expectations with regard to organizations and often depend on them, to some degree, for their welfare. Consequently, the decisions made by organizations often have an ethical dimension. Some people may view some decisions that are legal within society as unethical because they compromise an implied trust between the organization and its stakeholders. The next section provides a brief discussion of ethics and social responsibility.

ETHICS AND SOCIAL RESPONSIBILITY

As they relate to individuals, *ethics* are a personal value system that helps determine what is right or good. These values are typically associated with a system of beliefs that supports a particular moral code or view.[16] *Organizational ethics* are a value system that has been widely adopted by members of an organization. For example, Wal-Mart's values emphasize the worth of customers and employees, while Motorola has values that focus on participation and patriotism. To determine what the ethics of an organization are, a student can simply study the pattern of decisions in the organization to discover what or who is given priority.[17]

Sometimes the stated ethics of an organization differ from the actual values that guide organizational decisions. For example, an organization may publish an affirmative action statement that condemns prejudice in hiring and promotion decisions on the basis of sex or race. However, that same organization may not have a single minority member or female in its top management team. Thus, studying the pattern of promotion decisions over a few years can determine whether the stated ethical position differs from the actual behavior of the organization.

Embedded within the application of ethics found here is the notion of social responsibility. Social responsibility contains four major components: (1) economic responsibilities such as the obligation to be productive and profitable and meet the consumer needs of society; (2) a legal responsibility to achieve economic goals within the confines of written law; (3) moral obligations to abide by unwritten codes, norms, and values implicitly derived from society; and (4) discretionary responsibilities that are volitional or philanthropic in nature.[18]

Research evidence does not unequivocally support the idea that firms that rank high on social responsibility, based on the four components previously described, are necessarily any more or less profitable than firms that rank low.[19] However, firms that have an overall high rank in the four areas listed before (one of which is productivity and profitability) have achieved an end in itself. The old belief, espoused primarily by economists, that the only valid objective of a corporation is to maximize profits regardless of social consequences is no longer considered acceptable by most members of modern societies. This sort of philosophy can lead to, at best, shortsightedness and, at worst, disaster, to the extent that organizations forget their other obligations in the pursuit of short-run financial rewards. In addition, one business ethics expert argued that:

> there is a long-term cost to unethical behavior that tends to be neglected. That cost is to the trust of the people involved. Companies today—due to increasing global competition and advancing technological complexity—are much more dependent than ever upon the trust of workers, specialists, managers, suppliers, distributors, customers, creditors, owners, local institutions, national governments, venture partners, and international agencies. People in any of those groups who believe that they have been misgoverned by bribes, sickened by emissions, or cheated by products tend, over time, to lose trust in the firm responsible for those actions.[20]

The logic continues that trust leads to commitment, which leads to increased effort on the part of everyone associated with the firm. Committed effort is precisely what is needed to prosper in a complex world in which interdependence is increasing.

In summary, organizations that exhibit trustworthy behavior enjoy good reputations, a more committed effort by internal and external stakeholders to the organization, and eagerness on the part of stakeholders to conduct business. On the other hand, behavior that violates trust can lead to a poor reputation, legal suits, walkouts, and boycotts, as well as avoidance on the part of stakeholders to participate in transactions with the organization. The case of Manville is illustrative of this point.

> Nearly fifty years ago, employees and managers of Manville (then Johns-Manville) started to receive information that asbestos inhalation was associated with various forms of lung disease. Manville chose to ignore this information and suppress research findings. The company even went so far as to conceal chest X-rays from employees in their asbestos operations. When confronted about this tactic, a Manville lawyer was quoted as saying that they would let their employees work until they dropped dead, all in the interest of saving money. Eventually, this neglect of research findings and their own employees led to financial ruin for Manville.[21]

Concerning ethical decision-making, the approach of many business organizations seems to be to wait until someone complains before actions are taken. This is the type of attitude that resulted in the Savings and Loan crisis, the Bhopal explosion tragedy in India, and the explosion of the Space Shuttle Challenger. In each of these situations, the organizations involved could have avoided problems by being more responsive to warning signals from key stakeholders. History has taught us that many human-induced disasters and crises could be avoided if organizations were sensitive to what their stakeholders tell them.

Social responsibility and ethics become even more complicated as organizations cross international borders. Nevertheless, global forces are causing organizations to increase their international involvement. The final section of this chapter discusses some of these forces.

THE CASE FOR GOING GLOBAL

Most successful organizations find that their domestic markets are becoming saturated or that foreign markets offer opportunities for growth and profitability that often are not available domestically. Many forces are leading U.S. firms into the international arena (see Exhibit 1.5). Several of these forces are quite remarkable. Concerning profitability, Coke makes substantially higher profits in its foreign operations than it does at home.[22] Hasbro, the toy maker, also enjoys much higher prices and higher margins in other countries than it does in the U.S. McDonald's expects to see much greater growth in international markets than in U.S. markets. Some smaller, start-up firms find they can enter growing international markets more easily than they can fight for market share in saturated U.S. markets.

Changes in European markets, such as falling trade barriers, are among the most significant global changes. Although the process of economic unification in Europe is proceeding slowly, it is expected to lead eventually to increased productivity and reduced costs for European businesses. Furthermore, strategic alliances in the sector are expected to increase.[23] Eastern Europe, despite political turmoil, still offers substantial investment opportunities, due to low labor rates

---

Exhibit 1.5   *Forces Favoring Globalization*

Saturated domestic markets

Profitability of foreign markets

Falling trade barriers (i.e., EC 1992)

Newly industrialized countries (i.e., Korea, Taiwan, Spain) leading to increasing global competition and new market opportunities

Growing similarity of industrialized nations

Shift toward market economies (i.e., East Germany)

English becoming a universally spoken language

Globalization of capital markets

Availability of lower-cost resources (i.e., labor) in some foreign countries

Uniformity in technical standards

Opportunities to learn from foreign joint venture partners

Sources: Based on information contained in H. Henzler and W. Rall, "Facing Up to the Globalization Challenge," *McKinsey Quarterly* (Winter 1986): 52–68; T. Peters, "Prometheus Barely Unbound," *Academy of Management Executive* (November 1990): 70–84; M. E. Porter, ed., *Competition in Global Industries* (Boston: Harvard Business School Press, 1986): 2–3.

and untapped consumer markets.[24] Latin America, some authors have suggested, also offers substantial business opportunities.[25] Of course, Japan is already an economic superpower.

Now that Japanese consumers have gained purchasing power, the world economy is dominated by three regions called the "Triad" regions: North America, Europe, and the Pacific Rim. Some researchers have suggested that in order to remain competitive, larger organizations should be involved in all three regions.[26] The reason is simple. Often the best parts or technology does not exist in the home country. An organization may have to extend its ties to international markets to obtain the products, services, or knowledge necessary to be competitive in the world's markets.

Going global offers many new management challenges. The fact is that Europeans and the Japanese have different views of business and manage differently than American managers, although management techniques are slowly converging.[27] Most of the larger companies described in this book have substantial international business assets.

KEY POINTS SUMMARY

This chapter emphasized the important role of the strategic management process in modern organizations. Some of the most important points are:

1. The strategic management process includes the activities of internal and external analysis, establishment of strategic direction, development of strategies for the corporate and business levels of the organization, development and execution of an implementation plan, and the establishment of strategic controls.

2. The traditional process for developing strategy, sometimes called situation analysis, consists of analyzing the internal and external environments of the organization to arrive at organizational strengths,

weaknesses, opportunities, and threats (SWOT). The results are the basis for developing missions, goals, and strategies.

3. A deterministic view of strategy argues that the key role of managers is to determine which strategy will best fit environmental, technical, and human forces at a particular point in time, and then work to carry it out. However, according to the principle of enactment, organizations do not have to submit to existing forces in the environment. They can, in part, create their environments through strategic alliances with stakeholders, advertising, political lobbying, and a variety of other activities.

4. The deliberate view of strategy is that managers plan to pursue an intended strategic course. On the other hand, the emergent view argues that strategy simply develops or evolves from a stream of decisions. Managers learn as they go.

5. Stakeholder theory views the organization from the perspective of the internal and external constituencies that have an interest in the organization.

6. According to the resource-based view of the firm, an organization is a bundle of resources. The most important management function is to acquire and manage resources in such a way that the organization achieves sustainable competitive advantages leading to superior performance.

7. Social responsibilities include (1) economic responsibilities, (2) legal responsibilities, (3) moral obligations, and (4) discretionary responsibilities.

8. Many trends and influences are pushing firms to increase their involvement in international markets. Most larger firms have substantial global investments.

9. Ultimately, a firm's strategy is reflected in what the firm actually does, rather than what it says it will do. Strategic management processes are concerned with aligning intention with action.

END NOTES

1 S. Collet, "A Guide to Cisco's Acquisition and in S. Collet, "A Guide to Cisco's Acquisition and Investment Strategy," *Computerworld* (October 4, 1999): 20; J. Rendleman, "Cisco, Lucent Lay Groundwork for High-Speed Routing Plans," *PC Week* (July 12, 1999): 47; A. Serwer, "There's Something about Cisco," *Fortune* (May 15, 2000): 114–138.

2 R.E. Freeman, *Strategic Management: A Stakeholder Approach* (Boston: Pitman Publishing, 1984); M. Pastin, *The Hard Problems of Management: Gaining the Ethics Edge* (San Francisco: Jossey-Bass, 1986).

3 *New York Stock Exchange Annual Report*, New York Stock Exchange, 1990.

4 C.W. Hofer and D.E. Schendel, *Strategy Formulation: Analytical Concepts* (St. Paul: West Publishing, 1978).

5 J. Bourgeois, III, "Strategic Management and Determinism," *Academy of Management Review* 9 (1984): 586–596; L.G. Hrebiniak and W.F. Joyce, "Organizational Adaptation: Strategic Choice and Environmental Determinism," *Administrative Science Quarterly* 30 (1985): 336–349.

6 Bourgeois, "Strategic Management and Determinism," 589.

7 L. Smirchich and C. Stubbart, "Strategic Management in an Enacted World," *Academy of Management Review* 10 (1985): 724–736.

8 H. Mintzberg and A. Mchugh, "Strategy Formation in an Adhocracy," *Administrative Science Quarterly* 30 (1985): 160–197.

9 H. Mintzberg, "The Design School: Reconsidering the Basic Premises of Strategic Management," *Strategic Management Journal* 11 (1990): 171–196.

10 H. Mintzberg, "Learning 1, Planning 0: Reply to Igor Ansoff," *Strategic Management Journal* 12 (1991): 463–467.

11 Mintzberg, "Learning 1, Planning 0," 465.

12 N.J. Foss, C. Knudsen, C.A. Montgomery, "An Exploration of Common Ground: Integrating Evolutionary and Strategic Theories of the Firm," in C.A. Montgomery, ed., *Resource-Based and Evolutionary Theories of the Firm* (Boston: Kluwer Academic Publishers, 1995).

13 J.B. Barney, "Firm Resources and Sustained Competitive Advantage," *Journal of Management* 17 (1991): 99–120; J.B. Barney, *Gaining and Sustaining Competitive Advantage* (Reading, Mass: Addison-Wesley, 1997); J.S. Harrison, M.A. Hitt, R.E. Hoskisson and R.D. Ireland, "Synergies and Post-Acquisition Performance: Differences Versus Similarities in Resource Allocations," *Journal of Management* 17 (1991): 173–190; J.T. Mahoney and J.R. Pandian, "The Resource-Based View Within the Conversation of Strategic Management," *Strategic Management Journal* 13 (1992): 363–380; B. Wernerfelt, "A Resource-Based View of the Firm," *Strategic Management Journal* 5 (1984): 171–180.

14 Barney, "Firm Resources and Sustained Competitive Advantage"; Mahoney and Pandian, "The Resource-Based View."

15 D. Ulrich and D. Lake, "Organizational Capability: Creating Competitive Advantage," *Academy of Management Executive* 5 (1): 77–92.

16 L.T. Hosmer, *The Ethics of Management*, 2nd ed. (Homewood, Ill.: Irwin, 1991): 103.

17 This entire discussion of ethics as ground rules was strongly influenced by M. Pastin, *The Hard Problems of Management* (San Francisco, Jossey-Bass, 1986): 40–42.

18 A.B. Carroll, "A Three Dimensional Model of Corporate Social Performance," *Academy of Management Review* 4 (1979): 497–505.

19 K.E. Aupperle, A.B. Carroll, and J.D. Hatfield, "An Empirical Examination of the Relationship Between Corporate Social Responsibility and Profitability," *Academy of Management Journal* 28 (1985): 446–463.

20 L.T. Hosmer, "Response to 'Do Good Ethics Always Make For Good Business,'" *Strategic Management Journal* 17 (1996): 501. See also L.T. Hosmer, "Strategic Planning as if Ethics Mattered," *Strategic Management Journal*, Summer Special Issue, 15 (1994): 17–34.

21 S.W. Gellerman, "Why 'Good' Managers Make Bad Ethical Choices," *Harvard Business Review* (July/August, 1986): 85–90.

22 "As a Global Marketer, Coke Excels by Being Tough and Consistent," *The Wall Street Journal* (December 19, 1989): 1.

23 H. Weihrich, "Europe 1992: What the Future May Hold," *Academy of Management Executive* (May 1990): 7–18.

24 E.T. Yon, "Corporate Strategy and the New Europe," *Academy of Management Executive* (August 1990): 61–65.

25 J.I. Martinez, J.A. Quelch, and J. Ganitsky, "Don't Forget Latin America," *Sloan Management Review* (Winter 1992): 78–82.

26 K. Ohmae, "Becoming a Triad Power: The New Global Corporation," in H. Vernon-Wortzel and L.H. Wortzel, *Global Strategic Management: The Essentials*, 2nd ed. (New York: John Wiley and Sons, 1991): 62–74.

27 R. Calori and B. Dufour, "Management European Style," *Academy of Management Executive* (August 1995): 61–73.

CHAPTER

2

The External Environment

The Music Industry

Just like the steel and auto industries during earlier decades, the music industry is under siege. In recent years, the technological, economic, legal, and competitive forces have conspired to alter a decades-old business model. The traditional music recording and production companies in the $40 billion music industry are being forced to evolve from selling products to simply providing a service.

Music CDs each cost about $.50 to make, but retail for $15.00 or more. The $15.00 retail price covers the cost of production, marketing, distribution, royalties to the artists, and percentages for the record companies and the retailers. In a major settlement with record companies, the Federal Trade Commission recently concluded that consumers may have overpaid more than $450 million for CDs in the past three years. The agreement requires that record companies change their pricing policies.

The more significant threat to the traditional business model is technological change. The Internet has spawned a series of start-up companies that allow swapping and downloading of music files. Several companies, with Napster being the most famous, capitalized on the ease of transferring MP3 music files. The approach used by these companies is to simply act as a switchboard for matching up customers with their music interests, which allows users to copy music from other users free of charge.

As expected, Napster's activities have been challenged in court as a violation of copyright laws. A San Francisco federal judge ordered Napster to cease its music transfer operations. Napster has argued that it never takes possession of files or stores them on its server—it just moves the files from one customer to the other. Although the legality of the issue is still being assessed, the implications for the record companies are clear. Why should a record company produce millions of CDs then ship them via distributors all over the world? Why should retailers maintain an inventory of CDs when it is so easy to create a CD on the spot? What is to prevent a well-known music group with a young, Internet-savvy fan base—say, the Backstreet Boys—from just recording their own music then putting it out via their group's own Web site, circumventing record companies altogether and collecting all of the profits directly?

The implications are profound. In the future, record companies may just control access to copyrighted music rather than participate in production and distribution. According to one industry consultant, "The music business will become about growing the size of the crowd. It becomes more like radio or television." Payment to artists may be based on a royalty per download. Traditional retailers may be largely cut out of the loop—and, once established, artists may choose to access their market directly. As noted by *Time* magazine writer, Karl Taro Greenfeld, "Ultimately, it will be technology and economics, not lawyers and mega bands, that will call the tune in the music business. Already, record companies like Sony, Warner, Universal, EMI, and BMG are making plans to sell digital files of music, either as albums or tracks.[1]

This chapter is about the influence of the external environment on organizations. Although an organization cannot have much direct influence on its broad environment (i.e., society, the economy, technology, global politics), it can buffer itself from threats and take advantage of opportunities. On the other hand, the external stakeholders that compose an organization's task environment (i.e., customers, suppliers, competitors) are subject to substantial firm influence. As described in the previous example, the fundamental technological trends and the resulting economic trends, both of which are part of the broad environment, are largely beyond the influence of any one firm. The competitive implications—such as the threat of substitute business models like the Napster model, and the relationships with artists, distributors, and retailers—can be influenced by organizations within the music industry. Whether they treat these fundamental changes as threats or opportunities may determine their survival. We will now discuss the broad environment, followed by the task environment.

THE BROAD ENVIRONMENT

Forces in the broad environment can have a tremendous impact on a firm and its task environment; however, individual firms typically have only a marginal ability to influence these forces. In rare cases, individual firms can influence trends in the broad environment, as when innovations at Intel influence technological trends in the microprocessor, microcomputer, and software industries. In general, however, it is virtually impossible for one independent firm to dramatically influence societal views on abortion, policies on free trade with China, migration to the Sun Belt, the number of school-age children, or even the desirability of particular clothing styles. Consequently, although firms may be able to influence the broad environment to some degree, the emphasis in this book generally will be on analyzing and responding to this segment of the environment. The most important elements in the broad environment, as it relates to a business organization and its task environment, are global socio-cultural, economic, technological, and political/legal forces.

Socio-cultural Forces

A few of the major socio-cultural issues currently facing the United States are shown in Exhibit 2.1. Analysis of societal trends is important from at least four perspectives. First, because most of the other stakeholder groups are also members of society, some of their values and beliefs are derived from broader societal influences, which can create opportunities and threats for organizations. For example, societal interest in health and fitness has led to business opportunities in the home fitness and nutritional supplements industries, whereas concerns about smoking have set the stage for a regulatory and legal backlash against the tobacco companies.

Second, firms may reduce the risk of gaining a bad "ethical" reputation by anticipating and adjusting for socio-cultural trends. In the late 1990s, Bill Gates, the founder of Microsoft, was facing rising societal concern about the extraordinary profits generated by Microsoft and by his "unimpressive philanthropic record."[2] In 1999, he donated $3.35 billion to the William Gates Foundation, which provides grants for health and human services organizations, the Gates Learning

---

Exhibit 2.1   *Major Social Issues in the United States*

Role of government in health care and child care
Declining quality of education
Legality of abortion
Influence of World Wide Web
Importance and role of the military
Levels of foreign investment/ownership in the United States
Social costs of restructuring, especially layoffs
Pollution and disposal of toxic and nontoxic wastes
General increase in environmental awareness
Drug addiction
Continued migration toward the Sun Belt states
Graying of America
AIDS and other health problems
Major global issues
Immigration restrictions

Foundation, which gives software, computers, and services to libraries in low-income areas.[3] Some observers speculated that he was giving the money to garner sympathy as he was entering his antitrust investigation. In another example, the Denny's restaurant chain was known for many years as one of America's most racist companies. However, Ron Petty, Denny's CEO, introduced initiatives that turned the company into a model of multicultural sensitivity.[4] In 2000, after two years in the top 10, Denny's was number one on the list of Fortune's best companies for minorities.[5]

Third, correct assessment of socio-cultural trends can help businesses avoid restrictive legislation. Industries and organizations that police themselves are less likely to be the target of legislative activity. In 2000, Microsoft was judged to be a monopoly and ordered to break into two separate businesses. Although the judgment is under appeal at the time of this writing, the decision raises the question—could Microsoft have done something to avoid the investigation in the first place? Could they have anticipated and avoided the wrath of competitors and the attention of regulators? In another example of societal concerns about business practices, the United States Sentencing Guidelines (USSG), compulsory guidelines courts must use to determine fines and penalties when corporate illegalities are proven, were a direct response to public outcry over negligence on the part of businesses in preventing white-collar crime.[6]

The fourth reason why analysis of socio-cultural values is important is that demographic and economic changes in society can create opportunities for and threats to the revenue growth and profit prospects of an organization. For example, many baby boomer couples had babies later in life than their counterparts in past generations, causing a demographic trend toward older couples with children. In the 1990s, the higher levels of income of these more established "30- and 40-something" parents led to the development of higher quality baby accessories, clothing, and supplies, as well as new business opportunities in child care and specialized education. Seemingly unrelated industries, such as the motion picture and television industries, took advantage of these trends by producing many movies and television shows that centered on families and children. In the next several years, more of these aging baby boomers, who were born between 1945 and 1965, will be entering their wealthy empty-nest years and retiring. Their numbers and their wealth will continue to stimulate growth in recreational and leisure industries, and in luxury products and services. Furthermore, the baby-boomers' children have purchasing power greater than previous generations of children, stimulating demand for music, entertainment, and fashion. They are also entering colleges at a record pace—straining resources on college campuses. Demographic changes such as these can help direct organizational planning and are often at the core of any forecast of industry demand.

Not only must an organization assess the potential effects of socio-cultural forces on its business, it must manage its relationship and reputation with society at large. The media acts as a watchdog for society. It is a commanding force in managing the attitudes of the general public toward organizations. Executives have nightmares about their organizations being the subjects of the next *60 Minutes* program or some other news show. On the other hand, a well-managed media can have a significant positive impact on a firm's image.

Global Economic Forces

Economic forces can have a profound influence on organizational behavior and performance. Economic growth, interest rates, the availability of credit, inflation rates, foreign exchange rates, and foreign trade balances are among the most critical economic factors. Economic growth can also have a large impact on consumer demand for products and services. Consequently, organizations should consider forecasts of economic growth in determining when to make critical resource allocation decisions such as plant expansions. Inflation and the availability of credit, among other factors, influence interest rates that organizations have to pay. High interest payments can constrain the strategic flexibility of firms by making new ventures and capacity expansions prohibitively expensive. Low interest rates, such as those experienced in the U.S. in the late 1990s, coupled with fears that the Federal Reserve would raise rates, have led to volatile reactions in the stock market.

Foreign exchange rates are another major source of uncertainty. For global organizations, profit earned in a foreign country may turn into a loss due to unfavorable exchange rates. Finally, foreign trade balances are highly relevant to both domestic and global organizations because they are an indication of the nature of trade legislation that might be expected in the future. For example, the United States has a large trade surplus with the European Union (EU). As a result, American manufacturers who export to the EU are concerned about new protectionist legislation, such as high tariffs, that may be enacted to reduce the trade imbalance.[7]

The socio-cultural forces discussed in the last section often interact with the economic forces. In the United States, birthrates (a socio-cultural force) are low and, because of improved health care and lifestyles (another socio-cultural force), more people are living longer. This demographic shift toward an older population is influencing the economic forces in society. For example, the older population means that demand for premium services are high but, simultaneously, there are shortages of young workers to fill the entry-level jobs, which may drive up wage rates and lead to inflation. So, for example, a service firm tracking these trends may project that its demand will go up as it sells its services to the older customers, but its wage rates will go up as well, leading to lower unit profitability.

To assess the effect of the interdependent socio-cultural and economic forces, organizations often model their business environments using different scenarios. The scenarios are composed of optimistic, pessimistic, and most likely assumptions and interpretations of various economic and socio-cultural trend data collected for the process. Continuing with the previous example, the service firm may develop demand and wage rate scenarios as a way of considering several different possible future business environments. These scenarios can be updated as information becomes firmer, and they may be used for evaluating different courses of action, such as capacity expansions or investments in labor-saving technologies.

This brief discussion of economic forces indicates the importance of monitoring and forecasting events in the global economy. We now turn our attention to the role that technological forces play in the strategic management of organizations.

Global Technological Forces

Technological change creates new products, services, and, in some cases, entire new industries. It also can change the way society behaves and what society expects. The Internet, hand-held computers, direct satellite systems, and cellular telephones are technological innovations that have experienced extraordinary growth in recent years, leaving formerly well-established industries stunned, creating whole new industries, and influencing the way many people approach work and leisure. Computers and telecommunications technologies, for example, have played an essential role in creating the increasingly global marketplace.

Technology refers to human knowledge about products and services and the way they are made and delivered. Technologies typically evolve through a series of steps, and each step has its own set of implications for managers. When a new idea or technology is proven to work in the laboratory, it is called an *invention*. New inventions are made every day—corporate research laboratories, universities, and individuals invent new products, new processes, and new technologies all of the time. Only a handful of those inventions, however, are ever developed past the laboratory stage. When an invention can be replicated reliably on a meaningful scale, it is referred to as an *innovation*. Most technological innovations take the form of new products or processes, such as fax machines, air bags, and cellular phones. A *basic innovation*, such as the microprocessor, light bulb, fiber optics, or mapping of the human genome, impacts much more than one product category or one industry.

To avoid being blindsided by a new technology, organizations should monitor technological developments in industries other than their own and conduct brainstorming sessions about the possible consequences for their own products and markets. For example, drawing from the example at the beginning of the chapter, record companies might have considered the effect of digital sound transmissions via the Internet on their traditional business model before being caught off guard by new start-ups like Napster.

To help identify trends and anticipate their timing, organizations may participate in several kinds of technological forecasting efforts. In general, organizations may monitor trends by studying research journals, government reports, and patent filings. Another more formal method of technological forecasting is to solicit the opinion of experts outside of the organization. These experts may be interviewed directly or contacted as part of a formal survey, such as a Delphi study. A third method is to develop scenarios of alternative technological futures, which capture different rates of innovation and different emerging technologies. Scenarios allow an organization to conduct what-if analyses and to develop alternative plans for responding to new innovations.

In addition to forecasting, some organizations establish strategic alliances with universities or research companies to engage in joint research projects, which allows the companies to keep abreast of new trends. For example, most of the established pharmaceutical firms have partnered with small, innovative biotechnology research firms in order to capture the next generation of biotech-driven product and process technologies. Other organizations simply donate funds to universities for research in exchange for information about findings. The Partnership Data Net, a Washington-based information center on partnerships, lists about 3,000 partnerships between schools and businesses.[8] Akzo NV, the Dutch chemical giant with more than 11,000 employees at 161 locations in North America alone, created a massive partnership with 12 U.S. colleges that has paid healthy dividends in terms of new products.[9]

With a well-thought-out plan for monitoring technological trends, an organization can better prepare itself to receive early warnings about trends that will create opportunities and threats. Now we will turn our attention to the global political and legal forces in the broad environment of organizations.

Global Political/Legal Forces

Political forces, both at home and abroad, are significant determinants of organizational success. The stakes are often high. Concerns about monopoly business practices have garnered more attention from regulators in recent years. As previously discussed, Microsoft was the subject of a monopoly practices investigation and was determined by the courts to be a monopoly. Final actions are pending. Similarly, a proposed merger between WorldCom and Sprint, the telecommunications giants, came under intense scrutiny from antitrust officials. Government officials wanted Sprint to divest its $50 billion long distance services business as a condition for approval. Instead, the deal fell through.[10]

Governments provide and enforce the rules by which organizations operate. Even in the United States, which is considered a "free" market economy, no organization is allowed the privilege of total autonomy from government regulations. Governments can encourage new business formation through tax incentives and subsidies; they can restructure organizations, as in the cases of the AT&T breakup and the planned Microsoft breakup; and they can totally close organizations that do not comply with laws, ordinances, or regulations. Furthermore, alliances among governments provide an additional level of complexity for organizations with significant foreign operations. Nonprofit organizations are as subject to government intervention and regulation as for-profit organizations.

Although all organizations face some form of regulation, the trend is toward deregulation and privatization of industries worldwide. In Portugal, for example, the previously regulated, government-owned banking industry has moved toward privatization. In Eastern Europe, many industries are struggling to survive and prosper in an emerging free market economy. In the United States, the last 20 years has brought the deregulation of airline, banking, long distance telephone communication, and trucking industries. The once highly regulated utility industry is undergoing partial deregulation, which is opening up new opportunities but creating competitive threats as well. Regulation protected these industries from competition, but required set prices and strict operating procedures. With deregulation, existing industry competitors face turbulence and unpredictability. However, deregulation also provides opportunities for new firms to enter the market.

The amount of time and effort organizations should devote to learning about regulations, complying with them, and fostering good relationships with regulatory agencies and their representatives depends, in part, on the industry. Some laws and regulations pertain to only one industry, such as nuclear energy, whereas others, such as Food and Drug Administration (FDA) and Environmental Protection Agency (EPA) regulations, apply different regulations to different industries. Some regulations cut across industry boundaries and apply to all organizations, such as those promulgated by the Occupational Safety and Health Administration (OSHA). In some industries, such as pharmaceuticals and military and defense contracting, organizations employ entire departments of analysts that are dedicated to studying regulations and ensuring compliance.

In summary, social forces, the global economy, technology, and the global political/legal forces make up the broad environment, the context in which the firm and its task environment exist. The next section will discuss the task environment.

THE TASK ENVIRONMENT

The task environment consists of stakeholders with whom organizations interact on a fairly regular basis. These stakeholders include domestic and international customers, suppliers, competitors, government agencies and administrators, local communities, activist groups, unions, and financial intermediaries. Michael Porter, an economist at Harvard University, assimilated years of economic research into a simple model that helps determine the influence of the first three of these stakeholders—suppliers, customers, and competitors—on competition in an industry. His model will be presented in the next section.[11]

Competitive Forces

Michael Porter integrated the theory of industrial organization economics into a "user friendly" model of the forces that drive industry competition. *Industries* are often difficult to define, but in general they refer to a group of organizations that compete directly with each other to win orders or sales in the marketplace. Porter's model includes suppliers, customers, and industry competitors.

Competitors are further divided into three types: existing competitors, potential competitors, and indirect competitors. The influence of potential competitors on industry competition is determined by the strength of entry barriers, in other words, the forces that discourage new firms from entering the industry. Indirect competitors sell products that can be substituted for products sold by existing competitors, such as contact lenses and corrective surgery as substitutes for glasses. According to Porter, the five forces largely determine the type and level of competition in an industry and, ultimately, the industry's profit potential.[12] These forces are illustrated in Exhibit 2.2.

An entire industry (as opposed to a single organization) is placed in the center of the model. One of the most common errors made by new students of strategic management is placing an organization in the middle of the model instead of an industry group. When this happens, substitutes are treated as competing products, which is inconsistent with Porter's ideas concerning the power of substitutes in influencing competition in an industry. Next we will discuss the factors that determine the strength of each of these five forces.

Exhibit 2.2   *Porter's Five-Forces Model of Industry Competition*

Source: Reprinted with permission of The Free Press, a Division of Simon & Schuster, Inc., from *Competitive Advantage: Creating & Sustaining Superior Performance* by Michael E. Porter. Copyright © 1985, 1998 by Michael E. Porter.

Customers. Although all customers are important, some are more important than others. For instance, when retail giant Home Depot announced that it would no longer buy carpet from Shaw Industries (because Shaw, a carpet manufacturer, was moving into retail), Shaw's stock dropped by 11 percent in one day.[13] According to Porter, customers tend to exhibit a powerful force on competition in an industry if the following conditions exist:

1. There are a small number of customers. In this case, losing one customer makes a big difference.
2. The customers make high-volume purchases.
3. The purchases customers make from the industry are large relative to the amount expended for items from other industries. Here customers will expend considerable effort to shop for the best price.
4. The products customers are buying are undifferentiated (also known as standard or generic). This means that customers are not concerned about which company they buy from.
5. The customers earn low profits. Customers who earn low profits are under constant pressure to keep the costs of their purchases down.
6. The customers can easily get accurate information on the selling industry's costs and demand. This gives them a real edge during negotiations.
7. The customers can easily integrate backward and become their own suppliers. Both Sears and General Motors have been known to buy supplier companies when they are unhappy with pricing.
8. Customers can easily switch from one seller to another.

In combination, these forces determine the bargaining power of customers, that is, the degree to which customers exercise active influence over pricing and the direction of product development efforts. The large discount retailers such as Wal-Mart, Kmart, and Target are powerful because of high-volume purchases and the ease with which they switch from one manufacturer to another for many products.

Suppliers. Suppliers to industries provide equipment, supplies, component parts, and raw materials. The labor and capital markets from which firms draw their employees and investment funds are also a source of supply. Powerful suppliers can raise their prices and therefore reduce profitability levels in the buying industry. They can also exert influence and increase uncertainty for the buying industry by *threatening* to raise prices, reducing the quality of goods or services provided, or not delivering supplies when needed. In general, supplier power is greater under the following circumstances:

1. Only a few suppliers are available.
2. Few substitutes exist for the product or service that is supplied. (These first two conditions limit the ability of the buying industry to use alternative supply sources as a bargaining tool.)
3. Suppliers are not dependent on the buying industry for a large percentage of their total sales. This means that the loss of one sale is not very important.
4. Suppliers know that the buying industry must have the product or service that suppliers provide to manufacture their own products.

5. Suppliers have differentiated their products, which means that the buying industry is willing to pay more for certain brands.
6. Suppliers make it costly to switch suppliers. IBM built its mainframe business by making IBM mainframes incompatible with other brands, thus preventing buyers from switching.
7. Suppliers can easily integrate forward and thus compete directly with their former buyers.

These forces combine to determine the strength of suppliers and the degree to which they can exert influence over the profits earned by firms in the industry. The notebook computer industry, for instance, is one that is particularly susceptible to the power of suppliers. Most of the industry competitors purchase microprocessors, batteries, operating system software, and flat-panel displays from suppliers. Consequently, the manufacturing costs, performance characteristics, and innovativeness of the notebook computer are largely in the hands of suppliers.

Existing Competitors. In most industries, competitive moves by one firm affect other firms in the industry, which may incite retaliation or countermoves. Competitors jockey with each other for market share and for the favorable comments of investment analysts. In many industries, every new product introduction, marketing promotion, and capacity expansion has implications for the revenues, costs, and profits of other competitors. Overall profitability is most susceptible to negative pressures from competitive rivalry in industries characterized by the following:

1. Slow industry growth, which means that competitors must steal market share if they intend to grow.
2. High fixed costs, which mean that firms are under pressure to increase sales to cover their costs and earn profits.
3. Lack of product differentiation, which puts a lot of pressure on prices and often leads to price-cutting strategies.
4. A large numbers of competitors, which means that the total market must be divided in more ways.
5. High exit barriers, which means that firms may lose all or most of their investments in the industry when they withdraw from it. Therefore, they are more likely to remain in the industry even if profits are low.

In many industries, competition is so intense that profitability is suppressed to almost nothing, as has been the case at various times in the airline, small computer, and fast food industries.

Potential Competitors/Entry Barriers. Several forces determine the ease with which new competitors can enter an industry and, therefore, how many new entrants can be expected. New entrants increase competition in an industry, which may drive down prices and profits. They may add capacity, introduce new products or processes, and bring a fresh perspective and new ideas—all of which can drive down prices, increase costs, or both. Forces that keep new entrants out, providing a level of protection for existing competitors, are called *entry barriers*.

Examples of entry barriers that are found in many industries include the following:

1. Economies of scale, which occur when it is more efficient to produce a product in a larger facility at higher volume.
2. Large capital requirements, also known as start-up costs, can prevent a small competitor from entering an industry.
3. High levels of product differentiation, which means that some firms enjoy a loyal customer base, making it harder for a new firm to draw away customers.
4. High switching costs, which apply not only to suppliers, can also serve as an entry barrier protecting established firms in an industry.
5. Limited access to distribution channels, which may prevent new companies from getting their products to market.
6. Government policies and regulations that limit entry into an industry, effectively preventing new competition.
7. Existing firm possession of resources that are difficult to duplicate in the short term, such as patents, favorable locations, proprietary product technology, government subsidies, or access to scarce raw materials.
8. A past history of aggressive retaliation by industry competitors toward new entrants.

Taken together, these forces can result in high, medium, or low barriers. In industries with high entry barriers, few new firms enter the industry, which reduces the competitive intensity and stabilizes profits for industry incumbents. When entry barriers are low, new firms can freely enter the industry, which increases rivalry and depletes profits. Examples of industries that are traditionally associated with high barriers to entry are aircraft manufacturing (due to technology, capital costs, and reputation) and automobiles manufacturing (due to capital costs, distribution, and brand names). Medium-high barriers are associated with industries such as household appliances, cosmetics, and books. Low entry barriers are found in industries such as apparel manufacturing and most forms of retailing. One of the most powerful effects of the Internet has been the ability to circumvent traditional barriers to entry. For many Americans, Amazon.com is as synonymous with book retailing as Barnes and Noble. Amazon, however, never had to face the extraordinary expense of leasing or buying land, building large bookstores in premium retail locations, stocking and maintaining inventories in remote locations, and hiring and training a workforce experienced in the nuances of book retailing. They circumvented those barriers to entry by going straight to consumers with an exclusive Internet strategy.

Indirect Competitors/Substitutes. If organizations provide goods or services that readily substitute for the goods and services provided by an industry, those organizations become indirect competitors. For example, aspirin, ibuprofen, and acetaminophen are all substitute pain relievers. In the service sector, credit unions are substitutes for banks and bus travel is a substitute for airline travel. Close substitutes can place a ceiling on the price that an industry can be charged for a good or service. For example, if the price of naproxen (e.g., Aleve) pain reliever/fever reducer becomes too high, many consumers who typically prefer it may switch to aspirin, acetaminophen (e.g., Tylenol), or ibuprofen (e.g., Advil).

Although Porter does not explicitly address other factors in his original model, other stakeholder groups exist that can influence an industry's profitability. Special interest groups and government agencies, for example, take actions that cause organizations to invest money, which can influence cost structures and profits. For example, improvements in automotive fuel efficiency and safety are largely the result of pressures from consumer groups and regulators.

An analysis of the five forces is useful from several perspectives. First, by understanding how the five forces influence competition and profitability in an industry, a firm can better understand how to position itself relative to these forces, determine any sources of competitive advantage now and in the future, and estimate the profits that it can expect. Firm managers may also decide to alter the influence of the five forces by actions such as erecting higher entry barriers through large-scale economies or greater product differentiation, or by creating switching costs to encourage customer loyalty. Frequent-flyer programs that reward customers for loyalty to one airline are an attempt to battle price comparisons and ease of switching.

An organization can also analyze the five forces within an industry prior to entry or as a basis for deciding to leave the industry. As a result of such an analysis, a firm may conclude that an industry is not attractive because of low entry barriers, powerful suppliers or buyers, close substitutes, or the number and strength of current competitors. In general, a thorough understanding of the forces within an industry can help a firm better understand the industry's overall profit potential and those forces most likely to create opportunities and threats.

This completes our discussion of Porter's model, which we used to consider the power of several important stakeholder groups. The next section provides ideas concerning how to manage external stakeholders.

External Stakeholders and Environmental Uncertainty

In an effort to deal with the increasing complexity and competitiveness of the world economy, organizations are coming together in partnerships in increasing numbers. These partnerships come in many forms, such as joint ventures, consortia, and many types of informal alliances. Organizations interact with a large number of external stakeholders. One of the important strategic questions organizations face is deciding which stakeholders should become partners. Stakeholders that are high priority for partnerships are those that have a strong influence on the outcomes of the organization. For example, Toys 'R' Us will have a large influence on Mattel's profits due to the large orders that it places. Or, a newly appointed, aggressive government regulator may be able to dramatically alter the way a firm will operate. These types of stakeholders powerfully influence the environmental uncertainty that an organization faces.

Environmental uncertainty reduces a firm's ability to predict with confidence the future state of its environment, such as demand, competitor actions, new regulation, the cost of supplies, or the availability of labor. If the environment were highly predictable, the management task would be fairly simple and profits would be relatively easy to achieve. On the other hand, high levels of environmental uncertainty reduce an organization's ability to chart an effective course into the future. From this perspective, stakeholders that (1) contribute to the environmental uncertainty facing a firm or (2) are able to reduce the environmental uncertainty facing a firm, should be given higher priority for partnerships.[14] An example from the space industry demonstrates this point:

In the early '90s, Lockheed Space Operations Company (LSOC), a division of what is now Lockheed Martin, experienced a very high level of environmental uncertainty due to changes in the way the U.S. government was managing the space program. For years, the U.S. government had been putting increasing pressure on government agencies to reduce costs. Under one of its cost initiatives, the government decided that the many contracts associated with the space shuttle and rocket operations at Kennedy Space Center should be managed by one prime contractor.

Executives at LSOC, who were largely responsible for the space shuttle launch operations, were concerned that they might not win the bid to manage the Center due to the political clout of Rockwell. Rockwell had built the space shuttle and trained many of the astronauts who were now high-level government officials. To reduce the uncertainty associated with this situation, LSOC formed a joint venture with Rockwell to run the Kennedy Space Center. The joint venture, called United States Alliance (USA), was selected by the government from among several other contenders.

Partnering with External Stakeholders

Partnering tactics are not new. What is new is that they are being used with increasing frequency and with a broader base of stakeholders. Exhibit 2.3 contains some of the more traditional techniques for managing external stakeholders, as well as several examples of partnering strategies. The first column in Exhibit 2.3 lists a few traditional stakeholder management techniques, grouped by type of external stakeholder. These techniques are both common and essential, and they should be used where appropriate. Many of these techniques are intended to protect the organization from negative influences. However, recently the emphasis in stakeholder management has been shifting away from protecting the organization from the influence of external stakeholders toward treating stakeholders almost as if they are part of the internal organization (see the second column of Exhibit 2.3). The rest of this chapter presents a few examples that demonstrate how organizations can manage their task environments.

Efforts to partner with customers and suppliers often provide significant benefits. Many firms are involving strategically important customers and suppliers in product and process design, in quality training sessions, and in on-line production scheduling. For example, Digital Equipment Corporation (DEC) and Hewlett-Packard include suppliers on their product planning teams. DEC also asks managers to evaluate its suppliers as if they were part of the internal organization.[15] G&F Industries, a plastic components manufacturer, has dedicated an employee to Bose, one of its major customers. The employee works full time inside the Bose facility.[16]

To combat collapsing product and process life cycles and to get a jump on new emerging technologies, competitors also are joining forces in increasing numbers. Rival organizations are forming alliances for technological advancement, for new product development, to enter new or foreign markets, and to pursue a wide variety of other opportunities. For example, Goodyear and Michelin, the powerhouse tire makers, plan to join forces for a research and development operation and various other initiatives. Their agreement will involve sharing of licensed technologies, setting a common standard for run-flat tires (tires that run

Exhibit 2.3   *Examples of Tactics for Managing and Partnering with External Stakeholders*

Stakeholders	Traditional Management Tactics	Partnering Tactics
Customers	Customer service departments Marketing research Advertising On-site visits Product/service development Market development	Customer involvement on design teams Customer involvement in product testing Enhanced communication linkages Joint training/service programs Sharing of facilities Appointments to board of directors
Suppliers	Purchasing departments Encourage competition among suppliers Sponsor new suppliers Threat of vertical integration Long-term contracts	Supplier involvement on design teams Integration of ordering system with manufacturing Shared information systems Joint development of new products Appointments to board of directors
Competitors	Competing on the basis of differentiation, technology innovation, speed price cutting, market segmentation Intelligence systems Corporate spying and espionage*	*Keiretsu** Joint ventures for R&D or market development Collective lobbying efforts Informal price leadership or collusion* Mergers (horizontal integration)
Government Agencies-Administrators	Legal/tax departments Government relations departments Lobbying/political action committees Campaign contributions Personal gifts to politicians*	Joint or government sponsored research Joint ventures to work on social problems Joint foreign development projects Appointment of retired government officials to the board of directors
Local Communities-Governments	Community relations offices Public relations advertising Involvement in community service/politics Donations to government/charities organizations Gifts to local government officials*	Joint urban renewal programs Cooperative training programs Development committees/boards Employment programs Joint education programs
Activist Groups	Public/political relations efforts to offset or protect them from negative publicity Financial donations	Consultation with members on sensitive issues Joint ventures for research/research consortia Appointment of group representatives to board
Unions	Avoid unions through high levels of employee satisfaction Thwarting attempts to organize Hiring of professional negotiators Public relations advertising	Mutually satisfactory (win-win) labor contracts Contract clauses that link pay to performance Joint committees on safety and other issues Labor leaders appointed to board of directors and included in major decisions
Financial Intermediaries	Financial reports/audits Finance and accounting departments High-level financial officer	Inclusion in decisions requiring financial backing Appointments to the board of directors Shared ownership of new projects

*These tactics are of questionable ethical acceptability to some internal and external stakeholders in the United States and elsewhere.

after the air is gone), and introduction of a jointly developed, integrated wheel and tire system.[17] Rivals may also partner through a trade association, with the intention of pooling their resources to get the attention of potential customers, as is the case with the "Got Milk?" campaign.

In oligopolies, where a few major rivals dominate an industry, the major firms may cooperate with each other in setting prices. Formal price-setting cooperation is called *collusion*, and it is illegal in the United States and many other countries. However, firms may still cooperate informally by being careful not to drop prices enough to start a price war.

Organizations may form alliances with rivals in an effort to influence common stakeholders such as government agencies, activist groups, unions, or local communities. These alliances then become a part of the organization's *political strategy*, which includes all organizational activities that have as one of their objectives the creation of a friendlier political climate for the organization. Lobbying is part of a political strategy, but it is only a small part of the bigger political picture. Collective activity may include membership in trade associations, chambers of commerce, and industry and labor panels. Firms join associations to gain access to information and to obtain legitimacy, acceptance, and influence.[18] Finally, many organizations form alliances directly with government agencies and officials to pursue a wide variety of objectives, including basic research, finding answers to social problems, and establishing trade policies.

Although this section has focused primarily on stakeholders that are likely to be high priority, such as customers, suppliers, competitors, and government agencies and administrators, partnerships with some of the other stakeholders listed in Exhibit 2.3 have brought equally impressive results. For example, the New England Electric System (NEES) utility formed a partnership with the Conservation Law Foundation, a New England-based environmental organization, to deal with conservation, load management, and regulatory and rate adjustments. As a result of this collaboration, it is estimated that one-third of the planned power plants in the region will not have to be built until the year 2010, releasing this capital for other uses. New England Electric saved capital and the Conservation Law Foundation helped reduce, among other things, air pollution and respiratory problems in the affected areas. It was a win-win situation.[19]

This chapter has discussed methods that firms can use to analyze and, to the extent possible, manage their external environments through partnerships and other strategies. The final section will present a tool that helps organizations understand the strategies of their competitors.

STRATEGIC GROUPS

In some industries, groups of competitors are constrained by similar resource positions and follow similar strategies. The groups or clusters of similar competitors are called *strategic groups*. For example, in the steel industry, domestic steel companies are of two general types: integrated continuous mills and mini-mills. Traditionally, the two groups of competitors faced very different cost structures and competed in largely different market segments. In recent years, the integrated mills have invested in mini-mill technology, and the mini-mill firms have developed new technologies to enter previously inaccessible market segments. Over time, the resource positions and strategies are converging, and the sharp differences between strategic groups are eroding.

One way to keep track of strategic groups and their behavior over time is with a strategic group map such as the one in Exhibit 2.4. A *strategic group map* is constructed by plotting industry rivals based on two or more strategic dimensions that are important to strategy in the industry. The axes of a strategic group map should describe strategy and not performance. Therefore, variables such as pricing strategy, customer service approach, level of advertising, and product mix are appropriate, whereas return-on-assets and earnings-per-share are not. Furthermore, to reveal more about the industry, the dimensions should not be highly correlated with one another. Members of the same strategic group should end up in the same general location on the map.

Strategic group maps can help an organization understand the strategies of competitors. They may also highlight an area in the industry in which no firms are presently competing (an opportunity). Another helpful use is in tracking the evolution of an industry over time. If movement from one group to another is difficult, then it is likely that mobility barriers exist. Mobility barriers are similar to entry barriers, but exist between strategic groups within one industry.

Exhibit 2.4   *Strategic Group Map of Department Store and Specialty Retailing*

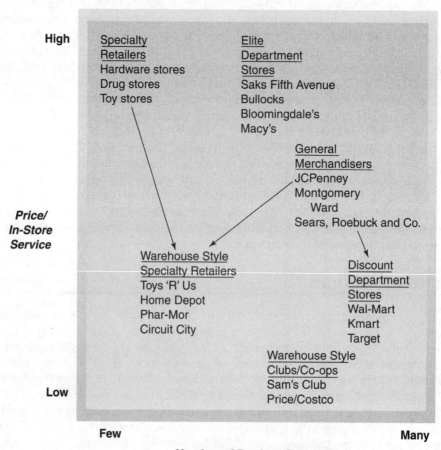

KEY POINTS SUMMARY

This chapter dealt with the external environment, which consists of the broad and task environments. The following are key points from this discussion:

1. The most important elements in the broad environment, as it relates to a business organization and its task environment, are socio-cultural forces, global economic forces, technological forces, and global political/legal forces. Organizations use a variety of techniques, including brainstorming, scenario development, surveys, and expert opinion to forecast changes in this environment.

2. One important distinction between the task and broad environments is that the task environment is subject to a high level of organizational influence, whereas the broad environment is not.

3. The task environment includes external stakeholders such as customers, suppliers, competitors, government agencies and administrators, local communities, activist groups, unions, and financial intermediaries.

4. The five primary forces that determine the nature and level of competition in an industry include the strength of customers, the strength of suppliers, the availability of substitutes, the strength of entry barriers, and forces that determine the nature of existing competition.

5. Organizations should use partnering tactics to manage external stakeholders that have a large influence on the environmental uncertainty facing the organization. On the other hand, traditional monitoring techniques can be used to anticipate the needs of lower-priority stakeholders.

6. Important partnering tactics include joint ventures and other forms of strategic alliances, the establishment of mutually beneficial contracts, various forms of stakeholder involvement in organizational processes and decisions, and the development of political alliances to promote a favorable task environment.

7. Strategic group maps can help organizations understand the strategies of their competitors.

END NOTES

1. D. Clark and M. Peers, "Music Companies Fight Back, Hoping Downloads for Fees Can Prove as Popular as Free," *The Wall Street Journal* (June 20, 2000): B1; L. Gomes, "Napster is Ordered to Stop the Music," *The Wall Street Journal* (July 27, 2000): A3; K.T. Greenfeld, "The Digital Reckoning," *Time* (May 22, 2000): 56.

2. D. Brittan, "Waiting for Uncle Bill," *MIT's Technology Review* 100(3) (1997): 69.

3. A. Serwer, "Bill Gates Gets Really Generous," *Fortune* (March 1, 1999): 35.

4. F. Rice, "Denny's Changes Its Spots," *Fortune* (May 13, 1996): 133–134.

5. M. Thomas, "Advantica Tops Fortune's List of Best Companies for Minorities," *The State* (June 27, 2000): 1.

6. D.R. Dalton, M.B. Metzger, and J.W. Hill, "The 'New' U.S. Sentencing Commission Guidelines: A Wake-up Call for Corporate America," *Academy of Management Executive* (February 1994): 7–16.

7. R.A. Melcher, "Europe, Too, Is Edgy about Imports From America," *Business Week* (January 27, 1992): 48–49.

8. S.A. Waddock, "Building Successful Social Partnerships," *Sloan Management Review* (Summer 1988): 18.

9. J. Vleggaar, "The Dutch Go Back to School for R&D," *The Journal of Business Strategy* (March/April 1991): 8.

10. "WorldCom, Sprint Continue Antitrust Discussions," *The Wall Street Journal* (June 23, 2000): B6.

11. M.E. Porter, *Competitive Strategy: Techniques for Analyzing Industries and Companies* (New York: The Free Press, 1980);

D.F. Jennings and J.R. Lumpkin, "Insights between Environmental Scanning Activities and Porter's Generic Strategies: An Empirical Analysis," *Journal of Management* 18 (1982): 791–803.

12. This section on competitive forces draws heavily on the pioneering work of Michael Porter. See M.E. Porter, *Competitive Strategy: Techniques for Analyzing Industries and Competitors* (New York: The Free Press, 1980): 1–33.

13. "Retail," *Orlando Sentinel* (February 1, 1996): C1.

14. W.P. Burgers, C.W.L. Hill, and W.C. Kim, "The Theory of Global Strategic Alliances: The Case of the Global Auto Industry," *Strategic Management Journal* 14 (1993): 419–432; J.S. Harrison and C.H. St. John, "Managing and Partnering with External Stakeholders," *Academy of Management Executive* (May 1996): 50–60.

15. R.M. Kantar, "The New Managerial Work," *Harvard Business Review* (November/December 1989): 85–92.

16. F.R. Bleakley, "Some Companies Let Suppliers Work on Site and Even Place Orders," *The Wall Street Journal*, (January 13, 1995): A1, A6.

17. C. Ansberry, "Goodyear, Michelin Hope to Raise Sales of Run-flat Tires," *The Wall Street Journal* (June 23, 2000): A12.

18. W.R. Scott, *Organizations: Rational, Natural, and Open Systems*, 3rd ed. (Englewood Cliffs, N.J.: Prentice Hall, 1992).

19. T.A. Hemphill, "Strange Bedfellows Cozy Up for a Clean Environment," *Business and Society Review* (Summer 1990): 38–45.

CHAPTER

3

The Internal Environment and Strategic Direction

Apple Computer

Steven Jobs has been described as one of the most charismatic leaders to ever head a company. He was one of the original founders of Apple Computer, and widely regarded as the visionary force behind the company that launched the microcomputer industry. The Apple strategy was centered on creative, user-friendly designs that made computers more like toys than business machines. In 1985, after he and his hand-picked CEO John Sculley differed on the direction of Apple, Steve Jobs was forced out of the company he created.

Following Jobs' departure, Apple experienced some good and bad years—then experienced stagnation and ultimately decline. Product innovations failed, strategies were inconsistent, market share fell, and morale plummeted. Sculley was eventually forced out, and a series of undistinguished CEOs followed. The company that used great design to change the dynamics of the computer industry was no longer a real competitor.

In 1997, Steven Jobs was invited back to Apple to execute a turnaround. Since his return, the company has undergone an extraordinary recovery. Jobs has restored the commitment to design and a culture of creativity. In the words of Fortune reporter, Christine Chen, Jobs is committed to "use the Internet to make Apple's competitors show up Wintel (Windows-Intel) PCs rather than merely staying even. … Jobs has marshaled the management team, the operational prowess, and the engineering skill that enable Apple to dream up and deliver genuinely innovative products and services quickly. Long known for its melodramatic, snafu-ridden, often downright dysfunctional culture, the company now routinely meets and even beats deadlines."

Jobs' leadership style is often described as charismatic, visionary, and harsh in the same breath. "No detail was too trivial to escape his scrutiny." He uses vivid metaphors and powerful communications skills to argue his vision for the future. In his words, "I don't want to toot our own horn too much, because it sounds arrogant, but the rest of the industry is trying to copy our every move again, just like in the '80s."[1]

In this chapter we turn our attention inside the organization: to the organization's resources and the executive managers who are responsible for developing those resources into capabilities and sources of competitive advantage. An executive such as Steven Jobs can have a profound influence on the way an organization is managed— the direction and strategy the organization will pursue, the culture or personality of the workforce, and the allocation of resources to build sustainable competitive advantages. The most successful organizations typically have excellent resources and managers and, like Apple in the year 2000, have a strong sense of direction. We will first discuss how internal resources and executive managers contribute to the strategic competitiveness of organizations, and then we will describe the tools organizations use to develop and communicate strategic direction.

THE INTERNAL ENVIRONMENT

Internal stakeholders include managers, employees, and owners, which in public corporations are represented by a board of directors. One of the most significant internal stakeholders is the chief executive officer (CEO). Most of the research indicates that CEOs have a significant impact on the strategies and performance of their organizations.[2] Certainly, CEOs like Steven Jobs at Apple, Michael D. Eisner at Disney, Bill Gates at Microsoft, or Andy Grove at Intel leave little doubt that much of an organization's success depends on the person at the top.

The Chief Executive Officer

The highest-ranking officer in a large organization can be called by a number of titles, but the most common is *chief executive officer*, or CEO. The CEO has primary responsibility for setting the strategic direction of the firm, although larger organizations are typically led by several high-ranking officers such as chief operating officers and vice presidents who form the *top management team*.

Top executives and managers perform a variety of functions both inside and outside of their organizations. Based on in-depth observations of managers at work, strategy scholar Henry Mintzberg concluded that these functions include figurehead, spokesperson, leader, resource allocator, monitor, liaison with outside groups, disseminator of information to internal stakeholders, disturbance handler, entrepreneur, and negotiator.[3] Most of these functions deal specifically with managing stakeholders.

The most important responsibility of a CEO is to exercise strategic leadership, which encompasses many of the functions identified by Mintzberg. The traditional view of leaders in organizations is that they set direction, make the important decisions, and rally the followers (usually employees). According to Peter Senge, a professor at MIT, this traditional view is particularly common in the West where leaders are often equated with heroes.[4] There are many examples of visionary decision makers in recent years. Lee Iaccoca of Chrysler, Steven Jobs of Apple Computer, Bill Gates of Microsoft, and Jeff Bezos of Amazon.com are just a few of the CEOs who are widely viewed as visionary leaders. It is common for organizations to incorporate stories about their great leaders in the myths and rituals that form the organizational culture.[5]

In the traditional model of leadership, the CEO decides where to go and then, through a combination of persuasion and edict, directs others in the process of implementation.[6] For many organizational scholars, the traditional view of the CEO and upper management as brilliant, charismatic leaders with employees who are "good soldiers" is no longer valid in many organization settings. Turbulent global competitive environments and multibusiness organizations are far too complex for one person to stay on top of all the important issues, or for one person to exhibit the same leadership style with every situation.[7]

Many organizational scholars believe that the true role of the CEO is to harness the creative energy of the individual, so that the organization as a whole learns over time.[8] In this capacity, the CEO has four primary responsibilities. First, he or she must create or design the organization's purpose, vision, and core values. Second, the CEO must oversee the creation of policies, strategies, and structure that translate purpose, vision, and core values into business decisions.

These first two responsibilities are consistent with what we expect of organizational leaders: they establish direction and purpose, and then install the management systems that coordinate decisions and actions.

It is with the third responsibility of leadership that a new role begins to emerge. Rather than directing, the CEO should create an environment for organizational learning by serving as a coach, teacher, and facilitator.[9] A learning environment is created by helping organizational members question their assumptions about the business and its environment: what customers want, what competitors are likely to do, which technology choices work best, and how to solve a problem. For learning to take place, members must understand that the organization is an interdependent network of people and activities. Furthermore, learning requires that members keep their work focused on creating patterns of behavior that are consistent with strategy rather than reacting haphazardly to problems. Leaders play the essential role in creating an environment where employees question assumptions, understand interdependency, see the strategic significance of their actions, and are empowered to lead themselves.[10]

Finally, CEOs and other managers must serve as stewards for their organizations: they must care about the organization and the society in which it operates. Organizational leaders must feel and convey a passion for the organization, its contribution to society, and its purpose. They should feel that "they are part of changing the way businesses operate, not from a vague philanthropic urge, but from a conviction that their efforts will produce more productive organizations, capable of achieving higher levels of organization success and personal satisfaction than more traditional organizations."[11] This concept is best illustrated with a quote from Stanley Gault shortly after he took over struggling Goodyear Tire and Rubber Company:

> People would say, "Why would you undertake this challenge?" Well, frankly, the decision was 98% emotional because Goodyear is the last major American-owned tire company. . . .Therefore, I decided that I was willing to change my life for three years if there was any way I could lead the charge to rebuild Goodyear.[12]

There is an on-going debate as to whether it is appropriate to try to match particular manager attributes to the type of strategy the firm is pursuing.[13] Some research suggests that strategies focused on cost reduction are best implemented by managers with production/operations backgrounds because of the internal focus on efficiency and engineering. The research also suggests that strategies focused on developing differences that customers will value need to be managed by marketing and R&D-trained executives because of the innovation and market awareness that are needed.[14] There is also some tentative evidence that strategic change or innovation in organizations is more likely to occur with managers that are younger (both in age and in time in the organization) but well educated.[15] Growth strategies may be best implemented by managers with greater sales and marketing experience, willingness to take risks, and tolerance for ambiguity. However, those same characteristics may be undesirable in an executive managing the activities of a retrenchment strategy.[16] Finally, when radical restructuring is required, a less-biased outsider may be needed.[17] Unfortunately, until additional research confirms or disproves these various findings, adherence to these prescriptions may be risky.

Other organizational scholars and consultants believe that leaders should employ different styles of leadership as situations change. Daniel Goleman, a leadership consultant with Hay/McBer, argues that leadership styles are not inherently ingrained in the individual, but can be changed to suit the situation. He believes that leaders should exhibit many styles and should seek to expand their repertory of leadership behaviors.[18] For example, in a crisis or situation requiring fast action, a leader may find it necessary to exhibit a coercive "do what I tell you" or "do what I do, now" style. These styles, while negative in the long run, may be required in some circumstances. More coaching and consensus-building styles are appropriate when attempting to improve employee performance, improve communication, stimulate creativity, and get valuable input from employees.

Boards of Directors and Agency Costs

Most larger companies, and smaller companies needing funds for growth, have issued stock. Therefore, their owners are the shareholders. If all of the stock is owned by a few individuals, often within the same family, the company is referred to as closely held or private. On the other hand, in larger, publicly owned companies, the interests of shareholders are protected by a board of directors, who are elected by the voting shareholders. The board of directors is responsible for hiring, firing, supervising, advising, and compensating top managers within the firm. Boards typically also reserve the right to reject major strategic decisions such as the development of a new line of business, mergers, acquisitions, or entrance into foreign markets.

Boards of directors play an important strategic role as monitors of conflicts of interest. As soon as ownership and management are separated, as is the case in most public organizations, the potential for conflicts of interest exists. Top managers become *agents* for the owners of the firm—they have a fiduciary duty to act in the owners' best interests. On occasion, top managers, as human beings, attempt to maximize their own self-interests at the expense of shareholders. When this occurs, it is called an *agency problem*.[19] Some examples of agency problems are shown in Exhibit 3.1.

One responsibility of boards is to monitor and prevent the potential for agency problems. For example, boards need sufficient power to both monitor and discipline CEOs. Vigilant boards are widely regarded as the best defense against conflicts of interest.[20] Even so, some business experts believe that many boards are negligent in their fiduciary duties associated with reprimanding or replacing top managers who are not acting in the best interests of shareholders, and they point to increasing incidence of shareholder suits against boards of directors as evidence of that concern.[21] In addition, big investors are putting lots of pressure on board members and directly on CEOs to initiate sweeping organizational changes that will lead to more accountability and higher performance.[22]

Many boards have responded to these and other forces by taking a more active role in corporate governance. Some years ago, John G. Smale, past CEO of Procter & Gamble and a 10-year veteran of General Motor's board of directors, was dissatisfied with GM's lackluster performance. He convinced other board members to elect him to the position of chairman of the executive committee, which effectively put him in control of GM. In what is now called a board revolt, he initiated the replacement of the CEO, which set GM on a new strategic course.[23] The GM

Exhibit 3.1   *Evidence of Agency Problems*

The following are a few commonly mentioned problems that may be evidence of agency conflicts:

High Salaries
It is in the best interests of CEOs to draw a high salary; however, these high salaries reduce the amount of earnings available to the shareholders. CEO compensation packages for the largest U.S. companies typically reach into the millions of dollars annually.

Current Expenses versus Future Investments
Since research and development expenditures reduce current earnings and often do not provide financial benefits for many years, CEOs who are compensated based on profitability levels have a built-in incentive not to approve research projects.

Status and Growth
Some power-hungry or status-conscious top managers may expand the size of their empires at the expense of organizational shareholders. For example, a few years ago Harding Lawrence led Braniff Airways to financial ruin through overzealous growth.

CEO Duality
CEO duality means that the CEO is also the chair of the board of directors. As chair, the CEO is in a strong position to ensure that personal interests are served even if the other stakeholders' interests are not.

---

board coup was followed by a wave of similar actions in several large companies, including IBM, Time Warner, American Express, and Westinghouse.[24]

The inclusion of several non-employee individuals (outsiders) on the board can help ensure that shareholder interests are well served. Outsiders were an important factor in the board revolt at GM. In fact, research indicates that the percentage of outsiders on the board of directors is increasing.[25] However, inclusion of outsiders may not be a potent force in reducing agency problems if external board members are personal friends of the CEO or other top managers. These types of relationships often limit the objectivity of outsiders.

The previous discussion demonstrated the importance of boards of directors in governing the behavior of top managers. However, boards can also play other important strategic roles, such as assisting in deciding strategic direction and in forming strategic alliances. Two recent studies, in fact, discovered higher performance in companies with boards that participated more actively in organizational decisions, compared to companies with "caretaker" boards.[26]

In 1999, Korn/Ferry International reported the results of an analysis of corporate board trends from 1973 to the present.[27] The study involved 14,000 CEOs, chairmen, and directors over several years. They concluded that boards have changed substantially since the 1970s. For example, the number of inside and affiliated outside directors in corporate boards has declined steadily since 1973. In the '70s, the typical corporate board had 10 and 15 members, with 8 or 9 inside directors who were either employees or providers of legal or accounting services. Today the average board is smaller, with about 11 members, 9 of whom are independent outsiders. The second major trend is increased prevalence of independent audit, compensation, and nominating committees on boards, composed of all outside directors. Also, boards are more likely to have processes for assessing CEO performance and their own director performance. Interestingly, McKinsey and Co. recently confirmed the findings of academic research when they reported the results of a survey that showed that institutional investors will pay a premium for good corporate governance practices, including mostly outside directors, formal evaluation processes, and compensation of directors through stock options.[28]

Employees and Culture

Employees and the way they are managed can be important sources of competitive advantage.[29] Many executives and human resource professionals believe that management of human resources will become more difficult in the next several years, but will bring a bigger pay-off than ever before. For example, in a survey of CEOs of large U.S. firms, 71 percent of the respondents pointed out the increasing importance of managing part-time, temporary, and contract workers as a major trend in the next decade.[30] In addition to being both specialized and mobile, the workforce is expected to be much more diverse demographically, ethnically, and geographically. These trends should affect job design and reward systems and increase the difficulty of molding an effective organizational culture. A possible upside to this difficulty, however, would be the competitive payoff accruing to firms capable of establishing and maintaining knowledge supply chains.[31]

An organization's culture, the system of shared values that guides employees, is another important component of the internal environment. Organization culture often reflects the values and leadership styles of the executives and managers and is, to a great degree, a result of the past human resource management practices, such as recruitment, training, and rewards.

An organization's culture can be its greatest strength or its greatest weakness. Some organizations have succeeded in creating cultures that are completely consistent with what the organization is trying to accomplish—high performance cultures. At Nucor Steel, the company's stated commitment to a low-cost strategy is supported by a culture that expects efficiency and tight fiscal policy. At Johnson & Johnson, the company's commitment to customers as its primary stakeholder is reflected in policy statements and adopted by employees. In other organizations, poor morale and a cynical attitude toward customers often undermine organizational performance. At Apple Computer, as described at the beginning of the chapter, organizational culture transitioned from positive to negative back to positive, as the leadership in the organization changed.

The first three sections of this chapter have described the human side of the internal environment. CEOs, other managers, the board of directors, employees, and the culture that ties these people together can all be sources of strength or weakness to an organization. The next section is a broader discussion of organizational resources in general and, specifically, how resources and resource management can lead to a sustainable competitive advantage.

Internal Resources and Competitive Advantage

The resources and capabilities that lead to competitive advantage are different in each industry and can also change over time. For example, researchers discovered that high-performing film studios during the period from 1936 to 1950 possessed superior property-based resources such as exclusive long-term contracts with stars and theaters. However, during the period from 1951 to 1965 knowledge-based resources in the form of production and coordinative talent and budgets were associated with high performance. They attributed these findings to the capabilities needed to deal with increasing uncertainty in the film industry.[32] Their study also demonstrates that organizational resources only result in a competitive advantage if they are uniquely valuable in the external environment. Chapter 1 introduced the concept of competitive advantage from uniquely valuable resources. We will now continue the discussion.

Uniquely Valuable Resources.   Chapter 1 described internal resources and capabilities as falling into four general categories: financial, physical, human, and organizational. In general, capabilities and resources become strengths leading to a *competitive advantage* if two conditions are met:

1. The resources or capabilities are *valuable*. They allow the firm to exploit opportunities and/or neutralize threats. For example, Sony has developed the capability to design, manufacture, and sell miniaturized electronics. This capability has value to external stakeholders—namely customers. Sony has applied this capability to numerous market opportunities such as stereos, tape players, disc players, televisions, and video cameras.

2. The resources or capabilities are *unique*. If an organization is the only one with a particular capability, then that capability may be the source of competitive advantage. If numerous organizations possess a particular resource or capability, then the situation is described as competitive parity—no company has the advantage. Note that uniqueness does not imply that only one organization possesses a capability or resource—only that few firms do.

In addition, the competitive advantage becomes sustainable over time if the following third condition is met:

3. The resources or capabilities are *difficult* or *expensive to imitate*. Competing firms face a cost disadvantage in imitating a resource or capability. The more difficult or costly a resource or capability is, the more valuable it is in producing a sustainable competitive advantage. In the case of a patent or a trademark that is enforceable, competing firms face an absolute cost disadvantage.[33] This is one of the potential problems with Internet businesses. The technological innovations that have spawned a flood of new e-tailers are widely available to everyone. It is difficult to create uniqueness, and even more difficult to protect it from imitation.

Exhibit 3.2 demonstrates how resources and capabilities become potential sources of sustainable competitive advantage. McDonald's, for example, has outperformed its competitors for many years because of superior locations (a physical resource), and a highly efficient operations system that delivers a consistent product at low cost (an organizational resource).

For a firm to realize an advantage from unique and valuable resources, the firm must also be organized to take advantage of it. For example, Xerox formed a research laboratory called PARC which, in the late 1960s and 1970s, developed an

Exhibit 3.2   *Organizational Resources and Capabilities Leading to Competitive Advantage*

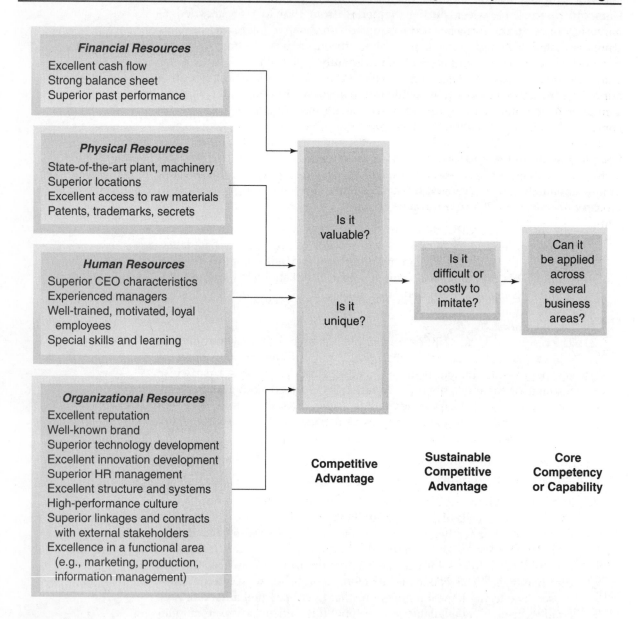

amazing assortment of technological innovations, including the personal computer, the "mouse," the laser printer, and Windows-type software. However, the company did not take advantage of many of PARC's innovations because it did not have an organization in place to do so. For instance, poor communications prevented most Xerox managers from knowing what PARC was doing, and a highly bureaucratic system mired a lot of the innovations in red tape.

If a resource or capability is valuable, unique, hard to imitate, and it also can be applied to more than one business area, it is called a *core competency* or *dis-*

tinctive competence.[34] Companies like Wal-Mart and Disney are masters at exploiting their sources of competitive advantage across different businesses. Disney has extended its unique and valuable animated characters through books, movies, theme parks, and television, showing a distinctive competence in creativity and "imagineering."

Most of the resources and capabilities that have been described are tangible. They can be seen, touched, and/or quantified.[35] However, some of the most important resources are hard to quantify. For many firms, the key to competitive advantage is to combine resources and develop capabilities that are hard to imitate. For example, a patent, which is tangible, may provide an organization with an advantage for a while. But the capability to quickly and accurately develop and introduce new products involves integrating the efforts of several resources: marketing (determining need), design and development engineers (creating the product, specifying raw materials), operations (arranging for raw materials and producing the product), and many others. These integrated resources and capabilities are particularly difficult for competitors to observe and imitate.

Organizational reputation and a well-known corporate brand are also hard to imitate. John Reed, CEO of Citicorp, would like to turn "Citibank" into "a worldwide consumer brand," establishing it, in effect, as the Coca-Cola or McDonald's of financial services. What goes with the brand equity that those companies have, and he covets, is the ability to set themselves above the competition, either in the prices they can obtain or quantities sold or both.[36] Disney also takes full advantage of its brand, which is one of its core competencies. According to Michael Eisner, CEO:

> We are fundamentally an operating company, operating the Disney Brand all over the world, maintaining it, improving it, promoting and advertising it with taste. Our time must be spent insuring that the Brand never slides, that we innovate the Brand, nurture the Brand, experiment and play with it, but never diminish it. Others will try to change it, from outside and from within. We must resist. We are not a fad! The Disney name and products survive fads![37]

Unique configurations of stakeholder relationships can also be very difficult, if not impossible, to imitate.[38] For example, Microsoft has developed a strong web of formal and informal relationships with some of its largest customers. While it may be possible for a company to create a product that is superior to one of Microsoft's products, it would be very difficult for that company to break into the unique configuration of relationships within which Microsoft operates. This type of advantage is also found in the more successful .com companies, such as Yahoo. Early entrants were able to establish critical relationships with hundreds of other companies, making it very difficult for new competitors to establish a competitive foothold.

Financial Resources. Financial resources also can be a source of advantage, although they rarely qualify as "unique" or "difficult to imitate." Nevertheless, strong cash flow, low levels of debt, a strong credit rating, access to low interest capital, and a reputation for creditworthiness are powerful strengths that can serve as a source of strategic flexibility. Firms that are in a strong financial position can be more responsive to new opportunities and new threats, and are under less pressure from stakeholders than their competitors who suffer financial constraints.

Among other things, financial analysis is used to indicate the ability of the firm to finance growth. For example, managers of a firm that has very high leverage (long-term debt) may have to be less ambitious in their strategies for taking advantage of opportunities. On the other hand, an organization with a strong balance sheet is well poised to pursue a wide range of opportunities. Strong financial resources are often hard to imitate in the short term. Financial analysis is also an important strategic tool used by managers in assessing their performance and identifying strengths, weaknesses, and trends. In general, financial analysis involves making two essential comparisons: (1) a comparison of the firm to its competitors, to determine relative financial strengths and weaknesses and (2) a comparison of the firm to itself over time, to show trends.

Firms often attempt to compare their expenses, investments, sources of income, and resulting profitability to competitors as a way of assessing the success of their strategies. A firm may observe that competitors are making more aggressive investments in R&D or paying higher wages to employees, which may heighten competitive intensity in the future. The findings from a competitor comparison must always be weighed against the goals of the firm. For example, a firm's investment in inventories may be higher than that of competitors for one of three reasons: (1) it is not as effective at managing inventories as competitors, which would be a cause for concern; (2) higher levels of inventories support its particular strategy (e.g., fast delivery and guaranteed availability); or (3) the items in inventory or accounting conventions are different, making a meaningless "apples and oranges" comparison.

Firms also track their own expenses and sources of income over time as a way of identifying trends. Poor financial trends are sometimes symptoms of greater problems. For example, a firm may discover that administrative costs are increasing at a faster rate than sales. This could be an indication of diseconomies of scale or the need for tighter controls on overhead costs or, on the contrary, part of a deliberate attempt by the firm to position itself now for future sales growth. Some of the most common ratios used in financial analysis are found in Exhibit 3.3.

Assessing Internal Strengths and Weaknesses

In evaluating the resources and capabilities of the organization, it is important to consider all of the various activities of the business and understand the role they play in building advantage and implementing strategies. Strategy should be based on what the organization does well relative to competitors *or* on the capabilities or resources the firm *wants to develop* that will create a competitive advantage in the future. Organizational constraints should be considered but should not place absolute limits on strategy. Instead, long-term organizational success often depends on developing new competencies.

Value Chain Analysis. Michael Porter developed a framework, called the value chain, which allows systematic study of the various value-adding activities of a business (see Exhibit 3.4).[39] Value chain analysis may be used to identify key resources and processes that represent strengths, areas that need improvement, and opportunities to develop a competitive advantage.

The *value chain* divides organizational processes into distinct activities that create value for the customer. The primary activities include inbound logistics,

Exhibit 3.3   *Commonly Used Financial Ratios*

Ratio	Calculation	What It Measures
Profitability Ratios		
Gross profit margin	$\dfrac{\text{Sales} - \text{COGS}}{\text{Sales}} \times 100$	Efficiency of operations and product pricing
Net profit margin	$\dfrac{\text{Net profit after tax}}{\text{Sales}} \times 100$	Efficiency after all expenses are considered
Return-on-assets (ROA)	$\dfrac{\text{Net profit after tax}}{\text{Total assets}} \times 100$	Productivity of assets
Return-on-equity (ROE)	$\dfrac{\text{Net profit after tax}}{\text{Stockholders' equity}} \times 100$	Earnings power of equity
Liquidity Ratios		
Current ratio	$\dfrac{\text{Current assets}}{\text{Current liabilities}}$	Short-run debt-paying ability
Quick ratio	$\dfrac{\text{Current assets} - \text{Inventories}}{\text{Current liabilities}}$	Short-term liquidity
Leverage Ratios		
Debt-to-equity	$\dfrac{\text{Total liabilities}}{\text{Stockholders' equity}}$	The relative amount of debt and equity financing (common measure of financial risk)
Total debt to total assets (debt ratio)	$\dfrac{\text{Total liabilities}}{\text{Total assets}}$	Percentage of assets financed through borrowing (also a common risk measure)
Activity Ratios		
Asset turnover	$\dfrac{\text{Sales}}{\text{Total assets}}$	Efficiency of asset utilization
Inventory turnover	$\dfrac{\text{COGS}}{\text{Average inventory}}$	Management's ability to control investment in inventory
Average collection period	$\dfrac{\text{Receivables} \times 365 \text{ days}}{\text{Annual credit sales}}$	Effectiveness of collection and credit policies
Accounts receivable turnover	$\dfrac{\text{Annual credit sales}}{\text{Receivables}}$	Effectiveness of collection and credit policies

operations, outbound logistics, marketing and sales, and service. ***Inbound logistics*** includes supply chain activities associated with acquiring inputs that are used in the product—warehousing, materials handling, and inventory control. ***Operations*** refers to transforming inputs into the final product through activities such as machining, assembly, molding, testing, and printing. ***Outbound***

Exhibit 3.4   *The Value Chain Including Support Activities*

Source: Adapted from Michael E. Porter, *Competitive Advantage: Creating and Sustaining Superior Performance*, (New York: The Free Press, 1985): 37. Adapted with permission of The Free Press, a division of Simon & Schuster. Copyright © 1985 by Michael E. Porter.

logistics are activities related to storing and physically distributing the final product to customers, such as finished goods warehousing, order processing, and transportation. *Marketing and sales* include processes through which customers can purchase the product and through which they are induced to do so, such as advertising, distribution of catalogs, direct sales, distribution channeling, promotion, and pricing. Finally, *service* refers to providing service to enhance or maintain product value, such as repairing, supplying parts, or installation.

Organizations also engage in activities that support these primary functions. These activities are placed above the primary activities in Exhibit 3.4. *Procurement* refers to the processes and activities involved in purchasing inputs and not to the inputs themselves or to the way they are handled once they are delivered. *Technology development* refers to product and process development processes and to organizational learning processes, which result in improved products and services and in improvements in the way organizational functions are performed.

Human resource management includes human-based activities such as recruiting, hiring, training, performance evaluation, employee development, and compensation. Finally, *administration* consists of general management activities such as planning and accounting. The dotted lines connecting most of the support activities with the primary activities demonstrates that they can be associated with each of the primary activities as well as support the complete chain. For example, technology developments are generally manifested in the products, services, and processes in the primary value-adding activities. Margin, which is on the right-hand side of the Exhibit 3.4, indicates that firms can achieve higher profit margins through the development of competencies and superior resources based on their value chain activities.

An organization can develop a competitive advantage (1) in any of the primary or support activities *or* (2) in the way they are combined *or* (3) in the way internal activities are linked to the external environment. The cumulative effect of value chain activities and the way they are linked inside the firm and with the external environment determine organizational strengths, weaknesses, and performance relative to competitors.

Functional Analysis. A thorough profile of the strengths and weaknesses of the major value-adding activities requires in-depth study of the specific actions, resources, and capabilities at the functional level. For example, an evaluation of marketing's value-adding performance and potential would consider the number and type of target customers, product positioning, product line mix, product line breadth, pricing strategies, promotion practices, and distribution channels. Each aspect would be characterized as a strength or weakness, then evaluated for its fit with current and future strategic plans. By identifying the specific strengths and weaknesses within each category of value-adding activities, plans can be developed for correcting or avoiding weaknesses and for cultivating and building strengths. A detailed framework for profiling organizational strengths and weaknesses is shown in the case analysis appendix.

We have concluded our discussion of organizational resources and capabilities, value-creation and competitive advantage, and processes for assessing strengths and weaknesses. We will now turn our attention to a discussion of strategic direction.

ESTABLISHMENT OF STRATEGIC DIRECTION

High-performing companies tend to have an organizational identity that is understood by both internal and external stakeholders. On the inside, a well-established organizational identity can provide guidance to managers at all levels as they make strategic decisions.[40] In addition, communicating strategic direction to external stakeholders can increase their understanding of the motives of the organization and may also facilitate the creation of alliances, since potential alliance partners have a greater ability to judge the existence of common goals. Strategic direction is established and communicated through tools such as missions, visions, business definitions, and enterprise strategies. Strategic direction also includes a general orientation toward growth.

Organizational Mission

An organization's mission provides an important vehicle for communicating ideals and a sense of direction and purpose to internal and external stakeholders. It also can help guide organizational managers in resource allocation decisions. Sometimes students of strategic management confuse the terms *mission* and *vision*. In general, organizational mission is what the organization is and its reason for existing, whereas vision is a forward-looking view of what the organization wants to become. For example, the mission and vision of MateriaLink, a business-to-business Internet company start-up, are as follows:

Mission: MateriaLink provides an electronic marketplace that allows buyers in Engine Procurement and Construction (EPC) companies worldwide to source, procure, and dispose of surplus and new materials in the most efficient manner possible.

Vision: MateriaLink is the premier electronic marketplace for project surplus, new and EPC industry information. We will be the preferred provider for all EPC and new materials transactions. We are committed to continuing to provide a site functionality that will enhance profitability and cut costs for our users.[41]

A vision statement is often included or embedded in the formal mission statement. In fact, a formal written mission statement often includes many or all of the elements of strategic direction: vision, business definition, enterprise strategy, and goals. Consequently, a mission is a catch-all statement of organizational purpose.

Organizations often prepare written mission statements as a way of communicating with the public. For example, mission statements are frequently included in annual financial reports to shareholders. Exhibit 3.5 contains the mission statement of Rhone-Poulenc Rorer, a global pharmaceutical organization that resulted from the 1990 merger of Rhone-Poulenc and Rorer. Their mission statement emphasizes their commitment to stakeholders and their ethical standards. The mission of Ashbridge Investment Management, in contrast, provides specific statements about what they do: "To preserve and enhance the wealth of our clients by employing an objective, analytical asset process and advising on relevant financial matters. We work with each client to develop a strategic investment policy which is then implemented to achieve long term financial goals."[42]

Exhibit 3.5   *Sample Mission Statement of Rhone-Poulenc Rorer*

Our Mission is to become the BEST pharmaceutical company in the world by dedicating our resources, our talents and our energies to help improve human health and the quality of life of people throughout the world.

Being the best means:
- Being the BEST at satisfying the needs of everyone we serve: Patients, healthcare professionals, employees, communities, governments and shareholders;
- Being BETTER AND FASTER than our competitors at discovering and bringing to market important new medications in selected therapeutic areas;
- Operating with the HIGHEST professional and ethical standards in all our activities, building on the Rhone-Poulenc and Rorer heritage of integrity;
- Being seen as the BEST place to work, attracting and retaining talented people at all levels by creating an environment that encourages them to develop their potential to the fullest;
- Generating consistently BETTER results than our competitors, through innovation and a total commitment to quality in everything we do.

Source: Annual report.

Business Definition

Derek Abell has argued that clear business definition is the starting point of all strategic planning and management.[43] A clear business definition provides a framework for evaluating the effects of planned change and for planning the steps needed to move the organization forward.

When defining the business, the question "What is our business?" should be answered from three perspectives: (1) Who is being satisfied? (2) What is being satisfied? (3) How are customer needs satisfied?[44] The first question refers to the markets that the organization serves, the second question deals with the specific functions provided to the customers identified in question 1, and the third question refers to the resource conversion processes and capabilities that the firm uses to provide the functions identified in question 2. In actuality, most mission statements also identify specific products or services provided by the organization. In this regard, a fourth question, which is an extension of the third question, can be stated as "What are our products and services?" This approach is, admittedly, marketing-oriented. Its greatest strength is that it focuses on the customer, a very important external stakeholder for most firms.

The *scope* of an organization is the breadth of its activities across markets, functions, resource conversion processes, and products. Some large organizations, such as General Electric and Nestlé, have a very broad scope. Other firms, including L.L. Bean and Nucor, have a narrower scope. Also, there are firms, such as McDonald's, that are very broad on one dimension (geographic markets served), but narrow on all the rest.

Exhibit 3.6 contains three examples of firms and their business definitions, organized around the four areas of a business definition—products and services, markets, functions served, and resource conversion processes (Church & Dwight is the 150-year-old manufacturer of Arm & Hammer baking soda). Notice that the concepts that have been discussed thus far apply equally well to both product and service firms.

Organizational Vision

Peter Drucker suggested that the business definition question should be stated not only as "What is our business?" but also as "What will it be?" and "What should it be?"[45] The second question refers to the direction that the organization is heading at the current time. In other words, where will the organization end up if it continues in its current course? The third question, "What should it be?" allows for modifications to the existing strategy to move the organization in an appropriate direction.

Unlike mission, which addresses an organization's purpose at the present time, an organization's vision is very future-oriented. An organization with a vision has a clear sense of what it wants to be in the future. For example, Bill Gates has a clear vision of how he expects his industry to evolve and the role he wants to play in it. He wants Microsoft to dominate the software systems that link all digital transactions and communications in business, entertainment, and leisure. That vision, which involves a very different "business definition" for the future, provides the framework for creating new businesses and forming new partnerships.

Exhibit 3.6   *Business Definitions of Well-Known Companies*

	Church & Dwight	Toys 'R' Us	Delta Airlines
Products and Services	Baking soda and related consumer products	Children's products	Air transportation
Markets	Grocery stores and bakeries	Children, grandparents, and parents	Business travelers, vacationers, and infrequent travelers
Functions Served	Odor absorbency, baking, cleaning	Availability, entertainment, clothing	Fast, long-distance transportation
Resource Conversion Processes	Chemical processing-packaging, promotion, and advertising	Buying, inventory management, distributing, limited service, promotion, and advertising	Flying, logistics, fleet management, baggage handling, reservations, promotion, and advertising

For many years, Wal-Mart's vision was to become the largest discount retailer in the U.S., a vision that was achieved shortly before Sam Walton's death. In the case of Wal-Mart, the organizational vision did not require a departure from the existing business definition, although it did require continued growth along the "markets served" dimension as new regions were entered. More importantly, Sam Walton and Wal-Mart illustrate how a well-articulated vision of what the company wants to be in the future can be a strong motivational tool. Once it is stated, it may be used to focus the efforts of the entire organization.[46] For example, plans, policies, or programs that are inconsistent with the corporate vision may need to be altered or replaced. A well-understood vision can help managers and employees believe that their actions have meaning. As we will discuss in later chapters, organizations develop specific goals, objectives, and action plans to focus their efforts on those areas that fit the business vision.

Enterprise Strategy and Ethics

One fundamental question an organization should ask in determining its purpose is "What do we stand for?" This question is the critical link between ethics and strategy. *Enterprise strategy* is the term used to denote the joining of ethical and strategic thinking about the organization.[47] It is the organization's best possible reason (assuming there is a reason) for the actions it takes. An enterprise strategy can contain statements concerning a desire to maximize stockholder value, satisfy the interests of all or a subset of other stakeholders, or increase social harmony or the common good of society.[48] For example, in the mission statement of Rhone-Poulenc Rorer (Exhibit 3.5), the enterprise strategy is to "help improve human health and the quality of life of people throughout the world." Some researchers have found that organizational mission statements containing the elements of an enterprise strategy are more likely to be found in high-performing than low-performing corporations.[49]

Enterprise strategy is a natural extension of the ethics of the organization, which are an extension of the values of key managers. The ethics of an organization are not just a matter of public statements. Ethical decision making is a way of doing business. An organization that specifically works to build ethics into its business practice, to develop and implement an enterprise strategy, will have a frame of reference for handling potential ethical problems.

Many organizations create a code of ethics to communicate the values of the corporation to employees and other stakeholders. For example, United Technologies states the following about its code of ethics:

> Our code of ethics, comprised of corporate principles and standards of conduct, governs our business decisions and actions. The integrity, reputation, and profitability of United Technologies ultimately depend upon the individual actions of our employees, representatives, agents and consultants all over the world. Each employee is personally responsible and accountable for compliance with our code.[50]

The United Technologies code of ethics, which is quite long, addresses specific standards of conduct the organization will exhibit in its dealings with customers, suppliers, employees, shareholders, competitors, and worldwide communities. Employees are encouraged to report violations to their supervisors or the Vice President for Business Practices. Clearly, a company like United Technologies expects members to maintain standards of ethical behavior that transcend minimum legal standards. To ensure that employees abide by the corporate code of ethics, some companies establish an ethics system, including an audit process to monitor compliance.

KEY POINTS SUMMARY

This chapter described internal stakeholders and the important roles they play in strategic management processes, followed by a discussion of strategic direction. The following are some of the most important points that were made:

1. The Chief Executive Officer (CEO) is the primary orchestrator of organizational vision and strategies. CEOs perform interpersonal, informational, and decisional functions in organizations, and influence the organization through their personal values and style of strategic leadership.

2. Owners in a for-profit, publicly held corporation, the shareholders, are typically represented by a board of directors, who have the responsibility to oversee the activities of organizational managers and ensure that shareholder interests are protected.

3. Agency problems can exist when boards of directors are weak in carrying out their supervisory responsibilities, when CEOs also serve as chairs of their own boards (e.g., CEO duality), or any time CEOs of other managers act in their own personal interests at the expense of shareholders.

4. Organizations need highly qualified employees if they are going to succeed in the global economy. Training and other human resource management activities are crucial to long-term competitiveness.

5. Other tangible resources that can lead to a competitive advantage include superior financial resources, excellent physical resources, and organizational resources such as excellent management systems and structures. Intangibles such as brands, business relationships, culture, and reputation are

harder to quantify but are some of the most important sources of competitive advantage.

6. For each potential resource or capability, the following questions should be asked: "Is it valuable?" "Is it unique?" "Is it difficult or expensive for competitors to imitate?" Finally, for potential sources of competitive advantage to become real, firms should be organized in such a manner that the full potential is realized.

7. The value chain may be used in determining the strengths and weaknesses of the different value-adding activities of the business and may be useful in identifying sources of competitive advantage.

8. A mission often contains statements concerning the basic purposes and broad goals of an organization, as reflected in its enterprise strategy, a vision of what it can become, and a definition of its business or businesses.

END NOTES

1 Burrows, "Apple," *Business Week* (July 31, 2000): 102–113; Christine Y. Chen, "Steve Jobs' Apple Gets Way Cooler," *Fortune* (January 24, 2000): 66.

2 S. Finkelstein and D.C. Hambrick, *Strategic Leadership: Top Executives and Their Effects on Organizations* (Minneapolis: West Publishing Company, 1996): Chapter 2.

3 H. Mintzberg, *The Nature of Managerial Work* (New York: Harper and Row, 1973).

4 P. Senge, "The Leader's New Work: Building Learning Organizations," *Sloan Management Review* 32(1) (Fall 1990): 7–24.

5 E.H. Schein, *Organization Culture and Leadership* (San Francisco: Jossey-Bass, 1985).

6 Nutt, "Selecting Tactics to Implement Strategic Plans," *Strategic Management Journal* 10 (1989): 145–161.

7 D. Goleman, "Leadership That Gets Results," *Harvard Business Review* (March/April 2000): 78.

8 Senge, "The Leader's New Work"; C.C. Manz and H. Sims, "SuperLeadership," *Organization Dynamics* 17, 4 (1991): 8–36.

9 Senge, "The Leader's New Work."

10 Senge, "The Leader's New Work"; Manz and Sims, "SuperLeadership."

11 Senge, "The Leader's New Work," 13.

12 J.M. Graves, "Leaders of Corporate Change," Fortune (December 14,1992): 104–114.

13 J.G. Michel and D.C. Hambrick, "Diversification Posture and Top Management Team Characteristics," *Academy of Management Journal* 35 (1992): 9–37; S.F. Slater, "The Influence of Style on Business Unit Performance," *Journal of Management* 15 (1989): 441–455; A.S. Thomas, R.J. Litschert, and K. Ramaswamy, "The Performance Impact of Strategy-Manager Coalignment: An Empirical Examination," *Strategic Management Journal* 12 (1991): 509–522.

14 V. Govindarajan, "Implementing Competitive Strategies at the Business Unit Level: Implications of Matching Managers to Strategies," *Strategic Management Journal* 10 (1989): 251–269.

15 K.A. Bantel and S.E. Jackson, "Top Management and Innovations in Banking: Does the Composition of the Top Team Make a Difference?" *Strategic Management Journal* 10 (1989): 107–124; C.M. Grimm and K.G. Smith, "Management and Organizational Change: A Note on the Railroad Industry," *Strategic Management Journal* 12 (1991): 557–562; M.F. Wiersema and K.A. Bantel, "Top Management Team Demography and Corporate Strategic Change," *Academy of Management Journal* 35 (1992): 91–121.

16 Gupta and V. Govindarajan, "Business Unit Strategy, Managerial Characteristics, and Business Unit Effectiveness at Strategy Implementation," *Academy of Management Journal* 27 (1984): 25–41.

17 B. Brenner, "Tough Times, Tough Bosses: Corporate America Calls in a New, Cold-eyed Breed of CEO," *Business Week* (November 25, 1991): 174–180.

18 D. Goleman, "Leadership That Gets Results," 78.

19 Weisbach, "Outside Directors and CEO Turnover," *Journal of Financial Economics* 20 (1988): 431–460.

20 Fama and M.C. Jensen, "Separation of Ownership and Control," *Journal of Law and Economics* 26 (1983): 301–325.

21 I.F. Kesner and R.B. Johnson, "Crisis In the Boardroom: Fact and Fiction," *Academy of Management Executive* (February 1990): 23–35.

22 M. Magnet, "Directors, Wake Up!" *Fortune* (June 15, 1992): 86–92.

23 A. Taylor, III, "The Road Ahead at General Motors," *Fortune* (May 4, 1992): 94–95; J.B. Treece, "The Board Revolt," *Business Week* (April 20, 1992): 31–36.

24 J.A. Byrne, "Requiem for Yesterday's CEO," *Business Week* (February 15, 1993): 32–33; C.J. Loomis and D. Kirkpatrick, "The Hunt for Mr. X: Who Can Run IBM?" *Fortune* (February 22, 1993): 68–72; A.A. Morrison, "After the Coup at Time Warner," *Fortune* (March 23, 1992): 82–90.

25 I.F. Kesner, B. Victo,r and B.T. Lamont, "Board Composition and the Commission of Illegal Acts: An Investigation of Fortune 500 Companies," *Academy of Management Journal* 29 (1986): 789–799; I.B. Kesner and R.B. Johnson, "An Investigation of the Relationship Between Board Composition and Shareholder Suits," *Strategic Management Journal* 11 (1990): 327–336.

26 W.Q. Judge, Jr. and C. Zeithaml, "Institutional and Strategic Choice Perspectives on Board Involvement in the Strategic Decision Process," *Academy of Management Journal* 35 (1992): 766–794; J.A. Pearce II and Shaker A. Zahra, "The Relative Power of CEOs and Boards of Directors: Associations with Corporate Performance," *Strategic Management Journal* 12 (1991): 135–153.

27 R.M. Ferry, "Boardrooms Yesterday, Today and Tomorrow," *Chief Executive (U.S.)* (March 1999): 44–48.

28 S. Webb, "Good Corporate Governance Will Spur Investor Premiums, According to Survey," *The Wall Street Journal* (June 19, 2000): B6.

29 W.C. Rapplege, "Human Capital Management: The Next Competitive Advantage," *Across the Board* 36 (September 1999): 39–48.

30 National Institute of Science & Technology, 1998.

31 J.J. Hughes, "Views of the Future," in R.L. Wolkoff, ed., *Next-Generation Manufacturing: A Framework for Action* (Bethlehem, PA.: The Agility Forum, 1997).

32 D. Miller and J. Shamsie, "The Resource-Based View of the Firm In Two Environments: The Hollywood Film Studios From 1936 to 1965," *Academy of Management Journal* 39 (1996): 519–543.

33 J.B. Barney, "Looking Inside for Competitive Advantage," *Academy of Management Executive* (November 1995): 49–61.

34 Barney, "Looking Inside for Competitive Advantage."

35 M.A. Hitt, R.D. Ireland, and R.E. Hoskisson, *Strategic Management: Competitiveness and Globalization* (Minneapolis: West Publishing Company, 1995): 73.

36 C.L. Loomis, "Citicorp: John Reed's Second Act," *Fortune* (April 29, 1996): 90.

37 Walt Disney Company, *1995 Annual Report*: 6–7.

38 J.H. Dyer, "Specialized Computer Networks as a Source of Competitive Advantage: Evidence From the Auto Industry," *Strategic Management Journal* 17 (1996): 271–291.

39 M.E. Porter, *Competitive Advantage: Creating and Sustaining Superior Performance* (New York: The Free Press, 1985): Chapter 2.

40 L.J. Bourgeois, "Performance and Consensus," *Strategic Management Journal* 1 (1980): 227–248; G.G. Dess, "Consensus on Strategy Formulation and Organizational Performance: Competitors in a Fragmented Industry," *Strategic Management Journal* 8 (1987): 259–277; L.G. Hrebiniak and C.C. Snow, "Top Management Agreement and Organizational Performance," *Human Relations* 35 (1982): 1139–1158; K. Labich, "Why Companies Fail," *Fortune* (November 14, 1994): 52–59.

41 "Mission and Vision," http://www.materialink.com/mission_vision.htm (July 5, 2000).

42 The Ashbridge Mission Statement, *Trusts and Estates* (August 1999): 59.

43 D.F. Abell, *Defining the Business: The Starting Point of Strategic Planning* (Englewood Cliffs, New Jersey: Prentice Hall, 1980): 169.

44 Abell, *Defining the Business: The Starting Point of Strategic Planning.*

45 F. Drucker, *Management—Tasks, Responsibilities, Practices* (New York: Harper and Row, 1974): 74–94.

46 D.J. Isenberg, "The Tactics of Strategic Opportunism," *Harvard Business Review* (March/April 1987): 92–97.

47 L.T. Hosmer, "Strategic Planning as if Ethics Mattered," *Strategic Management Journal* 15 (1994): 17–34; D. Schendel and C. Hofer, *Strategic Management: A New View of Business Policy and Planning* (Boston: Little, Brown, and Company, 1979).

48 R.E. Freeman and D.R. Gilbert, Jr., *Corporate Strategy and the Search for Ethics* (Englewood Cliffs, New Jersey: Prentice-Hall, 1988).

49 J.A. Pearce, II and F. David, "Corporate Mission Statements: The Bottom Line," *Academy of Management Executive* (May 1987): 109–115.

50 *Code of Ethics*, United Technologies, 1991.

CHAPTER

4

Business Strategy

Dell Computer

Dell Computer has remade itself before, and it will do it again. When Michael Dell started the company in a dorm room at University of Texas, Dell's strategy was to sell low-priced computers through mail order. Dell then transformed itself into a model of logistics management with a focus on rapid delivery of custom-assembled desktop and notebook computers for individual and business users. Dell has been praised by customers and business analysts as one of the few companies to master the logistics systems needed to support a high-volume, custom business.

But times are changing. As the editor of *High Tech Strategist* notes, "The party's over. Dell's the leader in a dying market." He is referring to the fact that desktop computers are now a slow-growth commodity. Even the top firm in the industry, Dell, has suffered drops in sales growth and a decline in profits.

For Dell, the changing industry conditions will require another change in strategy. *Forbes* reports, "The Internet, Michael Dell says, is pulling companies like Dell in two directions—toward the 'core,' where servers and huge storage systems reside, and the 'edge,' comprising PCs, cell phones, and hand-held devices. Dell won't fight the tug of war. He will move upstream, with a new line of servers and storage systems that will compete with Sun Microsystems. He'll also move downstream, selling low-cost PCs and reselling hand-held devices that other companies make. And he will move sideways into services . . . Web hosting and storage to drive new revenue streams. . . . Dell is in effect admitting what others have said for years . . . that it is not so much a PC manufacturer as a PC reseller. Dell has great one-to-one relationships with millions of customers around the world. Now it wants to use the Dell brand to sell those customers things other than computers."[1]

Business-level strategy defines an organization's approach to growth and competition in its chosen markets. Dell's growth strategy is to add products to its product line so that it can increase sales volume and enter new market segments. Dell's competitive strategy can be described as differentiation on the basis of service to customers and leveraging its brand name.

Some of the major strategic management responsibilities of business-level managers are listed in Exhibit 4.1. They include establishing the overall direction of the business unit, ongoing analysis of the changing business situation, selecting strategies for growth and for competitive positioning, and then managing resources to produce a sustainable competitive advantage. These responsibilities and the methods for carrying them out are similar in for-profit and nonprofit organizations.[2] This chapter will focus on selecting specific business-level strategies and developing distinctive competencies that lead to competitive advantages.

Exhibit 4.1   *Major Business-Level Strategic Management Responsibilities*

Major Responsibilities	Key Issues
Direction setting	Establishment and communication of mission, vision, ethics, and long-term goals of a single business unit
	Creation and communication of shorter-term goals and objectives
Analysis of business situation	Compilation and assessment of information from stakeholders and other sources
	Identification of strengths, weaknesses, opportunities, threats, sources of sustainable competitive advantage
Selection of strategy	Determination of growth strategy—internal strategies, external strategies, and level of aggressiveness
	Selection of a generic approach to competition—cost leadership, differentiation, focus, or best cost
	Selection of a strategic posture—specific strategies needed to carry out the generic strategy
Management of resources	Acquisition of resources or development of competencies leading to a sustainable competitive advantage
	Development of functional strategies and an appropriate management structure to support business strategy

Within single-business firms, and within each business unit of a multibusiness firm, managers must decide how to position the business to achieve its growth and profit targets. Business managers are involved with developing two categories of strategies: growth strategies and competitive strategies. *Growth strategies* are concerned with increasing the size and viability of the business over time. In planning growth strategies, managers are concerned with two key issues: (1) where do we allocate resources within our business in order to achieve growth, (2) what changes in business scope do we see as compatible with growth and overall strategic direction, and (3) how do we *time* our growth moves compared to competitors? *Competitive strategies*, on the other hand, are concerned with how the firm intends to position itself to create value for its customers in ways that are different from those of competitors. Strategies that involve the organization in new industries and new businesses are called corporate strategies. Corporate strategies are the subject of the next chapter.

GROWTH STRATEGIES

In designing growth strategies for a single business, managers must decide where to allocate resources and how, or if, to alter the scope (products, markets, functions served, and resource conversion activities) of the business. In general, single businesses may choose to pursue growth through internal or external investment or stabilize their growth through restricted investment. Internal growth, external growth, and stability strategies, and their implications for resource allocations and business scope, are the topics of the next three sections. All of these approaches are outlined in Exhibit 4.2.

Internal Growth Strategies

By investing its resources (i.e., time, money, people) internally, a business can pursue market penetration, market development, or product/service development. *Market penetration* entails investing in advertising, capacity expansion, and/or the sales force with the intent of increasing market share in the current business. This strategy requires no changes in the scope of the organization. On the other hand, *market development*, in which the organization seeks new market segments, or, *applications development*, which involves creating new applications of its products, both require a broadened definition of the markets or functions served. To support market development, firms may need to invest in market research, new marketing approaches, and a new sales force. In applications development, firms will invest in market research, product testing and qualifications, and new market strategies. For example, a nylon fabric manufacturer who sells fabric to windsuit manufacturers would likely have to invest in market and applications development in order to sell nylon fabric to tent or sleeping bag manufacturers.

Firms pursuing *product/service development* seek to *modify* existing products or *develop* new products/services for the purpose of selling more to existing customers or creating new market segments. In addition to changes in the scope of products/services, this type of development may require expanded definitions in markets, functions served, or the resource conversion process. Resource allocations focus on product/service development, applications development, basic research and development, and perhaps process development or market development, depending on the nature of new or modified products/services. For example, pharmaceutical companies continuously make investments in new and improved products. Johnson & Johnson manufactures an effective drug for the treatment of colon cancer that started out as a sheep wormer sold through veterinarians! Through product and applications development, the drug now serves a very different function and serves a completely different customer group. Consequently, the types of customers served and the functions served by a particular company's product/service line may change over time.

Product development efforts can also result in relatively minor changes, as in packaging. Heinz boosted ketchup and mustard sales when it began selling those products in plastic rather than glass bottles. The company hopes to stimulate sales of Star Kist tuna by moving from cans to plastic pouches.[3]

Exhibit 4.2   *Growth Strategy and the Scope of the Business*

Internal Growth Options

1. Market Penetration
   - Tactic: Increase market share in current business through advertising, promotions, stepped-up sales effort
   - Change in scope: None

2. Market Development
   - Tactic: Identify new market segments or new applications for products/services
   - Change in scope: Broaden definition of markets or functions served by products/services

3. Product/Services Development
   - Tactic: Modify existing products/services or develop new products/services for existing or potential customers
   - Change in scope: Definite change in products/services; possible changes in markets, functions served, or resource conversion processes

External Growth Options

1. Horizontal Integration
   - Tactic: Purchase company in same line of business
   - Change in scope: Extend market base; may also include other changes, depending on the company acquired

2. Strategic Alliances
   - Tactic: Create alliances with other organizations to achieve market position, product development, or process development
   - Change in scope: Extend products/services, markets, and functions served or alter resource conversion process

No-Growth or Slow-Growth Option

1. Stability
   - Tactic: Maintain the status quo (some firms may pursue this strategy temporarily during restructuring)
   - Change in scope: None

Virtually all business organizations follow internal growth strategies of some type. In general, market penetration strategies are successful in the early stage of an organization's life, when many customers are untapped. However, with growth and success, the organization must cast a wider net to find more customers and to sustain its growth. At that point, organizations will usually begin more aggressive investment in market development and product development to broaden their appeal to more and more customers. To help fuel growth and supplement their products and markets, some businesses look outside of the organization for investment opportunities and ideas. These external growth strategies are the subject of the next section.

External Growth Strategies

External growth strategies involve investing organizational resources in another company or business to achieve growth targets and include horizontal integration and joint ventures or alliances. As with internal growth strategies, external growth strategies involve making decisions about the priority of resource allocation and have implications for the scope of the single business or business unit.

Horizontal integration involves the acquisition of an organization in the same line of business. Typically, horizontal integration is accomplished for the purpose of gaining market share in a particular market, expanding a market geographically, or augmenting product or service lines. It involves *acquisition* of capabilities, market segments, or products lines, rather than *development* of them internally. The $75.7 billion merger of SmithKline Beecham with Glaxo Wellcome (each the product of an earlier merger) has resulted in the world's largest drug company. The new company will have sales of approximately $25 billion, over 100,000 employees, and global leadership positions in several pharmaceutical product lines. This is part of an industry-wide consolidation in the pharmaceutical industry designed to achieve scale effects and broader product lines in order to be better positioned to capitalize on future growth opportunities.[4] Horizontal integration is particularly common in industries that are undergoing consolidation, where new product and market opportunities are scarce, and growth must come by taking a share of a competitor's market.

The second external mechanism for achieving growth within a single business or business unit is through joint ventures or strategic alliances formed with other organizations to penetrate new domestic or foreign markets, develop new products and services, or improve existing processes for producing products and services. Formal contractual joint ventures as well as less formal strategic alliances are common in situations in which individual competing firms believe they are lacking a skill, technology, or capability that is needed to develop new products or markets. For example, General Motors is involved in several alliances that serve to extend its product line and its research capabilities. GM has created an on-line marketplace for auto suppliers' goods and services. Toyota is in talks to align with GM in their efforts. Isuzu, Suzuki, and Fuji are already involved. GM is also in an alliance with Honda for engine and transmission development and production.[5]

Ventures that penetrate new markets require a broadening of the market definition, while ventures to develop new products/services require changes to the products/services and perhaps functions also. Finally, ventures that seek to improve processes probably require changes in the resource conversion process.

External growth strategies often involve a significant investment or an acquisition of another firm and may involve creation of a new business division or business unit. Acquisitions and changes in organization structure are usually managed at the corporate level, even if the intention is to grow an individual business. Therefore, we will return to a discussion of mergers and acquisitions in Chapter 5—Corporate Strategy.

Stability Strategies

While most for-profit organizations actively seek growth, some organizations do not. They may be family-owned businesses, nonprofit organizations that are satisfied with the current level of operations, or they may simply be business organizations that are content with their share of a mature market. In these situations, no overt actions are taken to achieve growth. The prevalent theme of operations is "business as usual." These types of organizations maintain fairly level investments in marketing, operations, and services and only engage in enough R&D to maintain their share of the market.

Although this strategy may seem passive, in many situations it is perfectly logical and an appropriate use of investment funds. There are many situations in which investing for the objective of growth is ineffective. For instance, a firm may find itself in a mature, declining, or rigidly segmented market in which efforts to increase sales would cost more than they are worth. This situation is typical of industries with low profits, no growth, and high *exit barriers*. Exit barriers exist when the capital equipment and skills an organization possesses are not applicable to other businesses.[6] For example, the plants and equipment used by steel companies have almost no potential for other uses. Consequently, many steel companies are barely able to survive against the more successful mini-mill firms, but they do not close down because their entire investment would be lost.

Timing of Growth Strategies

A key issue in planning growth strategies is to determine the timing of particular growth moves relative to competitors. Based on field studies in four industries, Raymond Miles and Charles Snow classified firms into one of four categories based on the rate at which they changed their products and markets. They were able to identify four general categories.[7] *Prospectors* pursue what could be termed an offensive strategy. They aggressively seek new market opportunities and are willing to take risks. *Defenders*, on the other hand, are turf protectors that engage in little or no new product/market development. Their strategic actions are intended to preserve market share through reducing the impact of offensive moves by competitors. *Analyzers* occupy a position in between prospectors and defenders. They attempt to maintain positions in existing markets, while waiting to see what happens when a competitor introduces a new product or enters a new market. They then follow when the opportunity and the parameters for success are clearer. *Reactors* don't have a distinct strategy. They simply react to environmental situations.

The Miles and Snow classifications illustrate two fundamentally different positions with respect to growth. Prospectors aggressively pursue growth, while defenders tend to pursue stability. Analyzers pursue growth in areas that show substantial promise, usually after others have made an initial entry. In planning growth strategies, it is important to identify not only *what* should be done, but *when* it should be done as well. We will now turn our attention to a discussion of competitive strategies.

GENERIC COMPETITIVE STRATEGIES

In addition to planning the resource allocations necessary for growth, managers must decide the competitive positioning of the business. Growth and competitive strategies are tightly linked: only through successful competitive strategies will an organization have the fuel to make the growth strategies successful. Product and services strategies are as different as the organizations that create them. However, classifying competitive strategies into generic types helps firms identify common strategic characteristics.

In general, firms seek a competitive advantage either by offering (1) products or services that are different from those of competitors, and those differences are valued by customers, or (2) products or services that are standard, but produced at lower cost, or (3) a combination of the first two options, a hybrid competitive strategy called "best cost." Organizations also must decide how broadly their desired markets will be.[8] While some firms, like General Motors, market very broadly to most economic segments, other firms, like Porsche, "focus" on a particular segment of the market. Just like a broad market strategy, a focus strategy can be accomplished by offering differentiated products, producing at low cost, or through a combination of differentiation and low cost (best cost). The four generic strategies of low-cost leadership, differentiation, best cost, and focus will now be described in detail.

Cost Leadership

Firms pursuing cost leadership set out to become the lowest-cost providers of a good or service. The broad scope of cost leaders means that they attempt to serve a large percentage of the total market. Firms pursuing cost leadership include McDonald's and Panasonic. Generally, low-cost leadership allows a firm to compete by lowering prices when needed without becoming unprofitable. A low-cost leader can also price their products at the commodity or average industry price and reap larger profits than competitors.

To fully appreciate the significance of the low-cost leadership strategy, it is important to understand the factors that underlie cost structures in firms. Firms pursuing a low-cost strategy will typically employ one or more of the following factors to create their low-cost positions: (1) high-capacity utilization, (2) economies of scale, (3) technological advances, or (4) learning/experience effects.[9] These factors will now be explained.

High-Capacity Utilization.   When demand is high and production capacity is fully utilized, a firm's fixed costs are spread over more units, which lowers unit costs. However, when demand falls off, the fixed costs are spread over fewer units so that unit costs increase. This basic concept suggests that a firm capable of maintaining higher levels of capacity utilization, either through better demand forecasting, conservative capacity expansion policies, or aggressive pricing, will be able to maintain a lower-cost structure than a competitor of equal size and capability.

Economies of Scale.   The second major factor with the potential to lead to cost advantages is *economies of scale*. Economies of scale are often confused with increases in the "throughput" of a manufacturing plant or other facility. As described before, increases in capacity utilization that spread fixed expenses can lead to lower unit costs. However, true economies of scale are cost advantages associated with larger-sized facilities rather than with increased volume through an existing facility. For example, the cost of constructing a 200-bed hospital will not necessarily be twice the cost of building a 100-bed hospital, so the initial fixed cost per unit of capacity will be lower.

Other scale economies are also evident in many industries. Continuing with the previous example, the administrator of the larger hospital will not generally receive double the salary of the manager of the smaller facility. Also, activities such as X-ray and blood analysis laboratories, purchasing, and central supply typically do not require twice as much time, twice as much equipment, or twice as many employees. In addition, the purchasing manager of the larger hospital may be able to negotiate better volume discounts on supplies and equipment. In summary, the larger hospital may be able to achieve per-unit savings in fixed costs, indirect labor costs, and supply costs. If per-unit costs are not lower in the larger plant, then the company has *not* achieved economies of scale. In fact, *diseconomies of scale* occur when a firm builds facilities that are so large that the sheer administrative costs and confusion associated with the added bureaucracy overwhelm any potential cost savings.

Technological Advances.   Companies that make investments in *cost-saving technologies* are often trading an increase in fixed costs for a reduction in variable costs. While investments of this type are typically associated with the factory floor, it is just as common for investments to be made in office and service automation. For example, the automated distribution system at Wal-Mart, the automated ordering and warehouse system at Lands' End, and the reservation systems maintained by the major airlines all represent investments in technology that serve to lower overall costs and provide a degree of information and product control that was previously impossible.

Learning/Experience Effects.   A final factor that influences cost structures is *learning effects*. Freshmen often take a long time to register the very first time they register for classes. By the time they are seniors, however, they know how to get through the process much faster. When an employee learns to do a job more efficiently with repetition, then learning is taking place. The learning curve effect says that the time required to complete a task will decrease as a predictable function of the number of times the task is repeated. In theory, the time required to complete the task will fall by the same percentage each time cumulative production doubles. For example, a firm might see a 10 percent reduction in the time required to manufacture its products between the first and second unit of product, another 10 percent reduction between the second and fourth units, and another 10 percent reduction between the fourth and eighth units.

Clearly, dramatic time savings are achieved early in the life of a product. However, as the product matures, tangible cost savings from labor learning are harder to achieve because it takes longer to see a true doubling of cumulative volume. Also, learning effects do not just happen. They require a relatively labor-intensive process since people learn but machines do not. Learning effects only occur when management creates an environment that is favorable to both learning and change, and then rewards employees for their productivity improvements.

Experience effects are the same thing as learning effects but relate to indirect labor as well as direct production labor. For example, with experience a sales person becomes more efficient at identifying prospective clients and preparing sales presentations, and a purchasing manager becomes more efficient at negotiating supply agreements. In modern organizations, experience effects are even more important than direct labor learning effects because direct labor often represents less than 15 percent of total product costs. Much of the downsizing of middle management that we are seeing in industry today is an attempt to combine experience effects with economic gains from technologies (computer systems) to achieve a higher level of organization efficiency and effectiveness with fewer people.

Learning and experience effects can be described by a learning/experience curve such as the one found in Exhibit 4.3.[10] Following from the logic of these two curves, the market share leader should enjoy a cost advantage relative to competitors because of the extra learning and experience that has occurred by producing the additional output. This concept has led many firms to fierce competitive pricing in order to obtain the highest market share and thus move right on the curve as far as possible. As the curve flattens, however, it becomes increasingly difficult to gain cost advantages from learning and experience effects. The same sort of phenomenon exists with respect to economies of scale.

Companies that are able to achieve high-capacity utilization, economies of scale, economies of technology, and/or learning/experience effects may have the lowest costs, but do not have to charge the lowest prices. In other words, a *cost* leader does not have to be a *price* leader. If an organization is able to achieve the lowest cost, but charge a price that is the same as that of competitors, it will still enjoy higher profits. However, this strategy could potentially lead to a loss of the lowest-cost position if several customers switch to other brands, and the loss of sales reduces capacity utilization or learning and experience effects or undermines scale benefits.

There are several risks associated with too strong of a focus on a low-cost strategy. First, firms pursuing cost leadership may not detect required product or marketing changes because of a preoccupation with cost. Second, these firms run the risk of making large investments in plants or equipment only to see them become obsolete because of technological breakthroughs by competitors. Their large

Exhibit 4.3   *A Typical Learning/Experience Curve*

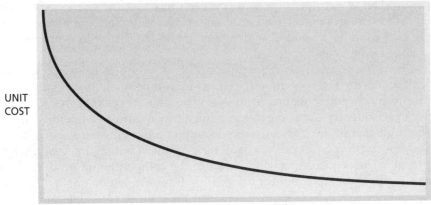

investments make them reluctant to keep up with changes that are not compatible with their technologies. Third, efforts to seek low costs may just go too far. ValuJet's "penny-pinching" allowed it to achieve a low-cost position in the airline industry. ValuJet passed the savings on to consumers and experienced unprecedented growth. However, their stinginess came under close scrutiny after the crash of ValuJet Flight 592 into the Florida Everglades. Federal investigators found some of ValuJet's procedures, especially maintenance procedures, unsafe and ultimately shut down the airline until safety concerns could be worked out.[11]

Differentiation

In differentiation strategies, the emphasis is on creating value through uniqueness, as opposed to lowest cost. Uniqueness can be achieved through product innovations, superior quality, superior service, creative advertising, better supplier relationships, or in many other ways. However, for a differentiation strategy to succeed, customers must be willing to pay more for the uniqueness of a product or service than the firm paid to create it. Competitive scope is still broad, which means that the differentiated product or service should be designed so that it has wide appeal to many market sectors. Examples of organizations that are pursuing differentiation strategies include Maytag through its highly reliable appliances, L.L. Bean through its quality products and well-managed mail-order services, BMW through its styling and performance, Coca-Cola through promoting its well-known brand name and reputation, and Amazon.com through its exclusive Internet-based book and gift retailing business and extremely high level of personalized, easy-to-use service.

Firms pursuing differentiation strategies can't ignore their cost positions. When costs are too high relative to competitors, a firm may not be able to recover enough of these additional costs through higher prices. Therefore, differentiators have to attempt to reduce costs in the areas that are not directly related to the sources of differentiation. The only way a differentiation strategy will work is if buyers value the attributes that make a product unique enough to pay a higher price for it or choose to buy from that firm preferentially.

Consequently, the major risks associated with a differentiation strategy center on the difference between added costs and incremental price. One risk is that customers will sacrifice some of the features, services, or image possessed by a unique product or service because it costs too much. Another risk is that customers will no longer perceive an attribute as differentiating. For example, customers may come to a point at which they are so familiar with a product that brand image is no longer important.

If a firm is successful at differentiation of its products or services, it will quickly become the target of imitative efforts by competitors. As competitors imitate, the formerly differentiating features will become commodity characteristics. Rivalry in an industry can make it very difficult to sustain a competitive advantage from innovation for very long. For example, competitors are able to obtain detailed information on 70 percent of all new products within one year after development.[12] Consequently, staying ahead of the competition in product development requires *constant* innovation. As one business writer put it, "For outstanding performance, a company has to beat the competition. The trouble is the competition has heard the same message."[13]

Best Cost

Porter referred to firms that are not pursuing a distinct generic strategy as "stuck-in-the-middle."[14] According to Porter, these uncommitted firms should have lower performance than committed firms, because they have no consistent basis for creating superior value and are not effective at implementing either strategy. He argued that firms that pursue one of the generic strategies exclusively will perform better because they can center all of their resources on becoming good at that strategy.

In recent years, it has become apparent that many firms have been successful at pursuing cost leadership and differentiation simultaneously. In some situations, the two strategies complement rather than detract from each other. It is well established that product quality and cost are complementary rather than conflicting strategies.[15] Furthermore, technological investments often allow firms to lower their costs while improving their performance on features that differentiate the company's products or services in the eyes of customers, just as ATMs improve access and availability of teller services while driving down direct labor costs. Over time, the profits generated from the successful pursuit of one element of strategy (i.e., low cost) allow investment in other elements such as differentiating features. Consequently, this middle-ground strategy is called "best cost," implying that it provides the most reasonable trade-off between low cost and differentiating features.[16]

Wal-Mart, for example, was successful at providing high-quality customer service in its industry at lowest cost. A key part of Wal-Mart's strategy is a technologically advanced distribution system that allows fast and efficient delivery of products.[17] McDonald's seeks a low-cost position through its efficient, highly automated operations, but also achieves the high levels of consistency over time that their customers value.

Some strategy scholars are now arguing that a combination of differentiation and low costs may be necessary to create a sustainable competitive advantage: "The immediate effect of differentiation will be to increase unit costs. However, if costs fall with increasing volume, the long-run effect may be to reduce unit costs."[18] Volume would be expected to increase because differentiation would make the product more attractive to the market. Then, as volume increases, costs will decrease. Jack Welch, CEO of General Electric, puts it this way:

> We're playing in a game where we'll show up and we'll be selling an engine against another engine competitor. Now, to get the deal, *you've got to have performance and all the other things*, but you'd better have low cost. And as you go around the world, and you want to sell turbines to developing countries, you'd better have a low cost base. Because in the end, you could have performance, you can have quality, but you'd better have cost (italics added).[19]

Anheuser-Busch has been very successful in creating brewing products that have a good image and high quality, yet A-B is a cost leader due to efficiencies created by high-volume production, distribution, and advertising. Kellogg, best known for breakfast cereals, enjoys a similar situation of low-cost production due to economies of scale combined with higher prices made possible due to differentiation through advertising and new product development.

The key to a best-cost strategy is simply supply and demand economics. For example, assume that three organizations manufacture hunting knives. The first firm pursues a low-cost strategy. It is able to produce a knife for $10 and sell 100,000 a year at $20, for a total profit of $1 million. On the other hand, the second firm uses a differentiation strategy. It produces a premium product with features that the market finds attractive. The premium product costs $40 to make. The firm can sell 50,000 at $60. The total profit is also $1 million, although the unit volume is half that of the low-price competitor. Both companies seem to be successful; however, they are each achieving success using a different generic strategy.

However, assume that a third company can create a very good product, through a variety of product and process technological advances, for $20. Further suppose that this product is almost as appealing as the product of the second firm. If the firm can sell 75,000 at $50, the total profit will be over $2 million and consumers will believe they are getting a great deal (saving $10). This is the essence of a best-cost strategy—finding a level of differentiation that will bring a premium price while doing so at a reasonable cost. Unlike a differentiation strategy in which the emphasis is on creating extra value or a low-cost strategy that stresses cutting costs, the best-cost strategy gives equal weight to both factors.

Focus

Focus strategies can be based on differentiation (differentiation focus) or lowest cost (cost focus) or a combination of differentiation and lowest cost (best-cost focus). The key to a focus strategy is providing a product or service that caters to a particular segment in the market. Firms pursuing focus strategies have to be able to identify their target market segment and both assess and meet the needs and desires of buyers in that segment better than any other competitor.

Cooper Tire and Rubber is an example of a company that pursues a cost focus strategy. Cooper is the only major tire company that does not sell tires to automobile manufacturers in the original equipment market (OEM). Instead, the company focuses on replacement tires. Cooper is very efficiency oriented: "Its low-rise corporate headquarters could pass for a 1950s suburban elementary school, right down to the linoleum floors and the flagpole out front. The annual report is printed in living black and white."[20] Cooper saves on R&D costs by copying the designs of OEM manufacturers instead of designing its own products. The cost focus strategy is so successful that Cooper provides the highest returns to its investors of any firm in the tire industry.

On the other hand, Japan Airlines pursues a differentiation focus strategy by catering to wealthy passengers. For example, the airline has invested $95,000 each in luxury bathrooms for its first-class cabins on its routes between Tokyo and New York. According to a JAL spokesperson, "Especially on long-distance flights, the toilet is something that leaves a deep impression." The larger bathrooms will feature piped-in music, soft lighting, a three-sided mirror, a window, and faucets that stay on so that passengers can wash both hands at once. A first-class round-trip ticket from Tokyo to New York costs $9,300.[21]

The risks of pursuing a focus strategy depend on whether the strategy is cost focus or differentiation focus. The risks of each of these strategies are similar to the risks faced by adopters of the pure strategies themselves. However, the focus strategy has two risks that are not associated with the emphasis on low cost or differentiation. First, the desires of the narrow target market may become similar to the desires of the market as a whole, thus eliminating the advantage associated with focusing. Second, a competitor may be able to focus on an even more narrowly defined target and essentially "outfocus the focuser."

Best-cost focus is another generic strategy that firms can pursue. However, this strategy is more difficult than a basic best-cost strategy because the narrow market focus means lower volume. At lower volume, it is hard to achieve low cost while still providing meaningful differentiation.

This completes our discussion of generic strategies. We have also devoted considerable attention on how to successfully implement those strategies. The final section provides a discussion of how the product life cycle can be used in formulating and implementing business strategies.

CHANGES IN STRATEGY OVER TIME

The product life cycle describes the stages most products—and industries—evolve through from creation to maturation. Study of product life cycle concepts can help an organization understand the dynamic nature of strategy. As a product moves through the stages of the life cycle, different strategies and organizational resources are needed to compete effectively.

The *product life cycle* portrays how sales volume for a product changes over its lifetime. For managers involved in strategy formulation and implementation, it is useful to have an understanding of the typical competitive and strategy changes that often accompany the different life cycle stages. As Exhibit 4.4 illustrates, demand for a product gradually builds during the *introduction stage*, as consumers come to understand the product and its uses. During the *growth stage*, demand greatly increases, which often attracts new competitors. Sales growth eventually begins to level off during the *maturity stage* of the life cycle. This slowing of growth can lead to a competitive "shake out" of weaker producers, resulting in

Exhibit 4.4   *The Product Life Cycle*

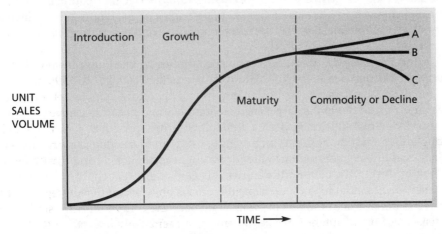

Note: A = Moderate Growth, B = Commodity, C = Decline

fewer competitors. During the *commodity* or *decline stage*, the demand curve can take many shapes. The traditional curve, representing decline, is labeled C in Exhibit 4.4. However, if the product becomes a commodity, which means that it is used in many other products or becomes a basic part of life for some consumers, demand may just level off, as in B, or may gradually increase over an extended time period, represented by A.[22]

Understanding the product life cycle not only helps an organization understand demand, but can also help the organization formulate strategies.[23] During the introduction stage, as demand for a product gradually builds, organizations are primarily concerned with survival—producing the product at low enough cost and selling it at a high enough price so that they will be able to sustain operations and enter the next stage of the life cycle. The competitive environment at this stage is often turbulent. Often customer needs for the new product are not that well understood and new firms enter with different product versions and new methods. Since businesses often lose money during this stage, this is a difficult challenge.

In the introduction stage, firms also attempt to produce a product that is of sufficiently high quality that they will be able to establish a good reputation in the market. The emphasis is often on research and development. Early producers sometimes enjoy a "first-mover advantage," because of the experience they are gaining, the image they have the opportunity to build, and the opportunity they may have to create entry barriers, such as patents or exclusive distribution channels.[24] There is some evidence to support these ideas.[25] In fact, products sometimes come to be associated with early innovators, as in the case of Scott towels, Scotch tape, Linoleum floor coverings, and Xerox machines.

During the growth stage, as demand greatly expands and the number of competitors increases, existing competitors may attempt to erect entry barriers by building plants that are large enough to enjoy economies of scale, locking in contracts for supplies or distribution of products, or differentiating products through advertising and new features or service. At this stage, products are much more standardized and competition tends to focus on product quality and availability. As growth begins to level off toward the end of the growth stage and as some firms fail to develop product characteristics that customers value or try to grow faster than their resources allow, a *competitive shakeout* usually occurs. Since the market is no longer growing at an increasing rate, the weaker competitors discover that they can no longer generate enough sales or profits to sustain themselves. They sell off their assets, declare bankruptcy, or are acquired by stronger competitors.

During the maturity stage, as demand continues to level off, efficient, high-volume production tends to dominate manufacturing strategy. A dominant design for the product has probably emerged, and therefore consumers typically focus on price and dependability. When an organization discovers a successful innovation, it is quickly incorporated into other firm's products. Consequently, product differentiation becomes increasingly difficult. Marketing, distribution efficiency, and low-cost operations gain increasing importance during this stage.

Finally, during the commodity or decline stage, tight cost controls leading to efficiency are essential to success. Since the product has become highly standardized at this point, price is still a very important basis for competition. Competition is intense, and firms may begin to drop out again, especially if demand takes the shape of curve C in Exhibit 4.4 and if exit barriers are low. Examples of exit barriers that might motivate organizations not to drop out include owning a lot of assets that can't be used for anything else, high costs of terminating contracts or tearing down buildings, or social costs such as laying off workers.[26]

To avoid the full effects of decline, firms may focus on a particular niche in the market that is still growing. Or innovative firms may be able to introduce a product that totally replaces the old product and makes it obsolete. For example, desktop computers and CDs have made typewriters and records obsolete. Finally, some organizations may just "hang on" until other firms have dropped out, at which time reduced competition can result in improved profitability and market share.[27] This is happening right now in the tobacco industry.

One of the lessons that we learn from the product life cycle is that organizations must adapt as their products move through the stages of evolution. Whereas product innovation and attempts to differentiate products may have value in the early stages, once a dominant design emerges, the focus of strategy must shift toward low costs and service, even if efforts to develop new products continue. As described in the Dell Computer example at the beginning of the chapter, Dell rode the product life cycle in desktop computers and was extremely successful. Now, however, the company must make a shift to earlier stage products for its product line in order to sustain revenues and must modify its competitive strategy to fit the competitive conditions.

The product life cycle concept is also applied to whole industries, which are identified by a basic product category such as automobiles or foods. Most industries in the U.S. have already matured and are represented by one of the three demand curves on the right side of Exhibit 4.4. This means that competition is fierce in most industries and that a careful analysis based on concepts found in this chapter is essential to success. However, even mature industries can experience growth in some product segments due to product innovations or other forms of differentiation that make older products undesirable or obsolete. Consequently, we come back to the notion that for the majority of firms, value creation through cost leadership or differentiation with controlled costs (or a focus strategy that emphasizes cost leadership or differentiation) is essential to higher-than-normal performance.

In summary, identification of the stage of the product/industry life cycle can provide strategic direction as firms develop their business-level strategies. As organizations fine-tune their strategies, they need to specify the distinctive competencies they will try to develop in order to achieve a competitive advantage.

KEY POINTS SUMMARY

This chapter dealt with business-level strategy, which defines an organization's approach to competing in its chosen markets. The following are important points from this chapter:

1. The responsibilities of business-level managers include establishing the overall direction of the business unit, ongoing analysis of the changing business situation, selecting growth and competitive strategies, and choosing a business-unit strategic posture.

2. Growth strategies are concerned with increasing the size and viability of the business over time. The primary issues with regard to growth are: (1) where do we allocate resources within our business in order to achieve growth, (2) what changes in business scope do we see as compatible with growth and overall strategic direction, and (3) how do we *time* our growth moves compared to competitors?

3. The four generic competitive strategies discussed in this chapter are cost leadership, differentiation, best cost, and focus.

4. Firms that are cost leaders actively pursue ways to produce products and services at the lowest possible cost. Low-cost leadership may be achieved through high-capacity utilization, scale economies, technological advances, and learning or experience effects.

5. Organizations that pursue differentiation attempt to differentiate their products or services in such a way that they have greater value to their consumers. Differentiation is often pursued on the basis of satisfying customers through higher quality, state-of-the-art research and development, superior human resources, or establishing a strong reputation and/or brand through advertising.

6. Best-cost strategies combine elements from both differentiation and low-cost leadership.

7. Focus strategies apply one of the generic orientations to a specific market niche.

8. An understanding of the product life cycle can assist in determining the distinct characteristics of a business-level strategy and how changes in industry growth rate and competitiveness will influence strategy choices.

END NOTES

1   D. Lyons, "Michael Dell's Second Act," *Forbes* (April 17, 2000): 208.

2   H.J. Bryce, *Financial and Strategic Management for Nonprofit Organizations* (Englewood Cliffs, New Jersey: Prentice-Hall, 1987).

3   J. Eig, "Heinz's CEO Unveils Plans to Stimulate Growth," *The Wall Street Journal* (June 16, 2000): B6.

4   "Smith Kline and Glaxo Agree to Merger," *The Wall Street Journal* (January 17, 2000): A3.

5   "Toyota Weights Joining GM in Web Supply System," *The Wall Street Journal* (January 6, 2000): B4.

6   K.R. Harrigan, "Deterrents to Divestiture," *Academy of Management Journal* 24 (1981): 306–323.

7   R.E. Miles and C.C. Snow, *Organization Strategy, Structure and Process* (New York: McGraw-Hill, 1978); R.E. Miles, C.C. Snow, A.D. Meyer, and H.J. Coleman, Jr., "Organizational Strategy, Structure and Process," *Academy of Management Review* 3 (1978): 546–562.

8   This discussion of generic strategies draws heavily from concepts found in M.E. Porter, *Competitive Strategy: Techniques for Analyzing Industries and Competitors* (New York: The Free Press, 1980): Chapter 2.

9   This discussion of factors leading to cost savings is based, in part, on R. Stagner, "Corporate Decision Making: An Empirical Study," *Journal of Applied Psychology* 53 (1969): 1–3.

10 W.J. Abernathy and K. Wayne, "Limits of the Learning Curve," *Harvard Business Review* (September/October 1974): 109–119; Boston Consulting Group, *Perspectives on Experience* (Boston: Boston Consulting Group, 1972); W.B. Hirschman, "Profit from the Learning Curve," *Harvard Business Review* (January/February 1964): 125–139.

11 A. Paszton, M. Branningan, and S. McCartney, "ValuJet's Penny-Pinching Comes Under Scrutiny," *The Wall Street Journal* (May 14, 1996): A2, A4.

12 E. Mansfield, "How Rapidly Does New Industrial Technology Leak Out?" *Journal of Industrial Economics* (December 1985): 217.

13 P. Ghemawat, "Sustainable Advantage," *Harvard Business Review* (September/October 1986): 53.

14 Porter, *Competitive Strategy*.

15 M. Walton, *Deming Management at Work* (New York: G.P. Putnam's Sons, 1990).

16 A.A. Thompson, Jr. and A.J. Strickland, Jr., *Strategic Management: Concepts and Cases*, 11th Edition (Boston: Irwin/McGraw-Hill, 1999).

17 T.C. Hayes, "Behind Wal-Mart's Surge, a Web of Suppliers," *The New York Times* (July 1, 1991): D1–D2.

18 C.W.L. Hill, "Differentiation Versus Low Cost or Differentiation and Low Cost: A Contingency Framework," *Academy of Management Review* 13 (1988): 403. See also A.I. Murray, "A Contingency View of Porter's 'Generic Strategies,'" *Academy of Management Review* 13 (1988): 390–400.

19 *Fortune*, "A Conversation with Roberto Goizueta and Jack Welch," (December 11, 1995): 98–99.

20 A. Talor, III, "Now Hear This, Jack Welch!" *Fortune* (April 6, 1992): 94

21 Associated Press, "Japan Airlines Puts Money in Toilet to Lure 1st-Class Travellers," *Orlando Sentinel* (May 8, 1996).

22 The term *commodity* to describe curves A and B was borrowed from R.H. Hayes and S.C. Wheelwright, *Restoring Our Competitive Edge: Competing Through Manufacturing* (New York: John Wiley and Sons, 1984): 203.

23 This discussion of strategy during the stages of product market evolution is based on C.R. Anderson and C.P. Zeithaml, "Stage of the Product Life Cycle, Business Strategy and Business Performance," *Academy of Management Journal* 27 (1984): 5–24; J.B. Barney and R.W. Griffin, *The Management of Organizations: Strategy, Structure, Behavior* (Boston: Houghton Mifflin, 1992): 229–230; Hayes and Wheelwright, *Restoring Our Competitive Edge*: Chapter 7; C.W. Hofer and D. Schendel, *Strategy Formulation: Analytical Concepts* (St. Paul: West Publishing, 1978): Chapter 5.

24 M.B. Lieberman and D.B. Montgomery, "First-Mover Advantages," *Strategic Management Journal* 9 (1988): 41–58.

25 M. Lambkin, "Order of Entry and Performance in New Markets," *Strategic Management Journal* 9 (1988): 127–140.

26 K.R. Harrigan and M.E. Porter, "End-Game Strategies for Declining Industries," *Harvard Business Review* (July/August 1983): 111–120.

27 Harrigan and Porter, "End-Game Strategies for Declining Industries."

CHAPTER

5

Corporate Strategy

In January 2000, Time Warner Inc., the world's largest media company, and America Online, Inc. (AOL), the world's biggest on-line company, announced their intent to join forces in the largest merger in history. AOL agreed to pay $156 billion in stock to Time Warner for 55 percent of the new company, which was to be called AOL-Time Warner. AOL founder and chairman, Steve Case, would serve as chairman of the new company. When it was announced, analysts expressed mixed feelings about the potential success of the proposed merger.

Why would these two powerhouses—from seemingly different industries—be interested in a merger? Management at both companies believed they were missing essential capabilities needed to succeed in the new digital economy. For AOL, Time Warner provides access to high-speed cable lines, the "pipe into the house" that is so valuable for Internet access. Time Warner also provides the 30 million subscribers to HBO and the all-news channel, CNN, which reaches a vast world market. For Time Warner, AOL provides a link to the future—where traditional print, voice, and broadcast media are interactive and delivered over the Internet.

As noted by *The Wall Street Journal*, "the mega-deal suddenly tears down the walls between old media and new, setting the stage for a huge collision of cultures and corporate fiefdoms." However, competitors of Time Warner and AOL complained that the new company would own 20 percent of all cable lines in the U.S. and control approximately 40 percent of the Internet access market. They were concerned that AOL-Time Warner would somehow restrict Internet availability. In response to these concerns, the Federal Trade Commission launched an antitrust investigation.[1]

This chapter deals with the functions top executives perform as they formulate corporate-level strategy, some of the tools they use (such as mergers and acquisitions), and theory concerning how corporate-level actions enhance the value of organizations. We will discuss the way business units can be related to each other and provide a rationale for building distinctive competencies based on similarities among them. Then we will describe specific tactics firms use to diversify.

At the corporate level, primary strategy formulation responsibilities include setting the direction of the entire organization, formulation of a corporate strategy, selection of businesses in which to compete, selection of tactics for diversification and growth, and management of corporate resources and capabilities. These responsibilities and the key issues associated with each responsibility are listed in Exhibit 5.1.

Exhibit 5.1   *Major Corporate-Level Strategic Management Responsibilities*

Major Responsibilities	Key Issues
Direction setting	Establishment and communication of organizational mission, vision, enterprise strategy, and long-term goals
Development of corporate-level strategy	Selection of a broad approach to corporate-level strategy—concentration, vertical integration, diversification, international expansion
	Selection of resources and capabilities in which to build corporate-wide distinctive competencies
Selection of business and portfolio management	Management of the corporate portfolio
	Emphasis given to each business unit—allocation of resources for capital equipment, R&D, etc.
Selection of tactics for diversification and growth	Choice among methods of diversification—internal venturing, acquisitions, joint ventures
Management of resources	Acquisition of resources or development of competencies leading to a sustainable competitive advantage
	Development of business-level strategies and an appropriate management structure for the corporation
	Development of an appropriate corporate structure

DEVELOPMENT OF CORPORATE STRATEGY

The three broad approaches to corporate strategy are concentration, vertical integration, and diversification. Also important to corporate strategy are tactics firms use to pursue these broad approaches, namely acquisitions and joint ventures. These five topics will form the basis for most of the discussion in this chapter.

Single Business/Concentration

Most organizations begin with a single or small group of products and services and a single market. This type of corporate-level strategy is called *concentration*. For instance, until recently, McDonald's was only engaged in one line of business, with limited backward integration to ensure a high level of quality for some of its raw materials (i.e., potatoes). The only real diversity pursued by McDonald's was geographic, since McDonald's operates worldwide. However, the same basic operating strategy is pursued at every McDonald's location in the world (although some of the food ingredients may change). In 2000, McDonald's announced the intention to create a business-to-business e-commerce company that would link food and service providers to fast food restaurants. This business represents an extension of McDonald's involvement in the fast food business and a way to leverage some of McDonald's strengths in supplier management. Federal Express, Domino's Pizza, Lands' End, and Delta Airlines are other examples of firms that participate in just one business.

Concentration strategies have sometimes been found to be more profitable than other types of corporate, or multibusiness, strategies.[2] Of course, the profitability of a concentration strategy is largely dependent on the industry in which a firm is involved. When the industry conditions are attractive, the strengths of a concentration strategy are readily apparent. First, a single business approach allows an organization to master one business and industry environment. This specialization allows top executives to obtain in-depth knowledge of the business and industry, which should reduce strategic mistakes. Second, since all resources are directed at doing one thing well, the organization may be in a better position to develop the resources and capabilities necessary to establish a sustainable competitive advantage. By concentrating on a single business, firms are able to concentrate on a focused set of strategies to achieve growth and profitability, as was discussed in Chapter 4.

Third, a concentration strategy can prevent the proliferation of management levels and staff functions that are often associated with large multibusiness firms and that add overhead costs and limit flexibility of business units. Fourth, a concentration strategy allows a firm to invest profits back into the business, rather than competing with other corporate holdings for the investment funds.

On the other hand, concentration strategies entail several risks, especially when environments are unstable. Since the organization is dependent on one product or business area to sustain itself, change can dramatically reduce organizational performance. The airline industry is a good example of the effects of uncertainty on organizational performance. Prior to deregulation in the airline industry, most of the major carriers were profitable. They had protected routes and fixed prices. However, deregulation and the ensuing increase in competition hurt the profitability of all domestic carriers. Since most of the major carriers were pursuing concentration strategies, they did not have other business areas to offset their losses. Consequently, several airlines were acquired or went bankrupt.

Product obsolescence and industry maturity create additional risks for organizations pursuing a concentration strategy. If the principal product of an organization becomes obsolete or matures, organizational performance can suffer until the organization develops another product that is appealing to the market. Some organizations are never able to duplicate earlier successes. Furthermore, since they only have experience in one line of business, they have limited ability to switch to other areas when times get tough. In the AOL-Time Warner example at the beginning of the chapter, AOL was facing obsolescence of its dial-up services as broadband and cable access received greater acceptance. Time Warner faced substitution of traditional media with Internet distribution methods.

Concentration strategies can also lead to uneven cash flow and profitability. While the business is growing, the organization may find itself in a "cash poor" situation, since growth often entails additional investments in capital equipment and marketing. On the other hand, once growth levels off, the organization is likely to find itself in a "cash rich" situation, with limited opportunities for profitable investment in the business itself. In fact, this may be one of the most important reasons that organizations in mature markets begin to diversify.[3] Having exhausted all reasonable opportunities to reinvest cash in innovation, renewal, or revitalization, organizational managers may look to other areas for growth.

Finally, a concentration strategy may not provide enough challenge or stimulation to managers. In other words, they may begin to get tired of doing the same things year after year. This is less true in organizations that are growing rapidly, since growth typically provides excitement and promotion opportunities.

Many successful organizations abandon their concentration strategies at some point due to market saturation, increased competition, or some other reason. Corporate strategy typically evolves from concentration to some form of vertical integration or diversification of products, markets, or resource conversion processes (see Exhibit 5.2).[4] Vertical integration and diversification are the topics of the next two sections. The final stage of Exhibit 5.2, restructuring, will be discussed in Chapter 7.

Vertical Integration

Vertical integration is the term used to describe the extent to which a firm is involved in several stages of the industry supply chain. A typical industry supply chain, which is illustrated in Exhibit 5.3, begins with *extraction* of raw materials such as timber, ore, and crude oil. In *primary manufacturing*, these raw materials are converted into commodities such as wood pulp and iron. Primary manufacturing sometimes involves the creation of components that are used to assemble final products, such as the engine, transmission, and brake systems used in automobiles. *Final product manufacturing* involves the creation of a product that is in its final form prior to consumption, such as the final assembly of an automobile. At this point branding becomes very important, since consumers associate brand names of final products with particular levels of quality, service, and reliability. Finally, *wholesaling* entails channeling final products to retail outlets and retailing consists of selling these products to the ultimate consumer. Some products bypass the wholesaling and/or retailing stages due to direct sale by the manufacturer to customers.[5] Also, as firms increase their use of the Internet to coordinate their buying activities, some wholesale distribution channels may be eliminated in some industries.

Exhibit 5.2   *The Development of Corporate-Level Strategy*

Exhibit 5.3 *Industry Supply Chain for Manufacturing Firms*

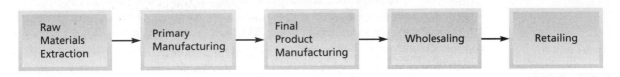

Source: Adapted from J.R. Galbraith and R.K. Kazanjian, *Strategy Implementation: Structure, Systems and Process,* 2nd ed. (St. Paul: West Publishing, 1986): 51.

Some industries, such as steel and wood products, contain firms that are predominantly vertically integrated. In other industries, such as apparel, vertical integration is limited and most organizations are only involved in one or a few stages. Firms may pursue vertical integration for a variety of reasons, including increased control over the quality of supplies or the way a product is marketed, better or more complete information about supplies or markets, greater opportunity for product differentiation through coordinated effort, or simply because they believe they can enhance profits through assuming one of the functions that was previously performed by another company.[6] For example, Walt Disney Co. and other entertainment giants like Viacom are involved in movie and television studios, movie distribution, broadcast and cable networks, theme parks, and retailing with the intention of controlling their product from concept to customers. *Transaction cost economics*, which is the study of economic exchanges and their costs, described in Exhibit 5.4, provides a cost perspective on vertical integration that helps explain when vertical integration may be appropriate.[7]

Exhibit 5.4 *Transaction Costs and Vertical Integration*

From a transaction cost perspective, firms can either negotiate on the open market for the products and services they need or they can produce these products and services themselves. If an organization can obtain required resources from a competitive open market without allocating an undue amount of time or other resources to the contracting process or contract enforcement, it is probably in its best interests to buy from the market instead of vertically integrating. However, when transaction costs are high enough to encourage an organization to produce a good or service in-house instead of buying it from the open market, a **market failure** is said to exist. The market is likely to "fail" under the following conditions:

- The future is highly uncertain. It may be too costly or impossible to identify all of the possible situations that may occur and to incorporate these possibilities into the contract.
- Only one or a small number of suppliers of a good or service exists, and these suppliers are likely to pursue their own self-interests.
- One party to a transaction has more knowledge about the transaction or a series of transactions than another.
- An organization invests in an asset that can only be used to produce a specific good or service, which makes use of the market difficult (asset specificity).

Sources: O.E. Williamson, *Markets and Hierachies: Analysis and Antitrust Implications* (New York: The Free Press, 1975); O.E. Williamson, *The Economic Institutions of Capitalism* (New York: The Free Press, 1985).

Research has not generally found vertical integration to be a highly profitable strategy relative to the other corporate-level strategies.[8] However, many of the firms that have been studied are old and large. They may have used vertical integration with success as their industries were forming. As one vertical integration expert explained, vertical integration can "lock firms in" to unprofitable adjacent businesses.[9] However, this does not mean that all vertical integration is unprofitable.

Furthermore, a recent study suggested that vertical integration may be associated with reduced administrative, selling, and R&D costs, but higher production costs. The researchers believe that the higher production costs may be a result of a lack of incentive on the part of internal suppliers to keep their costs down. Since the internal suppliers have a guaranteed customer, they do not have to be as competitive.[10]

Guarantee of an exclusive supplier arrangement can have the same consequences. For example, at the height of its popularity, the television program *Home Improvement*, produced by Disney subsidiary Walt Disney Television, was broadcast on ABC, which was purchased by Disney as a way to link a program supplier with a network distributor. In 1997, Wind Dancer Production, which also produced *Home Improvement*, sued production partner Touchstone, charging that the studio would not open up negotiations with other networks and had agreed to a special deal with ABC, foregoing a potentially higher price at another network.[11]

An important point to remember with regard to all of the strategies is that some companies are pursuing them successfully. Furthermore, vertical integration often requires substantially different skills than those currently possessed by the firm. In this regard, vertical integration is similar to unrelated diversification, a topic that will be discussed later in this chapter.[12] A firm that can master one stage of the industry supply chain will not necessarily excel at other stages. For this reason, many firms avoid vertical integration and move directly into some form of diversification.

Diversification Strategies

Diversification can be divided into two broad categories. *Related diversification* implies organizational involvement in activities that are somehow related to the dominant or "core" business of the organization, often through common markets or similar technologies. *Unrelated diversification* does not depend on any pattern of relatedness. Some of the most common reasons for diversification are listed in Exhibit 5.5.[13] They are divided into strategic reasons, which are frequently cited by executives in the popular business press, and personal motives that CEOs may have for pursuing diversification.

Unrelated Diversification. Large, unrelated diversified firms, such as General Electric and Hitachi, are often called *conglomerates*, since they are involved in a conglomeration of unrelated businesses. Most, but not all, research has demonstrated that unrelated firms have lower profitability than firms pursuing other corporate-level strategies.[14] There is also some evidence that unrelated diversification is associated with higher levels of risk than other strategies.[15] Unrelated diversification places significant demands on corporate-level executives due to increased complexity and technological changes across industries. In fact, it is very difficult for a manager to understand each of the core technologies and ap-

---

Exhibit 5.5   A Few Common Reasons for Diversification

Strategic Reasons

Risk reduction through investments in dissimilar businesses or less dynamic environments

Stabilization or improvement in earnings

Improvement in growth

Cash generated in slower growing traditional areas exceeds that needed for profitable invest
ment in those areas (organizational slack)

Application of resources, capabilities, and core competencies to related areas

Generation of synergy/economies of scope

Use of excess debt capacity (organizational slack)

Desire to learn new technologies

Increase in market power

Desire to turn around a failing business, leading to high returns

Motives of the CEO

Desire to increase power and status

Desire to increase compensation from running a larger enterprise

Desire to increase value of the firm

Craving for a more interesting and challenging management environment (boredom)

---

preciate the special requirements of each of the individual units in an unrelated diversified firm. Consequently, the effectiveness of management may be reduced.

Nevertheless, some firms have had success with unrelated diversification. Ford Motor is making literally billions of dollars each year in profits from its highly successful financial subsidiaries.[16] Also, General Electric, one of the biggest conglomerates in the world, has enjoyed many years of strong financial performance.[17]

Related Diversification. When an organization chooses to diversify from its original core business into other businesses, it often decides to enter an industry that seems to be similar or related to what it already knows. Most of the research on diversification strategies indicates that some form of relatedness among diversified businesses, rather than unrelatedness, leads to higher financial performance.[18] Also, a more recent study demonstrated that related diversification is also associated with reduced risk.[19]

Related diversification is based on similarities that exist among the products, services, markets, or resource conversion processes of two businesses. These similarities are supposed to lead to synergy, which means that the whole is greater than the sum of its parts. In other words, one organization should be able to produce two related products or services more efficiently than two organizations each producing one of the products or services on its own. The same reasoning applies to similar markets and similar resource conversion processes. For example, Johnson and Johnson is involved in a wide variety of diversified businesses; however, virtually all of them are related to converting chemical substances into drugs and toiletries.

Relatedness comes in two forms, tangible and intangible.[20] *Tangible relatedness* means that the organization has the opportunity to use the same physical resources for multiple purposes. Tangible relatedness can lead to synergy through resource sharing. For example, if two similar products are manufactured in the same plant, operating synergy is said to exist. Other examples of synergy resulting from tangible relatedness include (1) using the same marketing or distribution channels for multiple related products, (2) buying similar raw materials for related products through a centralized purchasing office to gain purchasing economies, (3) providing corporate training programs to employees from different divisions that are all engaged in the same type of work, and (4) advertising multiple products simultaneously.

Intangible relatedness occurs any time capabilities developed in one area can be applied to another area. When executed properly, intangible relatedness can result in managerial synergy.[21] For example, Toys 'R' Us developed skill in retailing that was directly applicable to Kids 'R' Us. Also, Campbell Soup has applied skills in manufacturing and packaging soup to a variety of other products. Synergy based on intangible resources, such as brand name or management skills and knowledge, may be more conducive to the creation of a sustainable competitive advantage, since intangible resources are hard to imitate and are never used up.[22]

Some types of relatedness are more imaginary than real. For example, the relatedness between oil and other forms of energy such as solar and coal proved illusive to several of the large oil companies, who experienced performance problems in these "related business ventures." In addition, even if relatedness is evident, synergy *has to be created*, which means that the two related businesses must fit together *and* that organizational managers must work at creating efficiencies from the combination process.[23]

Two types of fit are required: strategic fit and organizational fit. *Strategic fit* refers to the effective matching of strategic organizational capabilities. For example, if two organizations in two related businesses combine their resources, but they are both strong in the same areas and weak in the same areas, then the potential for synergy is diminished. Once combined, they will continue to exhibit the same capabilities. However, if one of the organizations is strong in R&D, but lacks marketing power, while the other organization is weak in R&D, but strong in marketing, then there is real potential for both organizations to be better off— if managed properly. *Organizational fit* occurs when two organizations or business units have similar management processes, cultures, systems, and structures.[24] Organizational fit makes organizations compatible, which facilitates resource sharing, communication, and transference of knowledge and skills.

Diversification Methods

Once an organization has decided to diversify, it can pursue one of three basic approaches: an internal venture to develop the new business on its own, an acquisition, or a joint venture.

Internal Ventures. An *internal venture* depends on the research and development activities of an organization. Since only the core organization is involved, management has greater control over the progress of the venture. Furthermore, proprietary information need not be shared with other companies, and all profits are retained within the organization. However, the risks of failure are high and even successful ventures take many years to become profitable.[25] Acquisitions are a much faster way to enter new markets. In fact, they are often considered a "substitute for innovation."[26] Joint ventures may not provide entry to new markets as fast as acquisitions, but they are a way for firms to share valuable skills and resources and spread risks across more than one company. Acquisitions and joint ventures will be discussed in the next two sections.

Mergers and Acquisitions. As an alternative to corporate venturing, some organizations choose to buy diversification in the form of acquisitions. *Mergers* occur any time two organizations combine into one. *Acquisitions*, in which one organization buys a controlling interest in the stock of another organization or buys it outright from its owners, are the most common types of mergers. Acquisitions are a relatively quick way to (1) enter new markets, (2) acquire new products or services, (3) learn new resource conversion processes, (4) acquire needed knowledge and skills, (5) vertically integrate, (6) broaden markets geographically, or (7) fill needs in the corporate portfolio.[27]

Unfortunately, most of the research evidence seems to indicate that mergers and acquisitions are not, on average, financially beneficial to the shareholders of the acquiring firm.[28] In one study of 191 acquisitions in 29 industries, researchers found that acquisitions were associated with declining profitability, reduced research and development expenditures, fewer patents produced, and increases in financial leverage.[29] Perhaps the most condemning evidence to date concerning mergers and acquisitions that were pursued to achieve diversification was presented by Michael Porter.[30] He studied the diversification records of 33 large, prestigious U.S. companies over the 1950–1986 period and concluded that the corporate strategies of most companies reduced, rather than enhanced, shareholder value. He discovered that most of these companies divested many more of their acquisitions than they kept. For example, CBS, in an effort to create an "entertainment company," bought organizations involved in toys, crafts, sports teams, and musical instruments. All of these businesses were sold due to lack of fit with the traditional broadcasting business of CBS.

Exhibit 5.6 provides several explanations for why acquisitions, on average, tend to depress profitability (at least in the short term). The mixed reactions of analysts following the announcement of the AOL-Time Warner merger reflect all of these concerns. Following the announcement, *The Wall Street Journal* ran an article titled, "Does Everybody Have to Own Everything?" Merger and acquisition analyst Morton Pierce argued against the logic of powerful companies tying themselves exclusively to one partner, "If I'm Time Warner and I own that kind of library (of content), should I ever worry I'm not going to get it out there? And, if I'm AT&T and I own cable, should I worry that content won't come to me?"[31]

Does this mean that all mergers are doomed to failure? Recently researchers have been able to identify factors that seem to be associated with successful and unsuccessful mergers. Unsuccessful mergers were associated with a large amount of debt, overconfident or incompetent managers, poor ethics, changes in top management or the structure of the acquiring organization, and diversification away from the core area in which the firm is strongest. The successful mergers were related to low-to-moderate amounts of debt, a high level of relatedness leading to synergy, friendly negotiations (no resistance), a continued focus on the core business, careful selection of and negotiations with the acquired firm, and a strong cash or debt position.[32]

Exhibit 5.6   A Few of Many Potential Problems with Mergers and Acquisitions

---

High Financial Costs

1. High premiums typically paid by acquiring firms. If a company was worth $50/share in a relatively efficient financial market prior to an acquisition, why should an acquiring firm pay $75 (a typical premium) or more to buy it?

2. Increased interest costs. Many acquisitions are financed by borrowing money at high interest rates. Leverage typically increased during an acquisition.

3. High advisory fees and other transaction costs. The fees charged by the brokers, lawyers, financiers, consultants, and advisors who orchestrate the deal often cost millions of dollars. In addition, filing fees, document preparation, and legal fees in the event of contestation can be very high.

4. Poison pills. These antitakeover devices make companies very unattractive to a potential buyer. Top managers of target companies have been very creative in designing a variety of poison pills. One example of a poison pill is the "golden parachute," in which target firm executives receive large amounts of severance pay (often millions of dollars) if they lose their jobs due to a hostile takeover.

Strategic Problems

1. High turnover among the managers of the acquired firm. The most valuable asset in most organizations is its people, their knowledge, and their skills. If most managers leave, what has the acquiring firm purchased?

2. Short-term managerial distraction. "Doing a deal" typically takes managers away from the critical tasks of the core businesses for long durations. During this time period, who is steering the ship?

3. Long-term managerial distraction. Sometimes organizations lose sight of the factors that lead to success in their core businesses because they are too distracted running diversified businesses.

4. Less innovation. Acquisitions have been shown to lead to reduced innovative activity, which can hurt long-term performance.

5. No organizational fit. If the cultures, dominant logics, systems, structures, and processes of the acquiring and target firms do not fit, synergy is unlikely.

6. Increased risk. Increased leverage often associated with mergers and acquisitions leads to greater financial risk. Acquiring firms also risk being unable to manage the newly acquired organization successfully.

Sources: Information in this table came from S. Chatterjee, M.H. Lubatkin, D.M. Schwerger, and Y. Weber, "Cultural Differences and Shareholder Value in Related Mergers: Linking Equity and Human Capital," *Strategic Management Journal* 13 (1992): 319–334; J.S. Harrison, "Alternatives to Merger—Joint Ventures and Other Strategies," *Long Range Planning* (December 1987): 78–83; J.P. Walsh, "Top Management Turnover Following Mergers and Acquisitions," *Strategic Management Journal* 9 (1988): 173–184; J.P. Walsh and J.W. Ellwood, "Mergers, Acquisitions, and the Pruning of Managerial Deadwood," *Strategic Management Journal* 12 (1991): 201–207.

Furthermore, researchers have discovered that the largest shareholder gains from merger occurred when the cultures and the top management styles of the two companies were similar (organizational fit).[33] In addition, sharing resources and activities was found to be important to post-merger success.[34] However, it is fair to say, "there are no rules that will invariably lead to a successful acquisition."[35]

Many of the diversification objectives sought by organizations through acquisitions are also available through strategic alliances and joint ventures, which are the topic of the next section.

Strategic Alliances and Joint Ventures. A *strategic alliance* is formed by two or more organizations to develop new products or services, enter new markets, or improve resource conversion processes.[36] When the arrangement is contractual and the alliance operates independently of the organizations that form it, then the alliance typically is called a *joint venture*. Strategic alliances are becoming increasingly popular.[37] Many of the partnerships with external stakeholders discussed in Chapter 2 are examples of strategic alliances and joint ventures.

AT&T has joint ventures with Philips, a leading European electronics and communications firm; Olivetti, a giant in European information processing; Lucky Goldstar, a manufacturer of communications equipment in Korea; Compania Telefonica Nacional de Espana, the Spanish telephone company; and three Taiwanese firms engaged in manufacturing switching equipment. Commenting on these alliances, James Olson, Chairman of the Board at AT&T, stated:

> We can't do everything everywhere—we will need to cooperate and partner with other companies. And we will have to concentrate our resources on activities that contribute to the success of our business and our long-term strategy.
>
> With partners that are established in the information industry overseas, AT&T will concentrate on bringing its evolving data networking capability to countries in the Triad (North America, Western Europe, and the Far East).[38]

Strategic alliances and joint ventures can help organizations achieve many of the same objectives that are sought through mergers and acquisitions. They can lead to improved sales growth and increased earnings or provide balance to a portfolio of businesses, which are some of the most commonly cited reasons for acquisitions.[39] For example, in 1980 Monsanto and General Electric formed a joint venture called Fisher Control International to make regulators and control valves. Within one year, their joint venture ranked second in sales in the growing process control equipment industry. Also, one of the largest and most profitable robot manufacturers in the world is a joint venture between GM and Fanuc Ltd. called GMF Robotics Corp.[40]

The strongest rationale for forming a joint venture is resource sharing. Since joint ventures involve more than one company, they can draw on a much larger resource base. The resources that are most likely to be transferable through a joint venture are:

1. *Marketing.* Companies can gain marketing information and resources not easily identified by outsiders, such as knowledge of competition, customer behavior, industry condition, and distribution channels.
2. *Technology.* Those participating in a joint venture can use technological skills and specific knowledge that is not generally available.
3. *Raw Materials and Components.* Some joint ventures are formed to have access to different elements of the manufacturing process.
4. *Financial.* Companies can obtain external capital, usually in conjunction with other resources.

5. *Managerial.* Joint venture participants can use specific managerial and entrepreneurial capabilities and skills, usually in conjunction with other resources.
6. *Political.* Some joint ventures are obligatory to enter developing countries; others are formed to gain political commitments.[41]

In addition to the advantages associated with resource sharing, joint ventures can enhance speed of entry into a new field or market because of the expanded base of resources from which ventures can draw. They also spread the risk of failure among all of the participants. That is, a failure will result in a smaller loss to each partner than it would to an organization that pursues the venture on its own. Consequently, compared to mergers or internal venturing, joint ventures are sometimes considered a less risky diversification option.

In spite of their strategic strengths, joint ventures are limiting, in that each organization only has partial control over the venture and enjoys only a percentage of the growth and profitability it creates. They create high administrative costs associated with developing the multiparty equity arrangement and managing the venture once it is undertaken.[42] As in mergers and acquisitions, lack of organizational fit can reduce cooperation and lead to venture failure. Furthermore, joint ventures entail a risk of opportunism by venture partners. Good written contracts can help to alleviate but cannot eliminate this risk.

Successful joint ventures and alliances require careful planning and execution. Managers should communicate the expected benefits of the venture to the important external and internal stakeholders so they will understand the role the alliance will play in the organization.[43] They should also develop a strategic plan for the venture, which consolidates the views of the partners about market potential, competitive trends, and potential threats. There are several additional steps which may be used to improve the likelihood of success:

1. Through careful systematic study, identify an alliance partner that can provide the capabilities that are needed. Avoid the tendency to align with another firm just because alliance-forming is a trend in the industry.
2. Clearly define the roles of each partner and ensure that every joint project is of value to both.
3. Develop a strategic plan for the venture that outlines specific objectives for each partner.
4. Keep top managers involved so that middle managers will stay committed.
5. Meet often, informally, at all managerial levels.
6. Appoint someone to monitor all aspects of the alliance and use an outside mediator when disputes arise.
7. Maintain enough independence to develop the company's own area of expertise. Avoid becoming a complete "captive" of the alliance partner.
8. Anticipate and plan for cultural differences.[44]

While each of the strategies described in this chapter have strengths and weaknesses, often the real key to success is execution. For example, General Electric gains higher-than-normal returns in spite of its unrelated diversification strategy and frequent use of acquisitions for growth. The next section describes a tool used by General Electric and other diversified companies to manage their portfolios of businesses.

PORTFOLIO MANAGEMENT

Portfolio management refers to managing the mix of businesses in the corporate portfolio. CEOs of large diversified organizations like General Electric continually face decisions concerning how to divide organizational resources among diversified units and where to invest new capital. Portfolio models are designed to help managers make these types of decisions.

In spite of their adoption in many organizations, portfolio management techniques are the subject of a considerable amount of criticism.[45] However, since they are still in wide use, this book would be incomplete without them. Keep in mind that they are not a panacea and should not replace other types of sound strategic analysis.

We will begin by describing the simplest and first widely used portfolio model, the Boston Consulting Group Matrix. The model has many shortcomings, stemming mostly from its simplicity. However, most of the other portfolio techniques are adaptations of it, and its simplicity makes it a good starting point. We will then describe a more complete model.

Boston Consulting Group Matrix

The Boston Consulting Group (BCG) Matrix, which is displayed in Exhibit 5.7, is based on two factors, industry growth rate and relative market share. Industry growth rate is the growth rate of the industry in which a particular business unit is involved. Relative market share is calculated as the ratio of the business unit's size to the size of its largest competitor. The two factors are used to plot all of the businesses in which the organization is involved, represented as Stars, Question Marks (also called Problem Children), Cash Cows, and Dogs. The size of the circles in Exhibit 5.7 represents the size of the various businesses of an organization. Remember that only one organization, comprised of many different business units, is plotted on each matrix.

The BCG Matrix is sometimes useful in planning cash flows. Cash Cows tend to generate more cash than they can effectively reinvest, while Question Marks require additional cash to sustain rapid growth, and Stars generate about as much cash as they use, on average.[46] According to the Boston Consulting Group, Stars and Cash Cows, with their superior market share positions, tend to be the most profitable businesses.[47]

Consequently, the optimal BCG portfolio contains a balance of Stars, Cash Cows, and Question Marks. Stars have the greatest potential for growth and tend to be highly profitable. However, as the industries in which Stars are involved mature and their growth slows, they should naturally become Cash Cows. Therefore, Question Marks are important because of their potential role as future Stars in the organization. Dogs are the least attractive types of business. The original prescription was to divest them.[48] However, even Dogs can be maintained in the portfolio as long as they do not become a drain on corporate resources. Also, some organizations are successful at positioning their Dogs in an attractive niche in their industries.

One of the shortcomings of the BCG Matrix is that it does not allow for changes in strategy due to differing environments. The standard BCG prescription is this: achieve high market share leadership and become a Star or a Cash Cow. The problem with this prescription is that it may only be valid for firms

Exhibit 5.7   *The Boston Consulting Group Matrix*

Source: B. Hedley, "Strategy and the Business Portfolio," *Long Range Planning* 10 (February 1977): 12. Copyright © 1977. Reprinted with permission from Pergamon Press Ltd., Headington Hill Hall, Oxford OX3 OBW, United Kingdom.

pursuing a low-cost leadership strategy. The use of market share as a measure of competitive strategy carries with it the implicit assumption that size has led to economies of scale and learning effects, and that these effects have resulted in competitive success through the creation of a low-cost position. Differentiation and focus competitive strategies are not incorporated into the model. Also, companies that are successful in pursuing focus strategies (through low cost or differentiation) in low-growth industries may be classified as Dogs even though their profit streams are strong. For example, Rolex would qualify as a Dog.

Other problems with the BCG Matrix are related to its simplicity. Only two factors are considered and only two divisions, high and low, are used for each factor. Also, growth rate is inadequate as the only indicator of the attractiveness of an industry. For example, some fast-growing industries have never been particularly profitable.[49] Market share, for all of the reasons stated previously, is also an insufficient indicator of competitive position. Other variables, such as corporate image, cost position, or R&D advantages, are likely to be equally or more important to the competitiveness of a business.

A common criticism that applies to many portfolio models, and especially the BCG Matrix, is that they are based on the past instead of the future.[50] Given the rate of change in the current economic and political environments, this criticism is probably valid. Finally, another problem that is inherent in all matrix approaches is that industries are hard to define.

In conclusion, the BCG Matrix is only applicable to firms in particular operating environments that are pursuing low-cost leadership strategies based on the experience curve. Nevertheless, the Matrix may help firms anticipate cash needs and flows. Numerous organizational managers and business writers have developed portfolio matrices that overcome some of the limitations of the BCG Matrix. One of these approaches will now be described.

The General Electric Business Screen

Virtually any variables or combination of variables of strategic importance can be plotted along the axes of a portfolio matrix. The selection of variables depends on what the organization considers important. Many matrices contain factors that are composites of several variables. One of the most famous of these, developed at General Electric, is illustrated in Exhibit 5.8. The GE model is referred to as the GE Portfolio Matrix, the Nine-Cell Grid, or the GE Business Screen.

Exhibit 5.8   *The General Electric Business Screen*

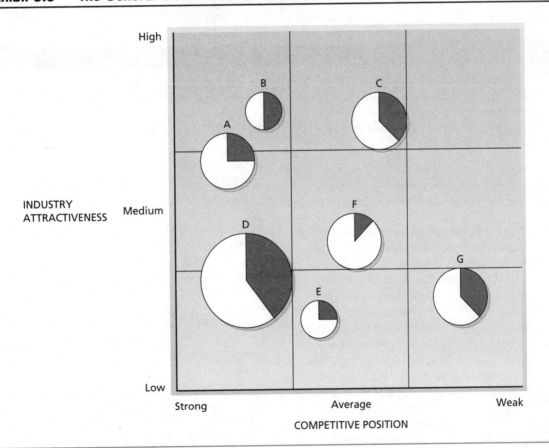

Source: C.W. Hofer and D. Schendel, *Strategy Formulation: Analytical Concepts* (St. Paul: West Publishing, 1978): 32.

In the GE Business Screen, the area in the circles represents the size of the industries in which each business competes. The slice out of the circle is the market share of the business unit in each of these industries. The variables that are used to assess industry attractiveness are typically derived from the objectives and characteristics of the organization (i.e., attitude toward growth, profitability, or social responsibility) and the industries themselves. Assessment of competitive position is based on a firm's position with respect to the key success factors in an industry.[51]

An organization would like to have all of its businesses in the top left cell. These businesses are called Winners. However, some of these Winners should be established businesses that are not growing rapidly so that a portion of their cash flow can be used to support developing winners.

The way an organization allocates its internal resources reconfirms its selection of businesses. For example, business units that are considered critical to the future success of an organization should receive high priority in resource allocation decisions, whereas unimportant businesses may receive only maintenance levels of support. From a portfolio management perspective, businesses that are in a strong competitive position in attractive industries should be given the highest priority.

In conclusion, while all portfolio management models have weaknesses and limitations, they provide an additional tool to assist managers in anticipating cash flows and making resource allocation decisions. The GE Business Screen, in particular, is flexible enough to accommodate a wide variety of indicators of industry attractiveness and competitive strength.

KEY POINTS SUMMARY

Corporate strategy focuses on the selection of businesses in which the organization will compete and on the tactics used to enter and manage those businesses and other corporate-level resources. Some of the most important points discussed in this chapter include the following:

1. At the corporate level, management responsibilities include direction setting, development of a corporate strategy, selection of businesses and management of the portfolio of businesses, selection of tactics for diversification and growth, and management of corporate-level resources.
2. The three broad approaches to corporate strategy are single business/concentration, vertical integration, and diversification, which is divided into two broad categories, related and unrelated.
3. Single business/concentration strategies allow an organization to focus on doing one business very well; however, a key disadvantage is that the organization is dependent on that one business for survival.
4. Vertical integration allows an organization to become its own supplier or customer. However, according to the theory of transaction cost economics,

if required resources can be obtained from a competitive open market without allocating an undue amount of time or other resources to the contracting process or contract enforcement, it is probably in the best interests of an organization to buy from the market instead of vertically integrating.

5. Research indicates that unrelated diversification is not a particularly successful strategy; however, some firms, such as GE, perform quite well with it.
6. Related diversification is a very popular strategy. Businesses are related if they share a common market, technology, raw material, or any one of many other factors. However, for a related diversification strategy to have its full positive impact, strategic and organizational fit is required.
7. Diversification can be accomplished through internal venturing, acquisition of existing businesses, or strategic alliances/joint ventures. Each of these tactics has advantages and disadvantages.
8. Portfolio models help organizations manage their portfolio of diversified businesses. Two examples are the Boston Consulting Group Matrix and the GE Business Screen.

END NOTES

1   T.E. Weber, M. Peeres, and N. Wingfield, "You've Got Time Warner!" *The Wall Street Journal* (January 11, 2000): B1.

2   R.P. Rumelt, *Strategy, Structure and Economic Performance* (Boston: Harvard Business School, 1974); R.P. Rumelt, "Diversification Strategy and Profitability," *Strategic Management Journal* 3 (1982): 359–369.

3   H.I. Ansoff, *Corporate Strategy: An Analytical Approach to Business Policy for Growth and Expansion* (New York: McGraw-Hill Book Company, 1965): 129–130.

4   A.D. Chandler, Jr., *Strategy and Structure: Chapters in the History of the Industrial Enterprise* (Cambridge, Mass.: MIT Press, 1962).

5   J.R. Galbraith and R.K. Kazanjian, *Strategy Implementation: Structure, Systems and Process*, 2nd ed. (St. Paul: West Publishing, 1986): Chapter 4.

6   K.R. Harrigan, "Formulating Vertical Integration Strategies," *Academy of Management Review* 9 (1984): 639.

7   O.E. Williamson, *Markets and Hierarchies: Analysis and Antitrust Implications* (New York: The Free Press, 1975) and *The Economic Institutions of Capitalism* (New York: The Free Press, 1985).

8   Rumelt, *Strategy, Structure and Economic Performance*; Rumelt, "Diversification Strategy and Profitability."

9   Harrigan, "Formulating Vertical Integration Strategies."

10   R.A. D'Aveni and D.J. Ravenscraft, "Economies of Integration Versus Bureaucracy Costs: Does Vertical Integration Improve Performance?" *Academy of Management Journal* 37 (1994): 1167–1206.

11   L. Rice, "Loot Time for Tool Time," *Broadcasting & Cable* (Oct. 13, 1997): 32–33; T.L. Stanley, "The 'Home Improvement' Producers Have Filed a Suit Against Their Production Partner, Walt Disney Television," *MediaWeek* (March 3, 1997): 9; J. Flint, "Disney Disses 'Home' Rule," *Variety* (March 3, 1997): 1.

12   R.E. Hoskisson, J.S. Harrison, and D.A. Dubofsky, "Capital Market Implementation of M-Form Implementation and Diversification Strategy," *Strategic Management Journal* 12 (1991): 271–279.

13   H.I. Ansoff, *Corporate Strategy: An Analytical Approach to Business Policy for Growth and Expansion* (New York: McGraw-Hill Book Company, 1965): 130–132; J.S. Harrison, "Alternatives to Merger—Joint Ventures and Other Strategies," *Long Range Planning* (December 1987): 78–83; C.W.L. Hill and G.S. Hansen, "A Longitudinal Study of the Cause and Consequence of Changes in Diversification in the U.S. Pharmaceutical Industry," *Strategic Management Journal* 12 (1991): 187–199; W.G. Lewellen, "A Pure Financial Rationale for the Conglomerate Merger," *Journal of Finance* 26 (1971): 521–537; F.M. McDougall and D.K. Round, "A Comparison of Diversifying and Nondiversifying Australian Industrial Firms," *Academy of Management Journal* 27 (1984): 384–398; R. Reed and G.A. Luffman, "Diversification: The Growing Confusion," *Strategic Management Journal* 7 (1986): 29–35.

14   A few examples of the many studies that demonstrate low performance associated with unrelated diversification are R. Amit and J. Livnat, "Diversification Strategies, Business Cycles, and Economic Performance," *Strategic Management Journal* 9 (1988): 99–110; R.A. Bettis and V. Mahajan, "Risk/Return Performance of Diversified Firms," *Management Science* 31 (1985): 785–799; D. Ravenscraft and F.M. Scherer, *Mergers, Selloffs, and Economic Efficiency* (Washington, D.C.: Brookings Institution, 1987); P.G. Simmonds, "The Combined Diversification Breadth and Mode Dimensions and the Performance of Large Diversified Firms,"

Strategic Management Journal 11 (1990): 399–410; P. Varadarajan and V. Ramanujam, "Diversification and Performance: A Reexamination Using a New Two-Dimensional Conceptualization of Diversity in Firms," *Academy of Management Journal* 30 (1982): 380–393. On the other hand, the following studies are among those that support the superiority of unrelated diversification: R.M. Grant and A.P. Jammine, "Performance Differences Between the Wrigley/Rumelt Strategic Categories," *Strategic Management Journal* 9 (1988): 333–346; A. Michel and I. Shaked, "Does Business Diversification Affect Performance?" *Financial Management* (Winter 1984): 18–25.

15   M.C. Lauenstein, "Diversification—The Hidden Explanation of Success," *Sloan Management Review* (Fall 1985): 49–55; M. Lubatkin and R.C. Rogers, "Diversification, Systematic Risk and Shareholder Return: A Capital Market Extension of Rumelt's 1974 Study," *Academy of Management Journal* 32 (1989): 454–465; M. Lubatkin and H.G. O'Neill, "Merger Strategies and Capital Market Risk," *Academy of Management Journal* 30 (1987): 665–684; M. Lubatkin, "Value Creating Mergers: Fact or Folklore?" *Academy of Management Executive* (November 1988): 295–302; C.A. Montgomery and H. Singh, "Diversification Strategy and Systematic Risk," *Strategic Management Journal* 5 (1984): 181–191.

16   A.B. Fisher, "Ford Rolls Out a Money Machine," *Fortune* (April 15, 1996): 48.

17   "A Conversation with Roberto Goizueta and Jack Welch," *Fortune* (December 11, 1995): 98–99.

18   A detailed review of this literature is found in R.E. Hoskisson and M.A. Hitt, "Antecedents and Performance Outcomes of Diversification: A Review and Critique of Theoretical Perspectives," *Journal of Management* 16 (1990): 468. More recent evidence is found in P.S. Davis, R.B. Robinson, Jr., J.A. Pearce, and S.H. Park, "Business Unit Relatedness and Performance: A Look at the Pulp and Paper Industry," *Strategic Management Journal* 13 (1992): 349–361 and in J.S. Harrison, E.H. Hall, Jr., and R. Nargundkar, "Resource Allocation as an Outcropping of Strategic Consistency: Performance Implications," *Academy of Management Journal* 36 (1993): 1026–1051.

19   M. Lubatkin and S. Chatterjee, "Extending Modern Portfolio Theory Into the Domain of Corporate Diversification: Does It Apply?" *Academy of Management Journal* 37 (1994): 109–136.

20   M.E. Porter, *Competitive Advantage: Creating and Sustaining Superior Performance* (New York: The Free Press, 1985): 317–363.

21   Ansoff, *Corporate Strategy*.

22   H. Itami, *Mobilizing Invisible Assets* (Cambridge, Mass.: Harvard University Press, 1987).

23   P.R. Nayyar, "On the Measurement of Corporate Diversification Strategy: Evidence From Large U.S. Service Firms," *Strategic Management Journal* 13 (1992): 219–235; R. Reed and G.A. Luffman, "Diversification: The Growing Confusion," *Strategic Management Journal* 7 (1986): 29–36.

24   D.B. Jemison and S.B. Sitkin, "Corporate Acquisitions: A Process Perspective," *Academy of Management Review* 11 (1986): 145–163.

25   E.R. Biggadike, "The Risky Business of Diversification," *Harvard Business Review* (May/June 1979): 103–111.

26   M.A. Hitt, R.E. Hoskisson, R.D. Ireland, and J.S. Harrison, "Effects of Acquisitions on R&D Inputs and Outputs," *Academy of Management Journal* 34 (1991): 693–706.

27 Lubatkin, "Value Creating Mergers: Fact or Folklore?"; J. Pfeffer, "Merger as a Response to Organizational Interdependence," *Administrative Science Quarterly* 17 (1972): 382–394; J.H. Song, "Diversifying Acquisitions and Financial Relationships: Testing 1974–1976 Behaviour," *Strategic Management Journal* 4 (1983): 97–108; F. Trautwein, "Merger Motives and Merger Prescriptions," *Strategic Management Journal* 11 (1990): 283–295.

28 One of the most active proponents of the view that mergers and acquisitions create value for acquiring-firm shareholders is Michael Lubatkin (see Lubatkin, "Value-Creating Mergers: Fact or Folklore?"). However, he recently reported strong evidence that contradicts his earlier conclusions in S. Chatterjee, M.H. Lubatkin, D.M. Schweiger, and Y. Weber, "Cultural Differences and Shareholder Value in Related Mergers: Linking Equity and Human Capital," *Strategic Management Journal* 13 (1992): 319–334. Other strong summary evidence that mergers and acquisitions do not create value is found in W.B. Carper, "Corporate Acquisitions and Shareholder Wealth," *Journal of Management* 16 (1990): 807–823; D.K. Datta, G.E. Pinches, and V.K. Narayanan, "Factors Influencing Wealth Creation From Mergers and Acquisitions: A Meta-Analysis," *Strategic Management Journal* 13 (1992).

29 M.A. Hitt, R.E. Hoskisson, R.D. Ireland, and J.S. Harrison, "Are Acquisitions a Poison Pill for Innovation?" *Academy of Management Executive* (November 1991): 20–35.

30 M.E. Porter, "From Competitive Advantage to Corporate Strategy," *Harvard Business Review* (May/June 1987): 59.

31 G.C. Hill and L. Landro, "Does Everybody Have to Own Everything?" *The Wall Street Journal* (January 12, 2000): B1.

32 M. Hitt, J. Harrison, R.D. Ireland, and A. Best, "Attributes of Successful and Unsuccessful Acquisitions of U.S. Firms," *British Journal of Management* 9 (1998): 91–114; J.B. Kusewitt, Jr., "An Exploratory Study of Strategic Acquisition Factors Relating to Success," *Strategic Management Journal* 6 (1985): 151–169; L.M. Shelton, "Strategic Business Fits and Corporate Acquisition: Empirical Evidence," *Strategic Management Journal* 9 (1988): 279–287.

33 Chatterjee, Lubatkin, Schweiger, and Weber, "Cultural Differences and Shareholder Value in Related Mergers"; D.K. Datta, "Organizational Fit and Acquisition Performance: Effects of Post-Acquisition Integration," *Strategic Management Journal* 12 (1991): 281–297; D.B. Jemison and S.B. Sitkin, "Corporate Acquisitions: A Process Perspective," *Academy of Management Review* 11 (1986): 145–163.

34 T.H. Brush, "Predicted Change In Operational Synergy and Post-Acquisition Performance of Acquired Businesses," *Strategic Management Journal* 17 (1996): 1–24.

35 F.T. Paine and D.J. Power, "Merger Strategy: An Examination of Drucker's Five Rules for Successful Acquisition," *Strategic Management Journal* 5 (1984): 99–110.

36 B. Boyrs and D.B. Jemison, "Hybrid Arrangements as Strategic Alliances: Theoretical Issues in Organizational Combinations," *Academy of Management Review* 14 (1989): 234–249; K.R. Harrigan, "Joint Ventures and Competitive Strategy," *Strategic Management Journal* 9 (1988): 141–158.

37 B.R. Barringer and J.S. Harrison, "Walking a Tightrope: Creating Value Through Interorganizational Relationships," *Journal of Management* 26 (2000): 367–403.

38 J.E. Olson and T.A. Cooper, "CEOs On Strategy: Two Companies, Two Strategies," *Journal of Business Strategy* (Summer 1987): 53.

39 J.S. Harrison, "Alternatives to Merger—Joint Ventures and Other Strategies," *Long Range Planning* (December 1987): 78–83.

40 C.E. Schillaci, "Designing Successful Joint Ventures," *Journal of Business Strategies* (Fall 1987): 59–63.

41 C.E. Schillaci, "Designing Successful Joint Ventures," *Journal of Business Strategies* (Fall 1987): 60. See also J. Hennart, "A Transactions Costs Theory of Equity Joint Ventures," *Strategic Management Journal* 9 (1988): 361–374.

42 Harrigan, "Joint Ventures and Competitive Strategy"; R.N. Osborn and C.C. Baughn, "Forms of Interorganizational Governance for Multinational Alliances," *Academy of Management Journal* 33 (1990): 503–519.

43 P. Lorange and J. Roos, "Why Some Strategic Alliances Succeed and Others Fail," *Journal of Business Strategy*, (January/February 1991): 25–30.

44 P. Burrows, "How a Good Partnership Goes Bad," *Electronic Business* (March 30, 1992): 87–89 and J.B. Treece and K.L. Miller, "The Partners," *Business Week* (February 10, 1992): 102–107.

45 R.A. Kerin, V. Mahajan, and P.R. Varadarajan, *Strategic Market Planning* (Needham Heights, Mass.: Allyn & Bacon, 1990): 94; J.A. Seeger, "Reversing the Images of BCG's Growth Share Matrix," *Strategic Management Journal* 5 (1984): 93–97; S.F. Slater and T.J. Zwirlein, "Shareholder Value and Investment Strategy Using the General Portfolio Model," *Journal of Management* 18 (1992): 717–732; R. Wensley, "PIMS and BCG: New Horizons or False Dawn," *Strategic Management Journal* 3 (1982): 147–158.

46 D.C. Hambrick, I.C. MacMillan, and D.L. Day, "Strategic Attributes and Performance in the BCG Matrix—A PIMS-Based Analysis of Industrial Product Businesses," *Academy of Management Journal* 25 (1982): 518.

47 Hambrick, MacMillan, and Day, "Strategic Attributes and Performance in the BCG Matrix."

48 B.D. Henderson, *Henderson On Corporate Strategy* (Cambridge, Mass.: Abt Books, 1979): 164.

49 C.W. Hofer and D. Schendel, *Strategy Formulation: Analytical Concepts* (St. Paul: West Publishing Company, 1978): 31.

50 Slater and Zwirlein, "Shareholder Value"; Seeger, "Reversing the Images."

51 Hofer and Schendel, *Strategy Formulation*, 73–76.

6

Strategy Implementation

At the turn of the century, Xerox is continuing to undergo a significant turnaround. Increasing competition from companies like Canon, coupled with the rapid growth in use of computers for basic printing functions, has caused their core copier business to suffer. In 1999, new CEO G. Richard Thoman articulated a new strategy that everyone believed made sense. It involved movement into printers and realignment of the sales representatives with the larger corporate customers. The idea was to move from selling products to selling integrated product and service solutions.

Unfortunately, Xerox's board concluded that Thoman "had the right strategic direction, but was not able to execute effectively." The restructuring of the sales group hurt morale. Many members of the sales organization felt they were being blamed for the company's performance problems. As the company's stock price lost 60 percent of its value in one year, morale continued to decline and the organization was faced with the potential defection of key employees in sales, product development, engineering, and manufacturing.

As the share price and morale continued to fall, Thoman resigned under pressure. He cited difficulty in making cultural changes at Xerox. He argued, "We didn't have any choice but to change aggressively." In referring to future initiatives, new president, Anne Mulcahy stated, "our execution will be as strong as our strategies."[1]

The previous example illustrates the extraordinary importance of effective strategy implementation. Until strategies are implemented, they are only ideas and intentions, with no real effect on the organization's direction. In the Xerox example, everyone agreed that the strategy was correct, but Thoman was unable to build commitment to and integrate the functional level initiatives required to change the organizational actions.

Strategy implementation typically goes hand-in-hand with strategy formulation, and we have made no attempt to create an artificial barrier between the two activities. However, two important implementation tools remain to be discussed and adding them to the earlier chapters would have made those chapters too long. The first of these tools is functional-level strategy. Business-level strategies are implemented through day-to-day decisions made at the operating level of the firm.[2] The competitive advantages and distinctive competencies that are sought by firms are often embedded in the skills, resources, and capabilities at the functional level. Functional strategies are the plans for matching those skills, resources, and capabilities to the business and corporate strategies of the organization. The second topic is organization structure.

FUNCTIONAL STRATEGIES

Some of the most successful companies of our time are operating in low-growth, moderately profitable industries and are pursuing strategies that are not unique. The reason for their extraordinary success is their attention to the details associated with strategy implementation. For example, one reason McDonald's continues to grow and profit at a time when other fast food chains have suffered is its fast, reliable service, clean restrooms and dining areas, and attentive, polite employees. Also, although two warehouse-style toy chains, Lionel and Child World, filed for Chapter 11 protection under federal bankruptcy law some years ago, Toys 'R' Us continues to prosper because of its attention to product line and inventory management, store location and appearance, and technological improvements that reduce operating costs.

The collective pattern of day-to-day decisions made and actions taken by employees responsible for value activities create *functional strategies* that implement the growth and competitive strategies of the business. In the following sections, we will discuss the responsibilities and patterns of decisions made by marketing, operations, R&D, information systems, human resources, and finance functions in organizations.

Marketing Strategy

One of the most critical responsibilities of marketing employees is to span the boundary of the organization and interact with external stakeholders such as customers and competitors. Marketing is responsible for bringing essential information about new customer needs, projected future demand, competitor actions, and new business opportunities into the organization as an input to plans for continuous improvements, capacity and workforce expansions, new technologies, and new products and services. Motorola makes the most of its technology by emphasizing the essential boundary-spanning role of marketing:

> Members of our sales force are surrogates for customers. They should be able to reach back into Motorola and pull out technologists and other people they need to solve problems and anticipate customer needs. We want to put the salesperson at the top of the organization. The rest of us then serve the salesperson.[3]

Marketing strategy evolves from the cumulative pattern of decisions made by the employees who interact with customers and perform marketing activities. To support growth strategies, marketing identifies new customer opportunities, suggests product opportunities, creates advertising and promotional programs, arranges distribution channels, and creates pricing and customer service policies which help position the company's products for the proper customer groups. If a company pursues a stability or retrenchment strategy within one of its businesses, the demands placed on marketing will change. Instead of pursuing growth, marketing may manage a reduction in the number of customer groups, distribution channels, and products in the product line—all in an attempt to focus on the more profitable and promising aspects of the business. Such was the case with Sturm Ruger & Co., a maker of guns for hunters, target shooters, and collectors. Facing a decline in the gun industry, the company decided it could no longer support wholesalers who also sold Smith & Wesson weapons. Fifty percent of its distributors agreed to supply Ruger guns only, which reduced the company's marketing costs and helped create a prestigious, hard-to-find image for its products.[4]

The competitive strategy of the firm also influences marketing decisions. Low-cost competitive strategies require low-cost channels of distribution and low-risk product and market development activities. If demand can be influenced by advertising or price discounts, then marketing may pursue aggressive advertising and promotion programs or deep price discounts to get demand to a level that will support full capacity utilization and economies of scale within operations, as when the soft drink companies advertise and discount their products. Differentiation strategies require that marketing identify the attributes of products and services that customers will value, price and distribute the product or service in ways that capitalize on the differentiation, and advertise and promote the image of difference.

Operations Strategy

Operations strategy emerges from the pattern of decisions made within the firm about production or service operations. The task of operations managers is to design and manage an operations organization that can create the products and services the firm must have to compete in the marketplace. An effective operations unit "is not necessarily one that promises maximum efficiency or engineering perfection, but rather one that fits the needs of the business—that strives for consistency between its capabilities and policies and the competitive advantage being sought."[5]

Operations managers, like marketing managers, must manage multiple stakeholder interests in their daily decision making. The total quality management (TQM) movement is a direct result of operations managers' neglect of their most critical stakeholders—customers. In the 1970s, many operations managers took the position, "We made it, now it is up to marketing to sell it." The cavalier attitude toward the concerns of customers led to systemic quality problems that undermined entire industries. Faced with fundamental change in their industries, many operations organizations implemented extensive total quality management and continuous improvement programs to help focus operations decisions on the needs of customers.

Growth strategies put pressure on the systems and procedures used to schedule customer orders, plan employee work arrangements, order raw materials, and manage inventories. Retrenchment strategies often target the activities of operations first: line employees are laid-off, equipment is idled, plants (offices and stores) are closed. In implementing an improvement program, an organization may choose to move to sole-source arrangements, which will increase dependency on one supplier and sever relationships with others. Differentiation strategies based on flexibility and high-quality service may require a flexible or temporary workforce, special arrangements with suppliers, and very high levels of training for employees. Major capital investments in new equipment depress earnings in the short run which lowers the earnings per share reported to stockholders. How operations handles these types of trade-off decisions can have a substantial influence on the performance of the firm.

Research and Development Strategy

In many organizations, R&D efforts are essential for effective strategy implementation. The strategy that emerges from the decisions and actions within R&D, engineering, and technical support activities is the *research and development strategy*. For example, a firm that is pursuing a market development growth strategy will invest in applications development so that its products can be tested and qualified for more uses. Fabric manufacturers, for example, put their industrial fabrics through extensive wear-testing to qualify them for everything from conveyor belts to tents to bandages. If the firm is seeking growth through product line development, the engineers and scientists within R&D will modify the product to improve its performance or extend its application to different markets. The wide-spread use of DuPont's Teflon fibers, coating, films, and membranes in everything from pots and pans to industrial equipment is the result of aggressive product development activities within the company.

Once products and entire product lines begin to mature, the focus of much of the R&D effort often shifts to process development.[6] While some product changes may still be required, the firm is primarily concerned with reducing its costs of production. Engineers and scientists work to improve processing methods and conditions and to design special-purpose equipment that can efficiently produce the company's products. For example, some of the R&D efforts within many computer and electronics firms have been redirected toward process development as product lines have matured and foreign competitors have achieved lower processing costs.

Information Systems Strategy

Since the early 1980s, the role of information systems in organizations has changed fundamentally. Before microcomputers, computer information systems were used primarily for accounting transactions and information record keeping. In the 1980s, computer technology and networks revolutionized the way organizations do business, and in the 1990s, the Internet continued the revolution with supply chain integration, new approaches to marketing and advertising, and new Internet-only competitors. In some organizations, an information systems department plans computer use organization-wide so that computer resources are compatible and integrated. However, as systems become more user-friendly and decentralized, many information system activities are being managed within other departments. The pattern of information systems decisions creates an *information systems strategy*. The purpose of the information systems strategy is to provide the organization with the technology and systems that, at a minimum, are necessary for operating, planning, and controlling the business. In some instances, well-designed integrated information systems serve as the foundation for a competitive advantage by allowing more aggressive cost management than competitors, by providing more effective use of timely market information, or by allowing integrated transactions within the supply chain of customers and suppliers.

In many organizations, computer information systems affect every aspect of business operations and serve a major role in linking stakeholders. With spreadsheet packages, expert systems, and other decision-support software, employees at the lowest levels of the organization have the information and the tools to make decisions that were once reserved to middle managers. Computer-aided design (CAD) systems help marketing, manufacturing, and R&D employees develop designs faster and with fewer errors. In computer-integrated manufacturing (CIM) environments, product designs and production schedules are linked directly to manufacturing equipment, which increases accuracy, flexibility, and speed in meeting customer orders. Direct linkages with suppliers help in managing just-in-time delivery arrangements. Real-time inventory systems linked to order-taking systems provide valuable information, which improves customer service. Direct computer linkages with customers provide real-time sales data that the organization may use to plan for the future.[7]

Some organizations have built their entire competitive strategy on effective use of information systems. At Toys 'R' Us, scanners are used to record sales data by product and by store. Store managers use the data to update inventory records and reorder products so that their in-stock position will be assured. The sales data from the hundreds of stores are transmitted daily to the corporate office where they are studied by product and by store to determine patterns and trends in customer buying behavior. Toys 'R' Us has made such effective use of its customer buying information that toy manufacturers regularly consult the company before scaling up to manufacture a new product.

Human Resources Strategy

The pattern of decisions made by managers about performance evaluation, selection, training, rewards, and benefits creates a *human resources (HR) strategy*. In the Xerox example described earlier, the planned changes in marketing strategy were not well coordinated with the management of the human resources. Human resources managers serve a coordinating role between the organization's management and employees, and between the organization and external stakeholder groups including labor unions and government regulators of labor and safety practices such as the Equal Employment Opportunity Commission and the Occupational Safety and Health Administration.

Although the HR staff serves as a resource, most of the actual HR decisions are made by line managers. All managers, whether they are involved in marketing, operations, R&D, or information systems, play the key roles in deciding employee performance levels, training needs, selection criteria, and salary levels.

Different industry environments and organizational strategies tend to reinforce different HR practices. In high-technology and growth organizations, employees are usually hired from outside the organization to fill positions at all levels, entry positions through top-level management. Compensation systems emphasize long-range performance goals, with frequent use of bonus and profit-sharing plans.[8] Therefore, in organizations pursuing growth strategies, like Microsoft in software and Merck in pharmaceuticals, the HR strategy focuses on hiring, training, and placing employees at all levels in the organization, and on developing performance-based compensation strategies.

Mature or cost-oriented businesses usually hire employees at the entry level and promote from within to fill higher-level positions. They are more likely to focus rewards on short-range performance goals and to include seniority issues in compensation systems.[9] Firms following retrenchment strategies must focus their HR priorities on programs for early retirements, structured lay-offs, skills retraining, and outplacement services.

As companies become more global, the challenges of managing human resources are mounting. The HR staff must determine what skills are needed to manage people of different cultures, recruit top candidates worldwide, create training programs and experiences that help employees appreciate other cultures, and conduct relocations worldwide.[10] Furthermore, they may need to create compensation strategies for employees who, because of their national culture, value different reward and benefit packages. For example, in cultures that value personal accomplishment, control of one's destiny, and independence such as the U.S. and Britain, compensation strategies may focus on individual performance. In cultures which value team accomplishment, sacrifice for others, and external control or fate, the rewards may focus on group measures and seniority.[11]

Financial Strategy

The finance and accounting functions play a strategic role within organizations because they control one of the most important resources needed to implement strategies: money. In implementing strategy, two sources of funds are needed: (1) large amounts of capital for growth and maintenance-related objectives and strategies, and (2) expense budgets to support the ongoing, daily activities of the business. The primary purpose of a *financial strategy* is to provide the organization with the capital structure and funds that are appropriate for implementing growth and competitive strategies.

The finance group decides the appropriate levels of debt, equity, and internal financing needed to support strategies by weighing the costs of each alternative, the plans for the funds, and the financial interests of various internal and external stakeholder groups. Finance also determines dividend policies and, through preparation of financial reports, influences how financial performance will be interpreted and presented to stockholders. In fact, financial reports may be the only contact some members of the investment community and most stockholders have with the organization.

Capital and expense budgets are an extremely important means for allocating funds to those departments, projects, and activities that need them to support strategies. All expenditures in capital and expense budgets should be linked back to the strategies of the firm. "The structure that a mature enterprise takes on at any point in time essentially represents the accumulation of a long series of prior resource allocation decisions. If a company wants to develop in a specific direction, it must make these resource allocation decisions in an organized fashion."[12]

The trade-offs that are embedded in financial decisions carry significant implications for strategy implementation. Should the firm pay earnings out in dividends to satisfy stockholders who want a fast return on their investment, or invest them back into the company to benefit employees, communities, and stockholders who want a longer-term increase in share price? In assessing expenses, investments, and earnings, should long-run or short-run performance be given more emphasis and how should that information be presented to stockholders and the investment community? Which internal stakeholder groups— marketing, operations, R&D, employees—should be most influential in capital allocation decisions?

Integrating Functional Strategies

Some researchers have found that in those firms where strategies were implemented effectively, employees worked as a coordinated system with all of their separate but interdependent efforts directed toward the goals of the firm.[13] Consequently, each functional area is one piece of a larger system, and coordination among the pieces is essential to successful strategy execution. Therefore, well-developed functional strategies should have the following characteristics:

1. *Decisions made within each function will be consistent with each other.* For example, if marketing chooses to spend a great deal of money creating a premium brand name for a new product, it should take advantage of distribution channels that allow the product to reach customers who will pay a premium price. If the wrong distribution channels are chosen, then the efforts spent on advertising, promotion, and product placement will be lost. Several years ago, one of the synthetic fiber producers allowed one of its best branded products to become associated with discount, low-quality garments and its investment in the trademark was lost.

2. *Decisions made within one function will be consistent with those made in other functions.* Unfortunately, it is common for the decisions made by one department to be inconsistent with those of another department. Marketing and operations frequently advocate very different approaches to the many interdependent decisions that exist between them. Left to their own devices, with no guidance from the organization, it is likely that marketing, over time, will make decisions that implement a differentiation strategy while manufacturing, over time, implements a low-cost strategy.

3. *Decisions made within functions will be consistent with the strategies of the business.* In a healthy business environment, marketing may pursue market share increases and revenue growth as its top priority. If the business environment changes—demand slows down and profits are squeezed— then the focus of marketing may have to change to stability and profit improvement over sales volume increases. Unless prodded by the organization, marketing may be very reluctant to change from its traditional way of doing business.[14]

The rapid success and subsequent decline of People Express Airlines is a good demonstration of what can happen when there is inconsistency in tactical decisions across departments or between a business strategy and functional strategies.

Following the deregulation of the airlines, Donald Burr started People Express as a low-cost commuter airline. In the beginning, every management decision supported low costs: aircraft were bought second hand, pilots kept planes in the air more hours per day than any other airline, terminal leases were inexpensive, and human resource policies required cross-training, encouraged high productivity, and rewarded employees with profit-sharing plans. In line with its no-frills commuter approach, the company did not book reservations or provide in-flight meals. The airline was extraordinarily successful with its strategy, and achieved the lowest cost position in the industry. However, with success, People Express began to alter its pattern of decisions and, over time, drifted from its low-cost strategy. It pursued longer routes, which pulled it into direct competition with the full-service airlines, even though it did not have the elaborate reservation systems and customer services. It contracted more expensive terminal arrangements and purchased new aircraft at market prices. The close-knit, high-performance culture that encouraged an extraordinary work pace in exchange for profit-sharing was undermined by rapid growth and too many new faces. Just a few years after its start-up, People Express was in serious financial trouble and was forced to sell out to another airline.

Value chain analysis, which was introduced in Chapter 3, is useful in planning the coordination of functional activities during strategy implementation. For managers, the key task of strategy implementation is to align or fit the activities and capabilities of the firm with its chosen strategy. An understanding of the linkages and interdependencies among the value-adding activities becomes critical. For example, in a firm pursuing a low-cost strategy, systemwide low costs are the goal. If the firm manages each activity independently, then what may appear to be a proper low-cost decision may, in fact, work to create higher systemwide costs. For example, if the firm purchases raw materials at the lowest possible price, it may actually be creating higher production costs because of the rework and extra handling required to accommodate lower-quality materials. In such a case, the decisions within each activity seem to fit the firm's strategy but, collectively, they do not. Exhibit 6.1 provides a summary of the functional strategy decision areas. It may be used as a tool for determining functional strategy needs and critiquing consistency among value-adding activities.

BUSINESS-LEVEL STRUCTURES

The *formal organizational structure* specifies the number and types of departments or groups and provides the formal reporting relationships and lines of communication among internal stakeholders. An organization's structure should be designed to support the intended strategy of the firm.[15] The underlying assumption is that a strategy-structure fit will lead to superior organization performance. When making decisions about how to structure an organization, it is important to remember the following:

1. Structure is not an end, but a means to an end. The 'end' is successful organizational performance.
2. There is no one best structure. A change in organization strategy may require a corresponding change in structure to avoid administrative inefficiencies, but the organization's size, strategies, external environment, stakeholder relationships, and management style all influence the appropriateness of a given structure. All structures embody trade-offs.[16]
3. Once in place, the new structure becomes a characteristic of the organization that will serve as a constraint on future strategic choices.
4. Administrative inefficiencies, poor service to customers, communication problems, or employee frustrations may indicate a strategy-structure mismatch.

In Chapter 5, we discussed the types of growth and competitive strategies available to businesses. When managers organize the activities of a business, they usually seek a structure that will support those growth and competitive strategies. Managers typically use one of four organization structures when grouping the activities of a single business or division: functional, product or market group, project matrix, or network. Each of the four structures, illustrated in Exhibit 6.2 (pp. 105–106), has important strengths and weaknesses that must be considered when making organization design decisions. The attributes of the four structures are summarized in Exhibit 6.3 (p. 107).

Exhibit 6.1   *Conducting a Functional Strategy Audit*

The functional strategy audit is a procedure for systematically reviewing the decisions in each of the functional areas to determine which ones should be changed to support the new strategy and needs of stakeholders. The format for the audit is shown.

	Current	Change Needed

Marketing Strategy Decision Areas
Target customers
   (few versus many, what groups, what regions)
Product positioning
   (premium, commodity, multiuse, specialty use)
Product line mix
   (a mix of complementary products)
Product line breadth
   (a full line offering of products)
Pricing strategies
   (discount, moderate, premium prices)
Promotion practices
   (directs sales, advertising, direct mail)
Distribution channels
   (few or many, sole contract relationships)
Customer service policies
   (flexibility, responsiveness, quality)
Product/service policies
   (premium quality, good price, reliable)
Market research
   (accuracy and frequency of information on customers
   and competitors)

Operations Strategy Decision Areas
Capacity planning
   (lead demand to ensure availability or lag demand to
   achieve capacity utilization)
Facility location
   (locate near suppliers, customers, labor, natural
   resources, transportation)
Facility layout
   (continuous or intermittent flow)
Technology and equipment choices
   (degree of automation, computerization)
Sourcing arrangements
   (cooperative relationships with a few versus competitive
   bid)
Planning and scheduling
   (make to stock, make to order, flexibility to customer
   requests)
Quality assurance
   (acceptance sampling, process control, standards)
Workforce policies
   (training levels, cross-training, reward systems)

(continued)

Exhibit 6.1   *(continued)*

	Current	Change Needed

R&D/Technology Strategy Decision Areas
Research focus
    (product, process, applications)
Orientation
    (leader versus follower)
Project priorities
    (budget, quality, creativity, time)
Linkages with external research organizations

Information Systems Strategy Decision Areas
Hardware capability and integration across the organization
    (mainframe, network, hardwire linkages, dial-up)
Software capability and integration across the organization
    (user support, compatibility, security, standardization)
Linkages with customers and suppliers
    (direct links, shared systems)
Investments in new technologies
    (Internet, bar-code scanners, satellite technology)
Strategic use of internal and external information
    (decision support, operations support, marketing
    support, forecasting)

Human Resources Strategy Decision Areas
Recruitment
    (entry-level versus experienced employees)
Selection
    (selection criteria and methods)
Performance appraisal
    (appraisal methods, frequency)
Salary and wages
    (relationship to performance, competitiveness)
Benefits
    (bonuses, stock-ownership programs, other benefits)
Personnel actions
    (disciplinary plans, outplacement, early retirements)
Training
    (types of training, availability to all employees)

Financial Strategy Decision Areas
Capital
    (debt versus equity versus internal financing)
Financial reporting to stockholders
Minimum return on investment levels
    (relationship to cost of capital)
Basis for allocating overhead costs
    (direct labor, machine use, sales volume, activity)

Exhibit 6.2   *Types of Business-Level Structures*

(a) *The functional structure.*

(b) *Product/market structure based on product groups.*

(continued)

Functional Structure

A *functional structure* (Exhibit 6.2a) is organized around the inputs or activities that are required to produce products and services, such as marketing, operations, finance, and R&D.[17] Organizations that are functionally structured usually have marketing, operations, finance, and R&D departments. The structure is centralized, highly specialized, and most appropriate when a limited product line is offered to a particular market segment and the needs of external stakeholders are relatively stable. The functional structure is oriented toward internal efficiency and encourages functional expertise. It is particularly appropriate in organizations that want to exploit economies of scale and learning effects from focused activities. Small and start-up businesses often employ functional structures very effectively. A functional structure can also be effective for a firm pursuing a market penetration strategy because organization scope (i.e., number of products and markets) and stakeholder requirements will be relatively stable over time.

Exhibit 6.2   *(continued)*

(c) The project matrix structure.

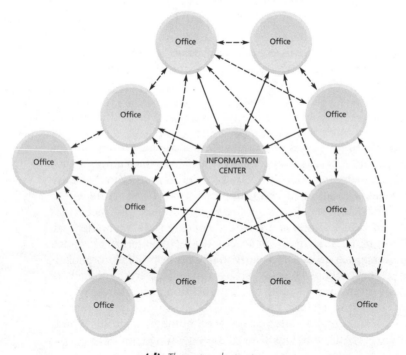

(d) The network structure.

Exhibit 6.3   *Attributes of Business-Level Structures*

	Functional	Product/Market	Project Matrix	Network
Organizing Framework	Inputs	Outputs	Inputs and outputs	Outputs
Degree of Centralization	Centralized	Decentralized	Decentralized with sharing	Very decentralized
Competitive Environment	Stable	Dynamic with external market pressures	Dynamic with external market pressures and internal technical pressures	Competitive conditions differ from region to region
Growth Strategy	Market penetration	Market or product development	Frequent new product/market development managed as project teams	Market penetration and market development

Product/Market Structure

A *product/market structure* organizes activities around the outputs of the organization system, such as products, customers, or geographical regions.[18] Exhibit 6.2b is an example of a product/market structure organized around product groups, but the other types of this structure are just as common. When a business pursues a product development strategy, it adds products to its product line and interacts with more customers, distributors, and suppliers. If the growth and complexity leads to administrative inefficiencies and confusion, then the business may need to shift from a functional structure to product divisions or groups. The more decentralized groups can handle the broader scope of activities and be more responsive to the diverse needs of customers.

Firms that pursue market development growth strategies also add complexity that may require a new structure. A firm that expands its business from a regional market base to a national market base may form new units around geographical market segments. For example, a restaurant chain or retail toy chain may be divided into units responsible for eastern and western regions. A firm that seeks out new customer groups and new product applications may reorganize around customer groups. For example, a soft drink company may divide its business into "fountain" and "retail" segments, with the fountain unit targeting its marketing and sales efforts to restaurants and theaters and the retail unit focusing on grocery and convenience stores. An architectural firm might organize around commercial, military, and residential projects.

Project Matrix Structure

A hybrid structure that combines some elements of both functional and product/market forms is called a *project matrix structure*. The project matrix structure is viewed by some as a transition stage between a functional form and a product/market group structure and by others as a complex form necessary for complex environments.[19] Either way, the many influences that simultaneously pull an organization toward functional forms and the more diverse product/market forms reach equilibrium in the matrix structure. Project matrix structures are most common in turbulent or uncertain competitive environments where coordination between different functional departments is extremely important and external stakeholder demands are diverse and changing.[20] Matrix structures can improve communications between groups, increase the amount of information the organization can handle, and allow more flexible use of people and equipment.[21]

In a matrix structure, the organization is simultaneously functional and either product, market, or project-oriented (see Exhibit 6.2c). Fluor Daniel, one of the world's largest engineering design and construction companies, employs a matrix structure.

> At Fluor Daniel, it is very common for design engineers to report to two or more managers: the project manager on a particular contract and the functional manager of their particular design area, such as electrical or mechanical systems. The dual reporting relationships of the matrix structure emphasize the equal importance of functional design performance and service on the particular project. The functional dimension encourages employees to share technical information from one project to the next (learning) and helps avoid unnecessary duplication of skills. The project dimension allows the organization to focus on serving the needs of the customer while simultaneously encouraging cooperation and coordination among the different interdependent functions.

Unfortunately, matrix structures can be disconcerting for employees because of the "too many bosses" problem. Not only is it difficult to balance the needs of the different lines of authority and coordinate among the many people and schedules, the sheer number of people that must be involved in decision making can slow decision processes and add administrative costs.[22] The overall complexity of the structure can create ambiguity and conflict between functional and product managers and between individuals.

Network Structure

Some organizations, particularly large integrated service organizations, use the network, or "spider's web" structure.[23] The *network structure* is very decentralized and organized around customer groups or geographical regions. As shown in Exhibit 6.2d, a network structure represents a web of independent units, with little or no formal hierarchy to organize and control their relationship. The independent units are loosely organized to capture and share useful information. Other than information sharing, however, there is little formal contact among operating units. When formal contact is needed, committees and task forces are created on an ad hoc basis. The network structure is particularly appropriate in knowledge-intensive industries where decentralization and duplication of resources are required to service the market, yet there are no manufacturing or technology economies of scale to drive centralization, such as large medical and legal practices, investment banking firms, and charitable institutions like United Way and Girl Scouts of America.

Arthur Andersen & Co. is an accounting firm with over 200 offices managed by over 2,000 partners in 54 countries. Using various computer systems, the company links its highly independent offices so they can share information. It maintains worldwide customer reference files and up-to-date resource information on tax rules, customers, court rulings, and professional standards. The files are updated regularly and distributed to each office.[24]

A network structure may not be appropriate when high levels of coordination and resource sharing are required since it represents an extreme form of decentralization, with executive-level management serving primarily an advisory function and lower-level managers controlling most decisions. The weaknesses of the network structure include the potential for lost control of the autonomous units and high costs from the extensive duplication of resources.

CORPORATE-LEVEL STRUCTURES

As organizations grow and pursue different business opportunities, administrative problems and complexity create pressures to break the organization into more manageable units. As part of the process of corporate strategy implementation, managers must structure and align the different business units. Earlier we discussed structuring *within* a business unit. In this section we are concerned with structuring relationships *among* an organization's businesses.

Depending upon the strategies that are being pursued, management may be interested in cultivating independence or interdependence among business units. *Independence* among units requires an organization structure that encourages separation and autonomy, as well as coordinating mechanisms that achieve hierarchical (between business units and top management) rather than lateral (among business units) coordination. An independent structure is appropriate when businesses are unrelated and managers only seek financial synergies.

When pursuing a related diversification strategy, managers try to convert the theoretical relatedness and fit of multibusiness strategies and strategic alliances into true synergistic relationships that benefit the organization as a whole. To exploit operational synergies, managers must structure relationships among businesses and partners in ways that encourage interdependence, and manage them over time with shared goals, shared information, shared resources, and cooperative program development.[25]

Four general types of structures are used by multibusiness organizations: multidivisional, strategic business unit, corporate matrix, and transnational. Exhibit 6.4 shows the issues that are raised when deciding among corporate-level structures.

Multidivisional

If an organization has a few businesses in its portfolio, management may choose a line-of-business or *multidivisional* structure, with each business existing as an autonomous unit. For example, a multidivisional organization may have an agricultural chemicals division, industrial chemicals division, and pharmaceuticals division. In this type of structure, a general manager—usually referred to as a divisional vice president—heads up each of the three divisions. Each division has its own support activities, including sales, accounting/finance, personnel, and

Exhibit 6.4   *Making the Corporate Structure Choice*

	Number of Businesses	Relatedness	Need for Coordination	Expected Synergy
Multidivisional	Few	Moderate/low	Moderate/low	Financial Limited operational
SBU	Many	Groups of related businesses	Moderate within SBU Low between SBUs	Limited operational within SBU Financial among SBUs
Corporate Matrix	Few or many	High	Very high	High operational synergies: cost, access, or innovation
Transnational	Many, in different nations	High	Very high	High operational synergies: cost, access, or innovation

research and development. Services that are common to all three businesses are housed at the corporate level, such as legal services, public relations, and corporate research. The multidivisional structure is appropriate when management of the different businesses does not require sharing of employees, marketing resources, or operations facilities.

The multidivisional structure, shown in Exhibit 6.5, has several advantages. By existing as a separate unit, each business is better able to focus its efforts on the needs of its particular stakeholders, without being distracted by the problems of other businesses. Corporate-level management is freed from day-to-day issues and able to take a long-term, integrative view of the collection of businesses. Corporate executives may monitor the performance of each division separately and allocate corporate resources for specific activities that show promise.

With the multidivisional structure, it is often difficult to decide which activities will be performed at the corporate level and which ones will be held within each division. Competition for corporate resources (R&D, legal, investment funds) may create coordination difficulties among divisions. Also, organizational efforts may be duplicated, particularly when the different businesses within the corporate portfolio are highly related. It may be that shared distribution channels or common process development could save costs for the two businesses, yet separation in the organization structure discourages cooperation. Although many firms use multidivisional structures when configuring the relationships between related businesses, the structure makes resource sharing and cooperation diffi-

Exhibit 6.5   *The Multidivisional Structure*

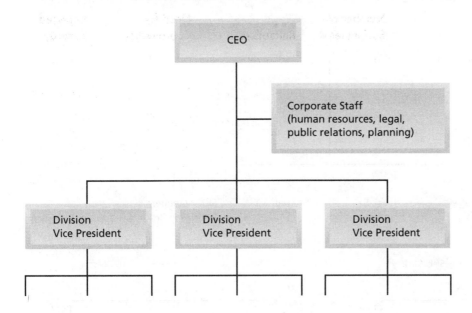

cult. Unfortunately, resource sharing and cooperation are necessary for synergy. Therefore, multidivisional corporate structures may interfere with the creation of synergies within organizations.

Strategic Business Unit

When an organization is broadly diversified with several businesses in its portfolio, it becomes difficult for top management to keep track of and understand the many different industry environments and business conditions. Management may choose to form *strategic business units* (SBUs) with each SBU incorporating a few closely related businesses. Each SBU is composed of related divisions, with divisional vice presidents reporting to an SBU or group vice president. If an organization becomes very large, it may combine strategic business units into groups or sectors, thus adding another level of management. An example of an SBU structure is shown in Exhibit 6.6.

The SBU structure makes it possible for top management to keep track of many businesses at one time. It allows decentralization around dimensions that are meaningful to the business, such as markets or technologies, so that the complexity will not overload top managers. The intent of the structure is to provide top management with a manageable number of units to keep track of and to force responsibility for decision making lower in the organization, near the important internal and external stakeholders. The difficulty of the SBU structure is that operating units, and therefore the customer, are even further removed from top management than in the multidivisional form. As with the multidivisional form, there is competition for corporate financial and staff resources which may create conflicts and coordination problems.

Exhibit 6.6   *The Strategic Business Unit (SBU) Structure*

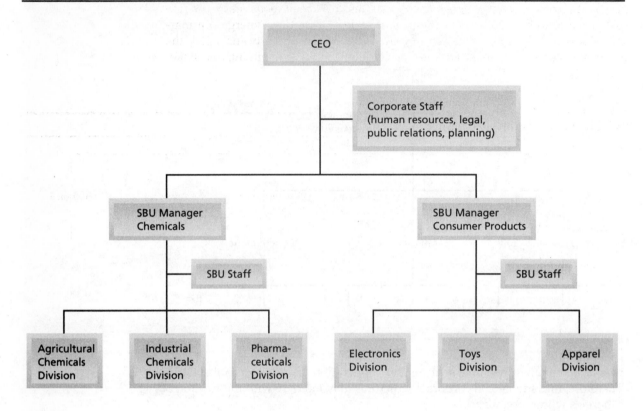

Corporate Matrix

The *corporate matrix* is the corporate-level counterpart to the project matrix structure described earlier. It is a way to achieve a high degree of coordination among several related businesses. Corporate matrix structures are used when the individual businesses within a corporation's portfolio need to take advantage of resource, information, or technology sharing in order to succeed in their industries. The corporate matrix structure tries to reach a balance between pressures to decentralize units closer to market and technological trends, and pressures to maintain centralized control to bring about economies of scope and shared learning.

3M is a global company with over 20 business units producing over 60,000 products in 55 countries. The organization structure is described by management this way:

> When people ask how we structure a corporation with such a disparate lot of variables, I begin by discussing 3M's matrix management structure. One side of the matrix represents the company's product divisions. Along the other axis are the international subsidiaries. For any business in an international subsidiary, responsibility is shared by the managing director of the subsidiary (who reports through area or regional vice-presidents to me as head of International Operations) and the product manager (who reports to the vice-president of his or her division).[26]

The corporate matrix structure is particularly appropriate for related diversification strategies and global strategies. For example, a consumer products firm that has businesses in beverages, snack foods, and packaged foods may use a matrix structure to capitalize on economies of scale and capture synergies in marketing and distribution, as shown in Exhibit 6.7. When properly managed, the corporate matrix structure improves coordination among different internal stake-

Exhibit 6.7   *Types of Corporate Matrix Structures*

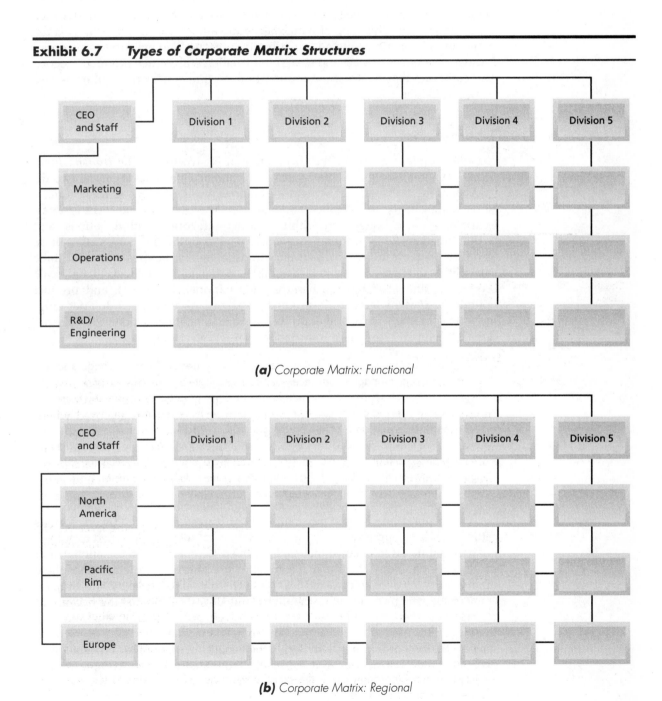

(a) Corporate Matrix: Functional

(b) Corporate Matrix: Regional

holders by forcing managers within related businesses to maintain close contact with each other. It can help the organization become more flexible and responsive to changes in the business environment and can encourage teamwork and participation.[27]

The corporate matrix form may also be effective in structuring an organization that produces several products that are all sold in several nations. A multinational organization may create a matrix structure that groups all products under each national manager and simultaneously groups all nations under each product manager. This type of matrix structure allows the firm to achieve a national focus in its marketing and distribution practices and encourages synergies through economies of scale and shared information within each product category. The corporate matrix structure applied to a multinational organization is also shown in Exhibit 6.7.

Transnational

A more complex version of the corporate matrix structure is the *transnational* form.[28] Whereas the global matrix structure organizes businesses along two dimensions, the transnational structure organizes businesses along three dimensions: nation or region, product, and function. The transnational form is an attempt to achieve integration within product categories, within nations, and within functions while simultaneously achieving coordination across all of those activities. Organizations which employ transnational structures can build three capabilities: responsiveness and flexibility at the national level, global scale economies, and learning which transcends national, functional, and product boundaries.[29] Many large multi-product global organizations, in industries ranging from computers to consumer products, are making the transition to a transnational structure. Xerox uses a transnational structure, as described:

> We have created an organization that by its very design forces managers to confront—and manage—the necessary tensions between autonomy and integration. . . . In a sense, we have turned the traditional vertically organized company on its side. At one end is technology, and we have retained an integrated corporate research and technology organization. At the other end is the customer. We have organized our sales and service people into three geographic customer-operations divisions, so that we can keep a common face to the customer. Between these two poles are the new business divisions. Their purpose is to create some suction on technology and pull it into the marketplace.[30]

The corporate matrix and transnational structures are plagued by one serious difficulty: sheer complexity may interfere with what they are designed to accomplish. It is difficult to balance the needs of the different functional, national, and product stakeholders. The unusual command structure can create an atmosphere of ambiguity, conflict, and mixed loyalties. The overall complexity and bureaucracy of the structure may stifle creativity and slow decision making because of the sheer number of people that must be involved. Furthermore, the administrative costs associated with decision delays and extra management may overwhelm the benefits of coordination.[31] To derive the benefits of any of the corporate-level or business-level structures, but especially those that are more complex, managers must take extra steps to ensure coordination.

KEY POINTS SUMMARY

In this chapter, we described the functional strategies and organization structures that are used in implementing strategies. The following points were discussed:

1. Strategies are implemented through the day-to-day decisions and actions of employees throughout the organization.
2. Management's challenge is to create a pattern of integrated, coordinated decisions that meets the needs of stakeholders and fulfills the planned strategy of the organization.
3. Functional strategies are represented by the pattern of decisions made by employees in marketing, operations, research & development, information systems, human resources, and finance. Managers must ensure that decisions within each area are consistent with each other, with other functions, and with the stated strategies of the firm.
4. In configuring the relationships among departments in a single business, organizations usually employ one of the following structures: functional, product/market group, project matrix, or network.
5. The functional structure encourages functional specialization and focus but discourages coordination between functions or departments.
6. The product/market group segments products and markets into smaller, more manageable subunits that may improve service to customers or economies of scale but result in resource duplication.
7. The project matrix structure employs a dual-reporting relationship that is intended to balance functional focus and expertise required for learning with responsiveness to customer needs. However, it may create ambiguity and slow decision making if managed improperly.
8. The network structure is a very decentralized form that is particularly well suited to geographically dispersed offices, stores, or units that, except for some sharing of information and operating policies, operate independently.
9. At the corporate level, multidivisional and strategic business unit structures divide businesses into divisions. While these structures focus the organization on the needs of its stakeholders, they make coordination and resource sharing among businesses, which are necessary to exploit operating synergies, very difficult.
10. Corporate matrix and transnational structures are intended to exploit economies, learning, and resource sharing across businesses; however, they require extra measures of coordination to avoid divided loyalties, slow decision making, and management conflicts.

END NOTES

1   J. Hechinger and J. Lublin, "Xerox's Thoman resigns under pressure," *The Wall Street Journal* (May 12, 2000): A3.

2   L.G. Hrebiniak and W.F. Joyce, *Implementing Strategy* (New York: Macmillan, 1984).

3   B. Avishai and W. Taylor, "Customers Drive a Technology-Driven Company: An Interview with George Fisher," *Harvard Business Review* (November/December 1989): 107–108.

4   J. Millman, "Steady Finger on the Trigger," *Forbes* (Nov. 9, 1992): 188–189.

5   R. Hayes and S. Wheelwright, *Restoring Our Competitive Edge: Competing Through Manufacturing* (New York: John Wiley and Sons, 1984): 30.

6   W.J. Abernathy and P.L. Townsend, "Technology, Productivity, and Process Change," *Technological Forecasting and Social Change* 7 (4) (1975): 379–396.

7   C. St. John, A. Cannon, and R. Pouder, "Change Drivers in the New Millennium: Implications for Manufacturing Strategy Research," *Journal of Operations Management* (in press).

8   C. Fisher, "Current and Recurrent Challenges in HRM," *Journal of Management* 15 (1989): 157–180.

9   Fisher, "Current and Recurrent Challenges in HRM."

10   N.M. Tichy, "Setting the Global Human Resource Management Agenda for the 1990s," *Human Resource Management* 27 (1) (1988): 1–18.

11   L.R. Gomez-Mejia and T. Welbourne, "Compensation Strategies in a Global Context," *Human Resource Planning* 14 (1) (1992): 29–41.

12   R.H. Hayes, S.C. Wheelwright, and K.B. Clark, *Dynamic Manufacturing* (New York: The Free Press, 1988): 61.

13   F.W. Gluck, S.D. Kaufman, and A.S. Walleck, "Strategic Management for Competitive Advantage," *Harvard Business Review* (July/August 1980): 154–161.

14   Hayes and Wheelwright, *Restoring our Competitive Edge: Competing Through Manufacturing.*

15   A.D. Chandler, *Strategy and Structure: Chapters in the History of the American Industrial Enterprise* (Cambridge, Mass.: The MIT Press, 1962).

16   P.R. Lawrence and J.W. Lorsch, *Organization and Environment* (Homewood, Ill.: Irwin, 1969): 23–39.

17 A.C. Hax and N.S. Majluf, *The Strategy Concept and Process: A Pragmatic Approach* (Englewood Cliffs, N.J.: Prentice Hall, 1991).

18 Hax and Majluf, *The Strategy Concept and Process: A Pragmatic Approach.*

19 J.R. Galbraith and R.K. Kazanjian, *Strategy Implementation: Structure, Systems, and Processes,* 2nd ed. (St. Paul: West Publishing, 1986).

20 R.L. Daft, *Organization Theory and Design,* 3rd ed. (St. Paul: West Publishing, 1989): 240.

21 R.C. Ford and W.A. Randolph, "Cross-Functional Structures: A Review and Integration of Matrix Organization and Project Management," *Journal of Management* 18 (1992): 267–294.

22 Ford and Randolph, "Cross-Functional Structures: A Review and Integration of Matrix Organization and Project Management."

23 J.B. Quinn, *Intelligent Enterprise* (New York: The Free Press, 1992).

24 Quinn, *Intelligent Enterprise.*

25 C.W.L. Hill, M.A. Hitt, and R.E. Hoskisson, "Cooperative Versus Competitive Structures in Related and Unrelated Diversified Firms," *Organization Science* 4 (1992): 501–521.

26 H. Hammerly, "Matching Global Strategies with National Responses," *The Journal of Business Strategy* (March/April 1992): 10.

27 Ford and Randolph, "Cross-Functional Structures: A Review and Integration of Matrix Organization and Project Management."

28 C.A. Bartlett and S. Ghoshal, *Managing Across Borders: The Transnational Solution* (Boston, Mass.: Harvard Business School Press, 1989).

29 C.A. Bartlett and S. Ghoshal, "The New Global Manager," *Harvard Business Review* (September/October 1992): 124–132.

30 R. Howard, "The CEO as Organizational Architect: An Interview with Xerox's Paul Allaire," *Harvard Business Review* (September/October 1992): 112.

31 Ford and Randolph, "Cross-Functional Structures: A Review and Integration of Matrix Organization and Project Management."

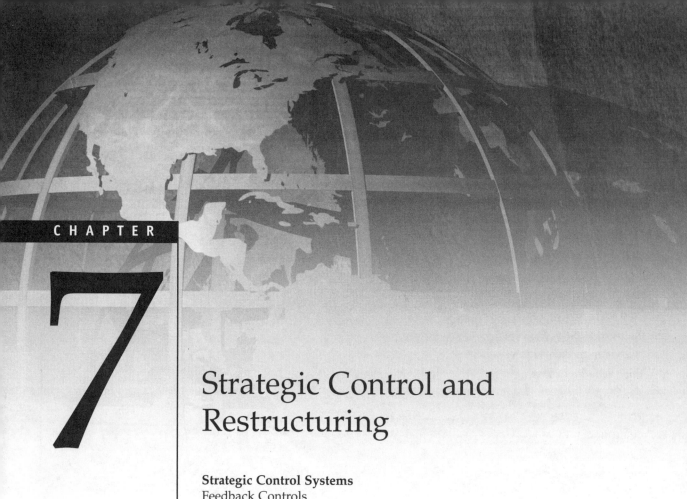

CHAPTER

7

Strategic Control and Restructuring

"To Fix Coca-Cola, Daft Sets Out to Get Relationships Right." This headline summarizes the challenge that Coca-Cola faces at the beginning of the new century. A serious "fix" is necessary and relationships with key constituents need mending. What happened, why, and what is Coke doing about it?

Coca-Cola controls 51 percent of the world market for carbonated drinks, and derives 80 percent of its profits from overseas markets. Even so, Coca-Cola just experienced an alarming series of negative events in Europe. Concerns about water quality used in soft drinks in Belgium turned into a public relations nightmare. Coca-Cola offended regulators when it attempted the acquisition of Cadbury Schweppes without European Union approval. Furthermore, the company is facing a decline in demand due to weakness in Turkey and Eastern Europe. To make matters worse, the head of the European Union antitrust area has accused Coke and its bottlers of anticompetitive practices. Coca-Cola has developed a reputation for aggressive, often arrogant, behavior in its dealings with the European communities.

The problems in Europe have reverberated through the U.S. organization as well, causing stock price concerns and morale problems with employees. CEO Douglas Daft is attempting to make changes. He initiated a series of labor cutbacks at the corporate headquarters in Atlanta to reduce costs and push more autonomy and control into the hands of local European employees. He replaced American managers in Europe with locals, and set out on a campaign to reestablish ties with regulators, bottlers, and the public.

The task before him is daunting. The cutbacks stunned Atlanta employees and fueled deeper morale problems. The increased autonomy and control for local bottlers have caused some of them to resent the increased duties, but Daft felt the changes were necessary. In his view, Coke made the mistake of seeing only what was acceptable in the U.S. "You've got to be able to look at things through their eyes."[1]

Effective control systems can reduce the probability that an organization will experience problems like those experienced at Coke. In the first half of this chapter, we will address the development of strategic control systems, which warn managers when performance is off target or when upcoming trends will affect organizational performance. In the second half, we will discuss the restructuring methods that may be used to reorient an organization that has either slipped out of control or that must realign itself with environmental trends.

STRATEGIC CONTROL SYSTEMS

From the perspective of top executives, a *strategic control system* is "a system to support managers in assessing the relevance of the organization's strategy to its progress in the accomplishment of its goals, and when discrepancies exist, to support areas needing attention."[2] Many existing control systems are based almost exclusively on accounting measures such as return on investment (ROI).[3] Since financial reporting requirements include figures for income, assets, and sales, managers can easily calculate ROI or related measures from existing data. In some organizations they are considered the only important measure of success. In the words of Roger Smith, former CEO of General Motors, "I look at the bottom line. It tells me what to do."[4]

Unfortunately, according to some control experts, accounting-based measures are "too late, too aggregated, and too distorted to be relevant for managers' planning and control decisions."[5] Lateness refers to the long lag times between the organizational transactions themselves and the dates financial reports come out. For example, some companies don't know they are in trouble until so much time has passed that the problem becomes very large. The aggregation problem simply means that accounting measures do not contain the detail that is necessary to make meaningful improvements to specific organizational processes. Finally, by relying too heavily on accounting information only, managers can develop a distorted view of organizational performance. Distortion is a particular problem when managers do not understand the effects of the policies that determine the way inventories, plant, and equipment are valued and the way overhead costs are allocated to various departments and divisions.

In addition, accounting-based financial measures can prompt managers to behave in ways that are counterproductive over the long run. For example, financial measures such as ROI, if given too much emphasis in the short run, discourage investments in long-term research and development projects because expenses must be paid out immediately while benefits may not accrue until many financial periods later.[6] Also, managers may shut down lines or cancel services that appear to be too costly, placing an emphasis on products and services that are most efficiently produced. These types of decisions are fine as long as customers don't prefer the more costly products and services. However, the end result is often that the overproduced "efficient" goods and services have to be sold at a discount to stimulate customer interest. Consequently, profit margins are eroded and the organization would have been better off keeping the lines or services that were dropped.

In a traditional accounting-based control system, control information tends to be collected at the top of the organization. Consequently, top executives possess all of the power to control organizational processes. These managers analyze the information and provide instructions to subordinates concerning expected levels of performance. This type of system assumes that organizational learning occurs at the top of the organization. Unfortunately, most top managers are too distant from the value-creating activities of their companies to understand or learn what needs to be done to improve long-run performance. This type of management is known as "management by remote control."[7] As a control expert put it:

> The chief problem with using accounting information to control operations—managing by remote control—is the tendency for businesses to lose sight of the processes by which people and customers make a company competitive and

profitable. What I believe has happened in American businesses since the 1950s is that managers and operating personnel at all levels have lost sight of people, customers, and processes as top management has turned everyone's attention to accounting results.[8]

Competitive forces in the global economy have led to the need for a more diverse set of control procedures. In particular, while traditional accounting-based controls do not necessarily need to be eliminated, they should be balanced with other types of controls. For example, "grass roots" or "bottom-up" controls leave as much information as possible as close to the customer as possible. For these types of systems to work, feedback from customers must be available to the workforce so that they can make the adjustments that are required for continuous improvement to organizational activities. Bottom-up approaches are, by their nature, flexible and adaptable to the peculiarities of particular systems.

The extreme case of "grass roots" control is a situation in which customers actually control the activities of the companies they are buying from. For example, Ito-Yokado Co., a company that manages 7-Eleven stores in Japan, controls the product mix, the manufacturing schedule, and the delivery of its most important supplies. "The moment a 7-Eleven customer in Japan buys a soft drink or a can of beer, the information goes directly to the bottler or brewery. It immediately becomes both production schedule and delivery schedule, actually specifying the hour when the new supply has to be delivered and to which of the 4,300 stores."[9] This process eliminates five or six wholesale levels. A little closer to home, Wal-Mart has similar practices with many of its suppliers. According to Peter Drucker, a very well-known business writer, these trends are a result of the availability of better information, "Now that we have real-time information on what goes on in the marketplace, decisions will increasingly be based on what goes on where the ultimate customers, whether housewives or hospitals, take *buying* action."

A comprehensive strategic control model is displayed in Exhibit 7.1. It illustrates three different types of control: feedback, concurrent, and feedforward. *Feedback control* provides managers with information concerning outcomes from organizational activities. *Concurrent control* provides managers with real-time information about processes and activities, so that deviations from plan can be identified before they can affect organizational results. It also includes behavioral controls such as bureaucratic systems and socialization processes. *Feedforward control* helps managers anticipate changes in the external and internal environments, based on analysis of inputs from stakeholders and the broad environment. We will now describe several types of feedback, feedforward, and concurrent control methods and some of their uses.

Feedback Controls

Exhibit 7.1 demonstrates that during the implementation stage of the strategic management process, managers should establish targets (e.g., specific objectives or goals) for activities and in areas that are critical to the success of a strategy and the attainment of organizational goals. A time frame for measuring performance is also established. When the appropriate amount of time has elapsed, performance is measured and compared against the targets that were established. If performance is within established tolerances for a certain factor, managers have learned that their expectations concerning performance for that factor are

Exhibit 7.1   The Strategic Control Process

possible, given current organizational and environmental conditions. However, if performance is out of the tolerance limits, managers should assess cause and effect in an effort to learn why.

Feedback control systems perform several important functions in organizations.[10] First, creating specific objectives or targets ensures that managers at various levels and areas in the organization understand the plans and strategies that guide organizational decisions. Second, feedback control systems motivate managers to pursue organizational interests as opposed to purely personal interests, because they know they will be held accountable for the results of their actions. Finally, feedback control systems help managers decide when and how to intervene in organizational processes by identifying areas that require further attention. Without good control systems, managers can fall into the trap of spending too much time dealing with issues and problems that are not particularly important to the future of the organization. Exhibit 7.2 provides a description of some common types of feedback controls.

As we mentioned in earlier chapters, the strategies an organization pursues should be directed toward fulfilling the strategic direction of the organization. Effective feedback controls are one way to help ensure that the strategies are indeed moving the organization in an appropriate direction. Exhibit 7.3 contains the

Exhibit 7.2   *Types of Feedback Controls*

1. **Budgets**: The targets in a budget are the revenue and expense accounts, and managers and employees are held responsible for variations that are greater than established tolerances. Sometimes tolerances are not stated, but are implied or are understood due to past budgeting processes. Budgets may also be used to evaluate the performance of managers; however, this procedure can be problematic because it may discourage investments in training, R&D, or new capital equipment due to their short-term impact on expense accounts. If a budget is used to evaluate managerial performance, organizations should consider adding back these types of investments before evaluation. Another alternative is to create separate accounts for longer-term investment programs that are independent of the rest of the budget.

2. **Ratio analysis**: Financial ratios such as return on investment (ROI) or a current ratio are measured against targets that are established on the basis of past performance or in comparison with competing firms. Although overdependence on this type of control can be dangerous to the long-term performance of firms, in some situations ratio analysis provides good control information. For example, a financial ratio such as the current ratio is important to managing working capital, and debt-to-equity ratio can tell an organization whether it is assuming too much financial risk.

   Sometimes corporate-level managers use ratios such as ROI to evaluate the performance of managers of individual business units. In those cases, top managers should consider adding back long-term investments before calculating ROI to discourage a short-term orientation in decision making. In related diversified firms, ROI-based rewards systems (financial controls) may be inappropriate because they encourage competition among business units instead of the cooperation that is necessary to achieve synergy. Also, because the operations of the various business units should be highly interconnected, it is hard to determine which unit is really most responsible for success. Therefore, in the case of a related diversified firm, ROI is probably an ineffective control measure as it relates to the rewards system.

   However, in an unrelated diversified firm, financial performance ratios may be appropriate for determining the performance of business unit managers. In this situation, organizational managers should only be held accountable for their own financial performance because linkages with other firms in the portfolio are uncommon. Consequently, ROI (after adjustments) may be an appropriate gauge of the performance of business unit managers in unrelated diversified organizations.

3. **Audits**: An audit measures firm conduct and outcomes against established guidelines. Financial audits control accuracy within accounting systems, based on generally accepted accounting principles (GAAP). Social audits control ethical behavior, based on criteria that are established either totally in-house or in conjunction with activist groups, regulatory agencies, or editors of magazines that compile this sort of information (e.g., Business and Society Review). Customer surveys may also be used to generate feedback for control as part of a customer service audit.

4. **Goals and objectives**: Goals and objectives provide performance targets for individuals, departments, and divisions. Specific operating goals are established to bring the concepts found in the mission statement to life—to a level that managers and employees can influence and control. One of the keys to effective goal setting is that the goals must be well integrated from level to level.

Exhibit 7.3   *Establishing a Feedback Control System*

Strategic Direction
Vision and Enterprise Strategy

	Customers (i.e., satisfied with products, safe, prefer to do business with organization)	**Owners (shareholders)** (i.e., high earnings, high share price stable earnings, increasing dividends)	**Employees** (i.e., satisfied, high self-esteem, stable employment, good attitude about company, excellent workers)	**Community** (i.e., excellent relationships, partners, benefit from firm activities)
Broad Goals Who will be affected and how will they be affected?				
Result Areas Which areas have greatest influence on accomplishment of broad goals?	**List Areas** (i.e., R&D, manufacturing, customer service, and marketing)	**List Areas** (i.e., R&D, finance, marketing, leveland type of diversification)	**List Areas** (i.e., training, scheduling, rewards, promotion)	**List Areas** (i.e., business planning, public relations, marketing, philanthropy)
Specific Targets What must be done in each area to accomplish the broad goals?	**Set Targets for Each Area**	**Set Targets for Each Area**	**Set Targets for Each Area**	**Set Targets for Each Area**
Time Frame Over what period of time will the target be accomplished?	**Establish Time Frame for Each Target**	**Establish Time Frame for Each Target**	**Establish Time Frame for Each Target**	**Establish Time Frame for Each Target**
Assignment Who will be responsible for ensuring completion?	**Assign a Manager to Each Target**	**Assign a Manager to Each Target**	**Assign a Manager to Each Target**	**Assign a Manager to Each Target**
Action Plan What actions will be necessary to ensure completion?	**Outline Specific Actions and Approximate Dates of these Actions**	**Outline Specific Actions and Approximate Dates of these Actions**	**Outline Specific Actions and Approximate Dates of these Actions**	**Outline Specific Actions and Approximate Dates of these Actions**

steps associated with establishing an effective feedback control system. These steps will now be described in detail.[11]

Establishment of Broad Goals. The major elements of strategic direction that drive an effective feedback control process are the vision, mission, and enterprise strategy. A vision articulates where an organization is heading or, more appropriately, where it should be heading. The mission contains a definition of the business and is therefore useful in controlling the scope of an organization's activities. For example, an organization might determine that it is too broadly diversified or not diversified enough to enhance financial performance. The enterprise strategy, an organization's purpose, helps articulate precisely what an organization intends to do for particular stakeholders, such as customers, employees, shareholders, or the community. Taken together, these elements of strategic direction provide a powerful tool for controlling an organization's processes. In essence, the key question is, "If we achieve our vision, who will be affected and how will they be affected?"

The stakeholder view of organizations presented in earlier chapters provides direction with regard to the stakeholders that are of greatest importance to an organization. Exhibit 7.3 contains examples for four stakeholder groups that most organizations would consider important—customers, owners (shareholders), employees, and the community. However, the list of important stakeholders will be different for each organization, as reflected by the organization's enterprise strategy and vision. For example, Harris Corporation has established specific goals for its suppliers. Other important stakeholders may include special interest groups, competitors (especially if cooperation is desirable), financial intermediaries, and unions. For nonprofit organizations, the list will include beneficiaries and donors.

Once high-priority stakeholders have been identified, the next step is to determine how they will be affected if the organization is successful in achieving its vision. Each stakeholder group will be associated with its own set of feedback controls. For example, those stakeholders who evaluate an organization's performance using financial targets will typically look to return on investment, cash flow, stock price, and stability of earnings. Customers, on the other hand, evaluate other types of information: pricing, innovation, quality, value, and customer service. Organizations may have a vision of becoming the preferred supplier of a good or services to their customers. From an internal stakeholder perspective, another set of "performance" indicators becomes important, such as cost controls, skill levels and capabilities, product line breadth, safety, on-time delivery, quality, and many others. High employee satisfaction may be a goal for some organizations, as well as a partnering attitude with respect to the community. What is important at this stage is that the broad goals are reflective of the strategic direction of the organization (see Exhibit 7.3).

Identification of Key Result Areas. The next step in the control process is to identify the areas of the organization that are key to accomplishing the broad goals that were set. For example, an organization may determine that to achieve broad customer goals such as satisfaction, safety, and loyalty, emphasis must be placed on research and development, manufacturing, customer service, and marketing. Accomplishment of shareholder goals may involve financial functions, marketing, research and development, and establishment of the appropriate level of diversification. Other examples are contained in Exhibit 7.3.

Establishment of Specific Targets and Time Frames. This phase of the control process identifies precisely what targets must be obtained in each key result area so that the broad goals will be obtained. Unlike the broad goals, these goals provide specific guidance concerning desired outcomes. Effective targets should have the following characteristics:

1. They are high enough to be motivating. If goals are set too low, employees will quickly achieve them and then spend too much time pursuing their own interests on company time.
2. They are realistic. If employees believe that goals are too high, they will become discouraged, which will reduce their motivation.
3. They are specific. Goals should be established for specific areas or even areas within areas. In other words, broad goals should be divided into smaller goals, which become the responsibility of specific departments and operating units.
4. They are measurable. While broad goals are more or less a permanent statement of organizational intent, goals can actually be obtained. Once they are achieved (or not achieved), it is the responsibility of management to reestablish, alter, or discard them. A goal such as, "The organization will be innovative," is not measurable. A better goal would be, "The organization will patent five new products in the next fiscal year."
5. They are understood by all affected managers and employees. If employees do not understand a goal, it is as if they never heard it. Effective communication of goals is essential to their attainment.
6. They are set through participative processes. If managers and employees who are affected by the goals participate in their creation, they will be more committed to them.
7. Feedback on performance is a part of the process. When goals are set and then forgotten, organizational members soon learn that they have no meaning.
8. Finally, they cover a specific time frame. Time periods are an essential factor in all good strategic planning.[12]

Assignment of Responsibility. If done correctly, the control process will result in many targets covering a wide range of organizational activities. The only way that anything will actually get done is if responsibility for these targets is assigned to specific managers who have responsibility for the various departments and activities within an organization. Assuming that the establishment of targets was a participative process, the managers that will ultimately be assigned responsibility were probably present when the targets were set. However, assignments should be formalized. For example, Greater Construction, a medium-sized construction company in the Orlando area, recently held an executive retreat. The retreat resulted in specific objectives that were to be accomplished by the next retreat (in six months). Before dismissing the meeting, the CEO assigned the objectives to each of the managers who were present. At the meeting six months later, nearly all of the objectives had been accomplished.

Development of an Action Plan. The final step in establishing a feedback control system is for each manager who has been assigned a target to develop a plan of action. The plan consists of the steps that each manager or his/her subordinates must take if the target is to be accomplished by the date specified. In some situations, it would be appropriate for the manager to submit the plan for approval. Also, some organizations combine the action plans into one document for distribution to all other managers. This provides a high level of accountability. For example, a large business unit within Lockheed Martin developed a six-month action plan that was approximately 40 oversized pages in length. The targets for each of the managers were contained in the plan, along with the schedule for completion.

Of course, this is not really the last step. As mentioned previously, follow-up with each of the managers is essential. In the case of Lockheed Martin, the action plan formed the basis for many of the discussions held between managers over the next six months. Also important is evaluating performance to assess cause and effect. As an example of assessing cause and effect, assume that a passenger airline has established an operating target that its planes should be 80 percent full over the next three months. At the end of the three-month period, performance is at 70 percent. Since performance is not on target, managers investigate. They discover that customer complaints and lost baggage both increased during the period. Now they have the information that they need to help correct the problem. If critical customer satisfaction data such as number of customer complaints and amount of lost baggage had not been collected in a timely fashion, managers would not have been in a position to identify problems fast enough to make corrections for the next period.

Concurrent Controls

As demonstrated in Exhibit 7.1, planning for concurrent controls occurs as a part of the implementation process. Concurrent controls are very similar to feedback controls, except that the time horizon is shortened to "real time." For example, the warning systems that are built into navigational equipment on an aircraft tell the pilot immediately if the aircraft has fallen below an acceptable altitude. It doesn't just feedback an aggregate report at the end of the flight telling the pilot how many times the aircraft fell below acceptable standards. That aggregate feedback information might be important for some uses—such as designing new navigational systems—but it would not be useful for the pilot. Within a business environment, real-time feedback is also useful in some instances, but would be a disadvantage in others. Real-time financial feedback, for example, would make managing a business much like operating on the floor of the stock market—frenetic. On the other hand, real-time controls in service delivery environments and in production environments can be very useful.

Some of the most common types of concurrent controls are those associated with production and service processes and with quality standards. Statistical process control involves setting performance standards for specific work activities. The employees performing the activities monitor their own performance and the "outputs" of their efforts. If their work is out of specification, they fix it before handing it off to someone else, as when an automotive worker "stops the line" to prevent a defective automobile from continuing to the next workstation. In those cases, real-time controls work to encourage autonomy and improve quality and efficiency. Other kinds of concurrent controls are those associated with inventory levels and order taking. For example, the more successful e-commerce companies, like Amazon.com and Buy.com, have real-time inventory systems that allow them to know when stock is low for a particular item so that a new order can be sent to their manufacturers as soon as needed. They also use real-time inventory controls to give customers specific information about what items will be shipped, on what day, and when the customer will receive them.

Another category of concurrent controls is associated with control of behavior. Within an organization, managers must depend on employees to perform their duties properly, even when management is not around. Behavioral controls work to encourage employees to comply with organizational norms and procedures. They are "real time" in that they influence employees as their jobs are being performed. Exhibit 7.4 describes two types of behavioral controls.

Feedforward Controls

As we mentioned at the beginning of this chapter, feedforward control systems help managers predict changes that may occur in their external and internal environments, based on analysis of inputs from stakeholders and the broad environment (see Exhibit 7.1). Good feedforward control systems are important because of *environmental discontinuities*, which are major, unexpected changes in the social, economic, technological, and political environments that necessitate change within organizations.[13] In other words, environmental change increases the need for organizational change and learning. However, even in stable environments, where environmental discontinuities play a minor role (i.e., production of commodities), feedforward control systems are essential to learning processes that allow organizations to move toward the accomplishment of their goals. Feedforward controls are an integral part of the strategic management process advanced in this book. Much of the distinction between the "strategic planning" of the 1960s and 1970s and the "strategic management" of today is the recognition of the importance of excellent control systems.

Exhibit 7.4   *Behavioral Controls*

Bureaucratic controls and *clan controls* are two common types of behavioral controls.

Bureaucratic controls: *Rules, procedures, and policies that guide the behavior of organizational members.* Rules provide standards or outline a specific way of doing something, such as check approval. A policy is a more general guide to action, and it provides a framework for decisions that are made routinely. One of the ways McDonald's achieves such a high level of control over its business is by establishing rules and policies that guide the daily decisions and actions of employees. Unfortunately, many companies do not see everyday rules, procedures, and policies as "strategic." However, because bureaucratic controls guide the decisions and actions of employees, they are a major determinant of how well strategies are implemented.

Clan controls: *Socialization processes through which an individual comes to appreciate the values, abilities, and expected behaviors of an organization.* Socialization also makes organizational members more inclined to see things the same way, by espousing common beliefs and assumptions that, in turn, shape their perceptions. Socialization processes for existing employees take the form of intensive training, mentoring relationships and role models, and formal organizational communications including the vision, mission, and values statements.

Strategic direction and strategies are established based on premises about the organization and its external environment, including the interests of stakeholders. These premises are assumptions about what will happen in the future. For example, an organization may plan to expand its manufacturing facilities over a period of five years based on the assumption that interest rates will remain approximately the same. If interest rates change dramatically, it could make the planned expansion unprofitable. Also, as discussed in earlier chapters, stakeholder needs and expectations can change—customers may want all transactions conducted over the Internet, suppliers may experience capacity shortages, communities may change their tax and zoning regulations—which will lead managers to evaluate the impact on existing strategies.

These types of situations demonstrate the need for premise control. *Premise control*, a type of feedforward control, involves periodically assessing the assumptions, or premises, that underlie strategic choices. The periodic reevaluation of assumptions is a foundation concept in the iterative, ongoing assessment of the environment in strategic management. Premise control helps organizations avoid situations in which their established strategies and goals are no longer appropriate.

The learning processes associated with *both* feedforward and feedback control form the basis for changes to strategic direction, strategies, implementation plans, or even the targets themselves, if they are found to be unreasonable given current conditions. In addition to the traditional measuring and monitoring functions, a recent study found that top managers use control systems to overcome resistance to change, communicate new strategic agendas, ensure continuing attention to new strategic initiatives, formalize beliefs, set boundaries on acceptable strategic behavior, and motivate discussion and debate about strategic uncertainties.[14] Control systems become one of the "tools of strategy implementation."[15]

So far this chapter has described types of control methods and issues surrounding them. Numerous control methods at multiple levels are necessary to keep an organization and its component parts headed in the right directions. However, they should be integrated in such a way that information can be shared. In other words, information from all parts of the organization should be accessible when and where it is needed to improve organizational processes. The next section discusses the development of comprehensive strategic control systems within organizations.

Comprehensive Strategic Control Systems

Rapidly advancing information technologies have made continuous improvements through control systems possible. Information systems can track large volumes of transactions, operating results, and external data efficiently, providing appropriate reports in a timely fashion to the right people. Unfortunately, few organizations currently make optimal use of available information technologies to control strategic processes.[16] However, rapid changes in an increasingly competitive global marketplace will make sophisticated strategic control systems a requirement for success in many industries in the future.

Comprehensive strategic control systems should include feedback, feedforward, and concurrent controls. To enhance the quantity and quality of organizational learning, these control systems should have the following characteristics:

1. Information generated by the control systems should be an important and recurring item to be addressed by the highest levels of management.
2. The control process should also be given frequent and regular attention from operating managers at all levels of the organization.
3. Data from the system should be interpreted and discussed in face-to-face meetings among superiors and subordinates.
4. The success of the control process relies on the continual challenge and debate of underlying data, assumptions, and strategies.[17]

A comprehensive strategic control system should provide feedback for ongoing, iterative adjustments in direction, resources allocations, and management priorities. When performance suffers, a strategic control system may provide early warnings of performance problems, but it cannot eliminate them completely. Unfortunately some managers find, through their control systems or too late, that their organization's performance does not fit with their expectations, or the expectations of their interested stakeholders. To correct an organization that has deviated sharply off course, managers must initiate some sort of restructuring. Restructuring is the topic of the next section.

STRATEGIC RESTRUCTURING

It is well known that no strategy or organization design works indefinitely. If a firm is successful with its strategies, that success *alone* will create a need for change, because the increases in sales volume and organization size will demand different management methods and organization structures. What is just as typical, however, is for customers, competitors, and technologies to interact to create a changing business environment, which will require that the organization make changes also. Unless a firm is the permanent sole participant in a no-growth industry (which is extremely unlikely), change is constant and should be assumed. The iterative, ongoing strategic management process described in this book, with its continuous scanning of the internal and external environments and its reevaluation of strategies and implementation methods, is all about the management of change over time. Recent restructuring at British Telecommunications is reflective of the changes organizations make to stay in touch with changes in their environments:

> British Telecommunications is undertaking a radical restructuring plan. The company has a policy of selling non-core assets and, therefore, intends to sell a network construction business. The company is also creating four new businesses to pursue different market segments, including an Internet business focusing on broadband services, an international mobile business, and an international directories and e-commerce business. Furthermore, the other assets in the U.K., Europe, and other regions will be re-grouped by market segment rather than by geography. The reorganization effort is prompted by two concerns: regulation of prices and increased competition. The restructuring splits the businesses into wholesale and retail divisions, leaving the retail division free of price regulation in the U.K.[18]

Researchers have observed that as organizations evolve over time they tend to move through a period of convergence, followed by a period of reorientation or radical adjustment, with a continuation of the convergence-reorientation cycle over time.[19] During the convergence stage, the organization makes minor adaptive changes to strategies, but for the most part follows a consistent approach. During this time, the structure and systems are stable, for the most part, and performance is acceptable.

For many organizations, the successes reinforce a certain way of doing business. During the convergence stage, managers develop certain mental models, or mindsets, about how the industry and the organization work. *Mental models* represent the knowledge managers have about the industry and the organization, and how specific actions relate to desired outcomes.[20] It is what they understand to be true about the organization and its industry. The mental models are derived from experiences, with past successes and failures contributing to the overall picture. As long as the premises that underlie these mental models do not change, the mental models represent useful experience that *should* be brought to bear on decisions. When premises do change, however, the established mental models may prevent the executives, managers, and employees from recognizing the *need* for change at all.

A few well-known examples will illustrate this point. In the automobile industry and minicomputer industry several years ago and in many retailing segments more recently, established management mental models have contributed to a sluggish response to industry change.[21] In both industries, the established competitors had achieved extraordinary, sustained success. They had effective strategies, useful structures, and strong cultures. When the assumptions underlying their industries changed, the existing competitors were slow to recognize what was happening. In the automotive industry, competitors failed to recognize the demographic, economic, and social trends driving demand for fuel-efficient economy cars, or the potential competitive threat from German and Japanese automakers. In the minicomputer industry, competitors failed to recognize that networked microcomputers would take the place of the mini. In retailing, bricks and mortar distributors and retailers have been shocked by the success of dot.com entrants.

Not only were these companies slow to recognize the need for change, they were also slow to make changes once the need was recognized. In other words, the out-of-sync mental models combined with established organizational structures, resources, and processes to create high levels of inertia, or reluctance to change course.

You should be asking yourself, "What about the feedforward control systems we read about in the last section? Why didn't these firms use the information that was available to them to question their own premises?" The answer is, for the most part, we don't know. The management of these firms did not recognize and respond to change until firm performance began to suffer. One of the limitations of human decision making is that often we succumb to perceptual distortion. The information that doesn't fit our preconceived mental model is just not seen at all. As one researcher recently described it, "The writing on the wall cannot be read. . . ."[22]

A period of convergence can continue indefinitely, as long as the industry conditions and organization characteristics are not significantly out of alignment.[23] However, when gradual drift results in a substantial misalignment or an environmental discontinuity does occur, the organization will be forced to reorient itself. A *reorientation* is a significant realignment of organization strategies, structure, and processes with the new environmental realities.[24] Transformation, renewal, reorientation, and restructuring are all words that describe the same general phenomenon: a radical change in how business is conducted.

As illustrated by the British Telecommunications example, many large companies experience changing circumstances that cause their corporate-level managers to "rethink" their organizations. Regardless of the reasons, restructuring typically involves a renewed emphasis on the things an organization does well, combined with a variety of tactics to revitalize the organization and strengthen its competitive position. Popular restructuring tactics include refocusing corporate assets on distinctive competencies, retrenchment, and organizational changes. In some extreme cases, a firm may be forced to consider reorganization under Chapter XI of the bankruptcy code, or a buyout. Organizations may use any one *or* a combination of these strategies in restructuring efforts.

Refocusing Corporate Assets

Refocusing activities generally are viewed favorably by external stakeholders such as the financial community.[25] Refocusing entails trimming businesses that are not consistent with the strategic direction of the organization. This type of refocusing is often called downscoping. *Downscoping* involves reducing diversification through selling off nonessential businesses that are not related to the organization's core competencies and capabilities.[26]

Researchers have discovered that most restructuring companies are moving in the direction of reducing their diversification as opposed to increasing it.[27] In essence, a *divestiture* is a reverse acquisition. One type of divestiture is a sell-off, in which a business unit is sold to another firm or, in the case of a leveraged buyout, to the business unit's managers. For example, Chrysler agreed to sell most of its aerospace and defense holdings to Raytheon.[28] In another move in the aerospace industry, Rockwell sold its aerospace and defense assets to Boeing.

Simple sell-offs are quickly being replaced by another form of divestiture called a spin-off. With a spin-off, current shareholders are issued a proportional number of shares in the spun-off business. For example, if a shareholder owns 100 shares of XYZ Company and the company spins off business unit J, the shareholder would then own 100 shares of XYZ Company and 100 shares of an independently operated company called J. The key advantage of a spin-off relative to other divestiture options is that shareholders still have the option of retaining ownership in the spun-off business. Spin-offs are extremely common when the stock market activity is trending upward. Ford spun off its Visteon auto parts division.[29] The merger of Bell Atlantic and GTE Corporation resulted in the spin-off of Genuity, a facilities-based provider of Internet infrastructure services.[30] Triarc decided to spin-off the Snapple Beverage Group, and Diageo PLC made a similar move with the Burger King chain.[31]

The businesses that should be divested during a restructuring include those that have little to do with the distinctive competencies of the organization. An obvious example is when Johnson & Johnson, the consumer-oriented drug and toiletry giant, sold their sausage casings company.[32] Lucent Technologies, a leading telecommunications equipment manufacturer, itself a spin-off from AT&T, has spun off several slow-growth parts of its business. It is now considering spinning off one of its fastest-growing, most profitable businesses, the microelectronics unit, for two reasons. First, some observers see a lack of fit with other aspects of Lucent's business. Argued telecom analyst, Jim Jungjohann, "This makes perfect sense. You have the world's leading manufacturer of fiber-optic components combined with integrated circuits—you don't find that anywhere else on Wall Street."[33] But, just as importantly, the spin-off could be worth $50 billion—which would provide much needed funds to Lucent.

Refocusing may also involve new acquisitions or new ventures to round out a corporate portfolio or add more strength in an area that is essential to corporate distinctive competencies.[34] For instance, Grand Metropolitan bought Pillsbury and simultaneously sold Bennigans and Steak & Ale restaurants in an effort to redefine its domain in the food processing industry.[35]

Retrenchment

Retrenchment is a turnaround strategy. It can involve such tactics as workforce reductions, closing unprofitable plants, outsourcing unprofitable activities, implementation of tighter cost or quality controls, or new policies that emphasize quality or efficiency.

Workforce reductions, sometimes called downsizing, have become commonplace in organizations in the U.S., as a response to the burgeoning bureaucracies in the Post WWII era. In June 2000, Ryerson Tull Inc., a metals and industrial plastics distributor and processor with sales of $2.8 billion, announced a major restructuring that would involve employee lay-offs. The lay-offs are part of an attempt to better integrate and achieve coordination among past acquisitions.[36]

The evidence is mounting that "downsizing does not reduce expenses as much as desired, and that sometimes expenses may actually increase."[37] Certainly, severance packages are one reason for the increase. Nabisco took a $300 million charge to cover its restructuring, while ConAgra spent $505 million. Also, many organizations cut muscle, as well as fat, through lay-offs. In addition, a study of "white-collar" lay-offs in the U.S. automobile industry found that most companies experienced problems such as a reduction in quality, a loss in productivity, decreased effectiveness, lost trust, increased conflict, and low morale.[38] Other studies have shown that the "surviving" employees experience feelings of guilt and fear that may hurt productivity or organizational loyalty.[39] It is not surprising, then, that the stock market often reacts unfavorably to announcements of major lay-offs.[40]

Chapter XI Reorganization

An organization that is in serious financial trouble can voluntarily file for Chapter XI protection under the Federal Bankruptcy Code: "Chapter XI provides a proceeding for an organization to work out a plan or arrangement for solving its financial problems under the supervision of a federal court. It is intended primarily for debtors who feel they can solve their financial problems on their own if given sufficient time, and if relieved of some pressure."[41] In spring 2000, two large computer distributors, Inacom Corporation and MicroAge, Inc., both filed for court protection under Chapter XI. Both firms were struggling with severe cash flow problems as more computer manufacturers chose to sell direct to their customers and prices for computers fell.[42]

One of the major disadvantages of Chapter XI is that, after filing, all subsequent managerial decisions of substance must be approved by a court. Thus, managerial discretion and flexibility are reduced. Also, in a recent study of firms that had voluntarily filed for Chapter XI protection, only a little over half of the firms were "nominally successful in reorganizing," and "two-thirds of those retained less than 50 percent of their assets on completion of the reorganization process."[43]

One organizational response to this problem is the *prepackaged reorganization strategy*. Firms using this strategy negotiate a reorganization plan with creditors *before* filing for Chapter XI. Consequently, the courts stay out of the picture until after a tentative agreement is reached.

Leveraged Buyouts

Leveraged buyouts (LBOs) involve the private purchase of a business unit by managers, employees, unions, or private investors. They are called leveraged because much of the money that is used to purchase the business unit is borrowed from financial intermediaries (often at higher-than-normal interest rates). Because of high leverage, LBOs are often accompanied by selling off assets to repay debt. Consequently, organizations typically become smaller and more focused after an LBO.

During the late 1970s and early 1980s, LBOs gained a good reputation as a means of turning around failing divisions. For instance, Hart Ski, once a subsidiary of Beatrice, was revived through an LBO led by the son of one of its founders. Also, managers and the union joined forces to turn around American Safety Razor, a failing division of Philip Morris. These LBOs benefited many of these organizations' stakeholders, including employees and local communities.[44]

However, some researchers have discovered that LBOs stifle innovation and research and development, similar to mergers and acquisitions.[45] Others have found that LBO firms have comparatively slower growth in sales and employees and that they tend to divest a larger proportion of both non-core and core businesses, compared to firms that remained public.[46] Also, some executives who initiate LBOs seem to receive an excessive return. For example, John Kluge made a $3 billion profit in two years through dismantling Metromedia following an LBO.[47] Consequently, some business people are starting to wonder if LBOs are really in the best interests of all stakeholders. Plant closings, relocations, and workforce reductions are all common results from LBOs. Not surprisingly, reports of failed LBOs are becoming more common. Successful LBOs require buying a company at the right price with the right financing, combined with outstanding management and fair treatment of stakeholders.[48]

Structural Reorganization

Organizational structure, which was discussed in detail in Chapter 6, can be a potent force in restructuring efforts. As organizations diversify, top managers have a more difficult time processing the vast amounts of diverse information that are needed to appropriately control each business. Their span of control is too large. Consequently, an organization that is functionally structured may move to a more decentralized product/market or divisional structure. The end result is more managers with smaller spans of control and a greater capacity to understand each of their respective business areas.

Ryerson Tull, the distributor mentioned earlier, initiated a significant change in its organization structure, with the purpose of saving $30 million annually.

They reorganized into 13 geographical divisions, each with three to seven service centers. They then centralized several administrative functions, including credit, accounting, and human resources staff functions. These changes are not part of a strategy change, but are an attempt to be more effective at integrating past acquisitions and in implementing current strategies.[49]

In an effort to increase control, some organizations are actually splitting their operations into multiple, public corporations. For example, Pepsico spun off its famous restaurants (Taco Bell, Pizza Hut, and Kentucky Fried Chicken) in order to focus more attention on beverages and snacks. On the other hand, some organizations restructure by becoming more centralized. For instance, British Petroleum collapsed its structure from 12 head offices to 1 head office to save costs. According to Robert Horton, former Chairman and CEO of British Petroleum, the savings were enormous.[50]

KEY POINTS SUMMARY

The following are some of the key points that were discussed in this chapter:

1. Strategic controls consist of systems to support managers in tracking progress toward organizational goals and ensuring that organizational processes and the behavior of organizational members are consistent with those goals.

2. Organizations should not rely exclusively on accounting-based, top-down controls because, according to some control experts, accounting-based measures are "too late, too aggregated, and too distorted to be relevant for managers' planning and control decisions. In addition, too much reliance on accounting-based financial measures can prompt shortsightedness among managers.

3. Feedback control provides managers with information concerning outcomes from organizational activities, which is then used as a basis for comparison with the targets that have been established.

4. Concurrent controls provide managers with real-time information for managing performance (e.g., process controls), or serve as a real-time source of influence over the behavior of employees (e.g., bureaucratic and clan controls).

5. Feedforward control helps managers anticipate changes in the external and internal environments, based on analysis of inputs from stakeholders and the remote environment.

6. The learning processes associated with all types of control form the basis for changes to strategic direction, strategies, implementation plans, or even the targets themselves, if they are found to be unreasonable given current conditions.

7. As a result of performance problems and/or pressure from stakeholders, many firms are now restructuring. The restructuring techniques that were described in this chapter included refocusing assets, retrenchment, Chapter XI reorganization, leveraged buyouts, and changes to organization structure. These methods can also be used in combination.

END NOTES

1   B. McKay, "To Fix Coca-Cola, Daft Sets Out to Get Relationships Right," *The Wall Street Journal* (June 23, 2000): B1.

2   P. Lorange, M.F. Scott Morton, and S. Ghoshal, *Strategic Control* (St. Paul: West Publishing Company, 1986): 10.

3   J.F. Weston and E.F. Brigham, *Essentials of Managerial Finance*, 7th ed. (Hinsdale, Ill.: The Dryden Press, 1985): 154.

4   A. Lee, *Call Me Roger* (Chicago: Contemporary Books, 1988): 110.

5   H.T. Johnson and R.S. Kaplan, *Relevance Lost: The Rise and Fall of Management Accounting* (Boston, Mass.: Harvard Business School Press, 1987): 1.

6   R.E. Hoskisson and M.A. Hitt, "Strategic Control and Relative R&D Investment in Large Mulitproduct Firm," *Strategic Management Journal* 6 (1988): 605–622.

7   R.H. Hayes and W.J. Abernathy, "Managing Our Way to Economic Decline," *Harvard Business Review* (July/August

1980): 67–77; H.T. Johnson, "Managing By Remote Control: Recent Management Accounting Practice in Historical Perspective," in P. Temin, ed., *Inside the Business Enterprise: Historical Perspectives on the Use of Information* (Chicago: The University of Chicago Press, 1991): 41–66.

8 H.T. Johnson, *Relevance Regained: From Top-Down Control to Bottom-Up Empowerment* (New York: The Free Press, 1992): 30.

9 This entire paragraph is based on P.F. Drucker, "The Economy's Power Shift," *The Wall Street Journal* (September 24, 1992): A1.

10 M. Goold and J.J. Quinn, "The Paradox of Strategic Controls," *Strategic Management Journal* 11 (1990): 43–57.

11 This discussion and our model are most heavily influenced by the work of R.E. Freeman, *Strategic Management: A Stakeholder Approach* (Boston: Pittman, 1984) and Robert S. Kaplan and David P. Norton, "Putting the Balanced Scoreboard to Work," *Harvard Business Review* (September/October 1993): 134–147.

12 G.P. Latham and E.A. Locke, "Goal Setting—A Motivational Technique That Works," *Organizational Dynamics* (Autumn 1979): 68–80; M.D. Richards, *Setting Strategic Goals and Objectives*, 2nd ed. (St. Paul: West Publishing, 1986); M.E. Tubbs, "Goal Setting: A Meta-Analytic Examination of Empirical Evidence," *Journal of Applied Psychology* 3 (1986): 474–475.

13 Lorange, Scott Morton, and Ghoshal, *Strategic Control*, 2–8.

14 R. Simons, "How New Top Managers Use Control Systems As Levers of Strategic Renewal," *Strategic Management Journal* 15 (1994): 169–189.

15 R. Simons, "Strategic Orientation and Management Attention to Control Systems," *Strategic Management Journal* 12 (1991): 49–62.

16 Goold and Quinn, "The Paradox of Strategic Controls."

17 Simons, "Strategic Orientation," 50.

18 "BT Responds to More Competition," *Communicate* (May 2000): 9.

19 C.J. Gersick, "Revolutionary Change Theories: A Multi-Level Exploration of the Punctuated Equilibrium Paradigm," *Academy of Management Review* 16 (1991): 10–37; M.I. Tushman and E. Romanelli, "Organizational Evolution: A Metamorphosis Model of Convergence and Reorientation," in E.E. Cummings and B.M. Staw, eds., *Research in Organizational Behavior* (Greenwich, Conn.: JAI Press, 1985): 171–222.

20 N.A. Wishart, J.J. Elan, and D. Robey, "Redrawing the Portrait of a Learning Organization: Inside Knight-Ridder, Inc.," *Academy of Management Executive* (February 1996): 7–20; J.P. Walsh, "Managerial and Organizational Cognition," *Organization Science* 6 (1995): 280–321.

21 A. Saxenian, *Culture and Competition in Silicon Valley and Route 128* (Cambridge, Mass.: Harvard University Press, 1994).

22 Gersick, "Revolutionary Change Theories," 22.

23 Gersick, "Revolutionary Change Theories"; Tushman and Romanelli, "Organizational Evolution."

24 Gersick, "Revolutionary Change Theories"; Tushman and Romanelli, "Organizational Evolution."

25 C. Markides, "Consequences of Corporate Refocusing: Ex Ante Evidence," *Academy of Management Journal* 35 (1992): 398–412.

26 R.E. Hoskisson and M.A. Hitt, *Downscoping: How to Tame the Diversified Firm* (New York: Oxford University Press, 1994): 3.

27 R.E. Hoskisson and R.A. Johnson, "Corporate Restructuring and Strategic Change: The Effect on Diversification and R&D Intensity,"

Academy of Management Executive (May 1991): 7–21; Hoskisson and Hitt, *Downscoping*.

28 J. Cole, "Chrysler Agrees to Sell to Raytheon Co. Bulk of Its Aerospace, Defense Holdings," *The Wall Street Journal* (April 8, 1996): A3; "Business and Finance," *The Wall Street Journal* (June 10, 1996): A1.

29 A. Bodipo-Memba, "Ford Unit Predicts Lower Profits as it Prepares for Spin Off," *Knight-Ridder/Tribune Business News* (June 2, 2000).

30 C. O'Connor, "Bell Atlantic/GTE Mega-Merger Creates First IPO Spin-Off," *The IPO Reporter* (June 19, 2000).

31 T. Catan, "Triarc Board Agrees to Beverage Division Spin-Off," *The Financial Times* (June 23, 2000): 30; J. Ordonez, "U.K.'s Diageo to Sell Burger King Stake," *The Wall Street Journal* (June 23, 2000): A3.

32 J. Weber, "A Big Company that Works," *Business Week* (May 4, 1992): 125.

33 D. Solomon, "Lucent May Shed Microelectronics Unit," *The Wall Street Journal* (June 16, 2000): B4.

34 M.A. Hitt, R.E. Hoskisson, and J.S. Harrison, "Strategic Competitiveness in the 1990s: Challenges and Opportunities for U.S. Executives," *Academy of Management Executive* (May 1991): 7–21.

35 R.L. Daft, *Organization Theory and Design*, 4th ed. (St. Paul: West Publishing Company, 1992): 94.

36 P. Burgert, "Ryerson Plans to Restructure into 13 Geographical Units," *American Metal Market* (June 9, 2000): 6.

37 W. McKinley, C.M. Sanchez, and A.G. Schick, "Organizational Downsizing: Constraining, Cloning, Learning," *Academy of Management Executive* (August 1995): 32.

38 K.S. Cameron, S.J. Freeman, and Aneil K. Mishra, "Best Practices in White-Collar Downsizing: Managing Contradictions," *Academy of Management Executive* (August 1991): 57–73.

39 J. Brockner, S. Grover, T. Reed, R. DeWitt, and M. O'Malley, "Survivors' Reactions to Layoffs: We Get By With a Little Help From Our Friends," *Administrative Science Quarterly* 32 (1987): 526–541.

40 D.L. Worrell, W.N. Davidson III, and V.M. Sharma, "Layoff Announcements and Stockholder Wealth," *Academy of Management Journal* 34 (1991): 662–678.

41 D.M. Flynn and M. Farid, "The Intentional Use of Chapter XI: Lingering Versus Immediate Filing," *Strategic Management Journal* 12 (1991): 63–64.

42 G. McWilliams, "Inacom Corp. Files for Chapter 11 After its Failure in Finding Buyer," *The Wall Street Journal* (June 19, 2000): B7.

43 W.N. Moulton, "Bankruptcy as a Deliberate Strategy: Theoretical Considerations and Empirical Evidence," *Strategic Management Journal* 14 (1993): 130.

44 K.M. Davidson, "Another Look at LBOs," *Journal of Business Strategies* (January/February 1988): 44–47.

45 A good review of these studies, of which there are seven, is found in S.A. Zahra and M. Fescina, "Will Leveraged Buyouts Kill U.S. Corporate Research and Development," *Academy of Management Executive* (November 1991): 7–21.

46 M.F. Wiersema and J.P. Liebeskind, "The Effects of Leveraged Buyouts On Corporate Growth and Diversification In Large Firms," *Strategic Management Journal* 16 (1995): 447–460.

47 K.M. Davidson, "Another Look at LBOs."

48 M. Schwarz and E.A. Weinstein, "So You Want to Do a Leveraged Buyout," *Journal of Business Strategies* (January/February 1989): 10–15.

49 Burgert, "Ryerson Plans to Restructure into 13 Geographical Units."

50 R. Calori and B. Dufour, "Management European Style," *Academy of Management Executive* (August 1995): 67.

CHAPTER

8

Strategic Challenges for the 21st Century

In 1981, Jollibee was an 11-store fast food chain based in the Philippines. That was the year McDonald's began its expansion into Manila. Observers expected Jollibee to fail.

Instead, CEO Ton Tan Caktiong studied everything about McDonald's—how tight, detailed operating procedures were used to control costs, quality, and service. Jollibee management incorporated as many of the operating procedures as possible—but tried to customize their menu and service to better suit the tastes and preferences of customers in the Philippines. The combination of the two—newfound efficiencies and tailored menu—was a success. Jollibee was able to expand its chain to 65 stores in the Philippines by 1990—faster than McDonald's.

When Jollibee ventured into new Asian and Middle Eastern markets in the early 1990s, it avoided encountering McDonald's head on. It focused on smaller markets, such as Guam and Vietnam, that had little in the way of fast food. It also continued to combine tight operating procedures with country-sensitive menus.

In the late 1990s, with 24 overseas stores in 10 countries, Jollibee was ready to take on the U.S. market. Three stores in San Francisco are up and running, sales well above forecasts. Seventeen additional stores are planned for California in the next 18 months.[1]

The Jollibee experience illustrates some important lessons.

The global marketplace is huge, there are significant opportunities even in industries dominated by large players, new market entrants could come from any country, and it is important to learn from those who enter markets early.[2]

The facts are that global expansion and awareness are rapidly increasing in all industrialized countries. In this chapter, we will discuss international expansion strategies and global business strategies, followed by a brief evaluation of several global markets. This chapter will end with a brief analysis of what the future may hold in store for businesses.

INTERNATIONAL EXPANSION

Organizations seem to evolve through four stages of international development.[3] In the first stage, the *domestic stage*, organizations focus their efforts on domestic operations, but begin to export their products and services, sometimes through an export department or a foreign joint venture. Toys 'R' Us, a fairly recent entrant into foreign markets, is currently in this stage. In the *international stage*, exports become an important part of organizational strategy. The organization typically forms international divisions to handle sales, service, and warehousing in the foreign markets. Marketing programs are custom-tailored to suit the needs of each country. Hasbro, the toy maker, is in this stage.[4]

In the third stage, the *multinational stage*, the organization has marketing and production facilities throughout the world. More than a third of firm sales originate overseas, and the organization has worldwide access to capital markets. Nike, the shoe distributor, is in the multinational stage, passing the point at which one-third of revenues come from non-U.S. sales.[5] Finally, in the *global stage*, the organization is no longer associated primarily with any one country. Global firms, such as Phillips N.V., Unilever, and Matsushita Electric, operate in as many as 40 countries or more.

Unfortunately, not all U.S. companies that attempt international expansion are really prepared for it. According to Sheth and Eshghi, experts on international strategy:

> Many companies become multinational reluctantly. They start off as export houses, and as international business grows and becomes a significant part of corporate revenues, they become more involved in foreign operations. However, the corporate culture still remains domestic, and the international division is treated as a stepchild. The situation becomes one of them vs. us . . . what is lacking is a true worldwide orientation in product design, manufacturing, and marketing functions.[6]

Structural inertia within U.S. companies has been a major impediment to their transformation into true global competitors. Historically, North American companies have been able to prosper by selling goods to the largest and richest market in the world. In the past, some managers considered overseas operations nuisances or simply organizational appendages that generated a few extra dollars in sales revenue.[7] Now, the world has changed. Since global competitors have invaded U.S. markets, U.S. companies must also learn to compete overseas.

International activities should be accompanied by a new mindset for all members of an organization, from top managers to the lowest-level employees. Where will this new global mindset come from? It has to start at the top of the organization. CEOs who want to create global organizations can start by expanding their organizational visions to include overseas operations. However, they should also assign specific individuals to monitor global stakeholder groups, economic trends, and markets and integrate this information into ongoing strategic management processes through the business intelligence system.

CEOs can create a sense of urgency in the organization by constantly discussing global customers, operations, strategies, and successes and failures with subordinates, the board of directors, employees, and the media. They will also want to make visits to global operations as a part of their regular routines. Finally,

CEOs can communicate the value of employees from countries that are outside of the home country by making sure that they are both hired and promoted as often as Americans.

Organizations are also sending some of their managers to special training programs to help increase their global awareness and vision. The University of Michigan recently provided an intensive, in-depth 5-week program for 21 executives from Japan, the United States, Brazil, Great Britain, and India to help them become global thinkers. They first made the participant more aware of the differences that existed between them. Then they helped them to work out these differences. The training program was so successful that organizers are planning to make it an annual event.[8]

Global Strategies

Throughout this book, we have provided many examples of non-U.S.-based firms in an effort to demonstrate that strategic management principles apply to all firms, regardless of origin. Nevertheless, significant differences exist between U.S. and other markets. This section will help demonstrate how firms can take advantage of the differences associated with participating in global markets and industries.

Global Product/Market Approach. One of the key issues facing top managers as their organizations pursue international development is selection of a product/market approach. A *multidomestic strategy* entails handling product design, assembly, and marketing on a country-by-country basis by custom tailoring products and services around individual market needs. On the other hand, organizations pursuing a *global strategy* produce one product design and market it in the same fashion throughout the world.[9]

Bausch & Lomb successfully adopted a multidomestic strategy to significantly increase its global market share:

> The key to global success for Bausch & Lomb is to "Think globally, act locally," by letting country managers make their own decisions. This strategy was applied in Bausch & Lomb's Ray Ban division. In Europe, Ray Bans tend to be flashier and costlier than in the U.S. In Asia the company redesigned them to better suit the Asian face and sales took off. This strategy has paid off. Ray Ban commands an awesome 40% of the world market for premium-priced sunglasses.[10]

Multidomestic strategies are intuitively appealing from a stakeholder point of view, since they emphasize the satisfaction of segmented customer needs. However, customization may add more costs to the products or services than can be successfully recaptured through higher prices. A well-known marketing scholar, Theodore Levitt asserts that:

> . . . well managed companies have moved from emphasis on customizing items to offering globally standardized products that are advanced, functional, reliable—and low priced. Multinational companies that concentrated on idiosyncratic consumer preferences have become befuddled and unable to take in the forest because of the trees. Only global companies will achieve long-term success by concentrating on what everyone wants rather than worrying about the details of what everyone thinks they might like.[11]

As a counter argument, some researchers explain that a global product/market strategy is only appropriate if (1) there is a global market segment for a product or service; (2) there are economic efficiencies associated with a global strategy; (3) there are no external constraints, such as government regulations, that will prevent a global strategy from being implemented; and (4) there are no absolute internal constraints either.[12]

Some organizations are now pursuing a hybrid *transnational* product/market *strategy*. An international counterpart to the best cost strategy discussed previously, a transnational strategy entails seeking both global efficiency and local responsiveness. This difficult task is accomplished through establishing an integrated network that fosters shared vision and resources while allowing individual decisions to be made to adapt to local needs.[13]

Global Expansion Tactics. Firms can apply a variety of expansion tactics as they pursue global opportunities. Among the most common are:

1. *Licensing*. Selling the right to produce and/or sell a brand name product in a foreign market.
2. *Franchising*. This is the services counterpart to a licensing strategy. A foreign firm buys the legal right to use the name and operating methods of a U.S. firm in its home country.
3. *Exporting*. Transferring goods to other countries for sale through wholesalers or a foreign company.
4. *Joint Venture*. Cooperative agreement among two or more companies to pursue common business objectives.
5. *Greenfield Venture*. Creation of a wholly owned foreign subsidiary.[14]

Some organizations combine these tactics in interesting ways. For example, Molson Breweries, a joint venture between Toronto's Molson Companies and Australia's Foster's Brewing Group, brews Miller Genuine Draft under license from Miller Brewing Company.[15] If that isn't confusing enough, Miller Brewing Company is actually a subsidiary of Philip Morris.

Among the most important criteria when deciding on an option for international growth are cost, financial risk, profit potential, and control. In general, moving down the list of alternatives from 1 to 5 entails greater cost and greater financial risk but also greater profit potential and greater control. Consequently, these alternatives represent a trade-off between cost and financial risk on the one hand, and profit and control on the other. Of course, this is a gross generalization. Some of the options, such as joint venture, are hard to judge on the basis of these four criteria because the exact nature of the agreement can vary so widely from venture to venture.

Enhancing Global Business-Level Strategies. Organizations that are involved in multiple global markets have advantages available to them in pursuing their business-level strategies. Examples of the many options available for improving competitive position vis-à-vis cost leadership through a global strategy include the following:

1. *Cost reductions through foreign assembly or manufacturing*. Many firms are currently shipping components to foreign countries for assembly by low-cost laborers. Some companies are also having some of their manufacturing done in foreign countries.

2. *Branding of finished products that are subcontracted to low-cost foreign manufacturers.* Nike designs shoes but does not manufacture them. They are manufactured in third world countries according to Nike specifications.

3. *Global sourcing (the purchase of low-cost foreign components or raw materials).* Many U.S. firms buy Japanese semiconductors or Japanese steel for use in their products.

4. *Expanding markets leading to economies of scale.* Some companies could not grow large enough to enjoy the lowest possible production costs on the basis of domestic demand alone. However, expansion into foreign markets can lead to significant increases in demand.

5. *Transfer of technological know-how through joint venture (learning from competitors).* Some foreign firms are more efficient than U.S. firms in producing similar products. Joint ventures with these firms may provide opportunities to learn new technologies that can lead to significant cost reductions.[16]

Global strategies can also lead to competitive advantages through differentiation. Some strategies for doing this include:

1. *Distribution of foreign products in the U.S.* American firms can purchase elite products from foreign manufacturers for sale in the U.S. This strategy is easy to imitate unless the companies sign a contract that provides the American firm exclusive rights to market the product in the U.S.

2. *Sale of U.S. products in foreign countries.* In some countries, American products command a premium price because of the image they convey. For example, Coca-Cola Co. enjoys higher operating profits in Japan than in the U.S.

3. *Superior quality through joint venture.* Just as U.S. companies can learn cost-saving technologies through joint ventures, they can also learn how to better differentiate their products through higher quality or some other unique feature.

4. *Licensing of product technology from abroad.* Joint venture is not the only way to learn new technologies. U.S. firms sometimes have the option of licensing product technologies to differentiate their present products.[17]

Many risks are also associated with global expansion. Organizations face the risk that citizens in some countries may not be receptive to some foreign products because of prejudices they hold against the countries in which they were produced. The same sort of risk applies to service firms. Also, the risks associated with managing international joint ventures and currency translations were discussed previously. These are only a few of many potential risks. Wise selection of countries in which to pursue opportunities can reduce costs and risks associated with global expansion. We will now discuss how to select a country for investment.

Foreign Business Environments

Significant changes in the global environment have created great opportunities for organizations that are willing to take a risk and wait patiently for returns. For example, Eastern Europe may have up to a quarter of the world's undiscovered oil, about equal to what's left in the Middle East. Russia and surrounding countries possess more natural gas than anyone else. Dozens of companies are

rushing to help bring this oil to market, however, as in the Chevron case, insta-
bility in the region makes investment recovery difficult and risky. Furthermore,
OPEC (the Organization of Petroleum-Exporting Countries), fearing that a new
force in oil will reduce its own power, is considering offering seats in its cartel to
Russia, Kazakhstan, and Azerbaijan.[18] Oil is not the only risky business in
Russia. Although Russia's many regions are working to attract funds from foreign investors, investments often bring unexpected problems. For example, a
British steel maker that bought Kazakhstan's largest steel plant had to negotiate
for two months to get more than a dozen old KGB agents to leave their elec-
tronically sophisticated corner office in the factory.[19] Furthermore, communist
ideals are still popular and some Russian officials are working to reverse business privatization.[20]

The problems associated with business ventures in Russia are similar to those
found in most developing countries—an unstable government, inadequately
trained workers, low levels of supporting technology, shortages of supplies, a
weak transportation system, and an unstable currency. Firms also have to struggle
with managing stakeholders that are typically very different—in values, beliefs,
ethics, and in many other ways—from stakeholders found in the home country.

Firms that are "first movers" into developing countries may be able to develop stakeholder-based advantages such as long-term productive contractual
and informal relationships with host-country governments and organizations
that followers won't have the opportunity to develop. For example, Spanish firms
took huge risks by making major investments in Latin America during a wave of
privatizations; however, they are now firmly entrenched in one of the world's
fastest-growing regions. According to one large Spanish bank executive with significant investments in Latin America, "It's not a new frontier for Spanish companies because we discovered America in 1492. But it's a growth frontier. It's a financial rediscovery of the Americas."[21] Closer to the U.S., the recent defeat of the
Institutional Revolutionary Party (PRI) in Mexico, after 71 years in power, is likely
to bring a more open and supportive business climate.[22]

Another region with a lot of potential for U.S. expansion is Asia. The "Pacific
Century" refers to a forecast that the world's growth center for the 21st Century
will shift across the Pacific Ocean to Asia. Asia is already the world's biggest consumer of steel and the second fastest-growing market for automobiles. China
alone has over 1 billion potential consumers, and television sets and beer are increasingly popular.[23] In response to the huge market potential, Motorola is doubling its stake in China. Also, Atlantic Richfield, referred to as "the lucky company" by the Chinese, completed a $1.13 billion gas pipeline project off the
southeast coast of China with very few problems.

Nevertheless, many companies are not so lucky. Rampant corruption and a
culture that considers counterfeiting "cool" can make business dealings difficult.
Furthermore, Chinese/American relations are often strained due to China's poor
human rights record and its unwillingness to conform to American policies on issues such as copyright protection and arms sales to politically unstable countries.[24] To make matters worse, anti-U.S. sentiment is surging in China:

> According to a recent survey of youths, 90% said they feel the U.S. behaves
> "hegemonistically," with expansionist aims, towards China. When the roman-
> tic movie, *Bridges of Madison County* played here, film authorities were inun-
> dated with phone calls complaining about "unhealthy capitalist lifestyles" of

the lead characters, who engage in adultery. Even fast-food restaurants like McDonald's have come under attack for undermining children's health.[25]

Reforms in China are currently progressing slowly, and it is hard for Westerners to forget the blood that was spilled in Tiananmen Square as pro-democracy student protesters faced off against hard-line government forces.[26] However, according to many experts, China is headed toward capitalism, and it is already too late to turn back.[27] Already, money and management from Hong Kong, Taiwan, and Singapore are transforming South China.[28]

In addition to China, other Asian countries hold great potential. The newly industrialized economies (NIEs) of South Korea, Taiwan, Hong Kong, and Singapore have been experiencing growth in real gross domestic product at a level that is nearly twice that of the EC, Japan, and the U.S.[29]

Finally, changes in Europe have made it increasingly important for U.S. companies to be involved there. The demise of some trade barriers among European countries has created a more open market of 340 million consumers.[30] Reduction in trade barriers and the acceptance of a single currency (the Euro) by most of the economically powerful nations in Europe means that companies involved in Europe can better take advantage of regional variations in wage rates and the cost of raw materials, which can lead to lower costs. Also, differentiation is easier to achieve because organizations can draw freely from the technological strengths of each nation. Organizations that have businesses in Europe already enjoy the advantages of a typically well-educated workforce, a well-developed infrastructure, a sophisticated level of technology, and high consumer demand—all factors that are associated with "first-world" countries. The recent changes in Europe make the EC even more attractive for investment.

Evaluating Foreign Investments. Many characteristics must be evaluated when considering a foreign country for investment. Many of them fall within the general areas of the remote environment, including the social environment, the economy, the political/legal environment, and the state of technology. Other characteristics are related to specific industries and markets. Questions concerning each of these factors are listed in Exhibit 8.1, which is a useful tool for evaluating a potential country.

The wrong answers to any of the questions in Exhibit 8.1 can make a country less attractive. The following are some examples that demonstrate this point: (1) an unstable government can greatly increase the risk of a total loss of investment; (2) an inefficient transportation system can increase total product costs to prohibitively high levels; (3) inadequate school systems can result in poorly skilled workers, which may not have the ability to manufacture technical products; (4) a slowly growing GNP could mean that consumer demand will be sluggish; (5) high foreign tax rates can virtually eliminate profits; and (6) if the local currency is not translatable into U.S. dollars, the organization will have a tough time removing profits from the country.

Answers to the questions should also be judged based on the type of activity the organization is considering. For example, a high per capita income is favorable if the organization is only going to sell U.S. products in the foreign market (export). On the other hand, low per capita income could mean that wages are very low, which is positive if the organization is only considering foreign manufacturing or assembly.

**Exhibit 8.1   *Examples of Questions to Ask
about a Potential Foreign Market***

Social Forces
What currently are the hot topics of debate? How well organized are special interest groups
with regard to the environment, labor, and management issues? Are current policies or behaviors of the organization likely to be offensive in the new host country? What is the attitude of
potential consumers toward foreign products and services? Will there be significant cultural
barriers to overcome? How difficult is the language? How old is the population? What other
differences could cause difficulty for the organization?

The Economy
What is the inflation rate? How large is the gross national product (GNP)? How fast is it growing? What is the income per capita? How much impact does the global economy have on the
domestic economy? How high is the unemployment rate? What actions does the government
take to fuel economic growth? What is the trade balance with the United States? Can the currency be exchanged for the home currency? How high are interest rates? Is the financial sector
well organized? How expensive are the factors of production?

Political/Legal Environment
What is the form of government? How much influence does the government have over business? Is the government stable? What is the government's attitude toward private enterprise
and U.S. firms? What is the home government's attitude toward the foreign government? How
high are tax rates compared with rates in the home country? How are taxes assessed and collected? How high are import and export taxes? What is the nature of the court system? Is legal
protection available through incorporation or a similar form?

Technology
Is the country technologically advanced? Do schools and universities supply qualified workers?
Are the required skills available in sufficient quantity? Are suitable information systems available? Is the infrastructure sound (e.g., roads, transportation systems)? Is an appropriate site
available?

Industry Specific
How large is the industry? How fast is it growing? Is it segmentable? How many competitors
are there? How strong are they? What is the relative position of industry participants in relation
to suppliers and customers? Are substitute products available? What is the primary basis for
competition? Is it possible to reach the market through a joint venture?

Competitive Advantages of Nations. Michael Porter, whose name should now
be familiar to you, expanded his analyses of competitive environments to include
the global economy. In his book, *The Competitive Advantage of Nations*, he developed arguments concerning why some nations produce so many stellar companies in particular industries.[31] For example, Germany is the home base for several
top luxury car manufacturers and Switzerland has many leading companies in
pharmaceuticals and chocolate. He explains that four characteristics of countries
actually create an environment that is conducive to creating globally competitive
firms in certain business areas. The four characteristics are:

1. *Factor Conditions.* These are endowments enjoyed by specific nations such as uncommon raw materials or laborers with specific skills that can lead to advantages in particular industries. Other factor conditions that can lead to advantage are superior factor-producing mechanisms such as excellent schools or universities.
2. *Demand Conditions.* If buyers of a product or service in a particular country are among the most discriminating and demanding in the world, competitors in that industry have to work harder to please them.
3. *Related and Supporting Industries.* If suppliers to an industry are the very best in the world, their excellence is passed on to the buyers who use their products. Advantages can also be obtained if firms in related industries are also global leaders.
4. *Firm Strategy, Structure, and Rivalry.* Sometimes the management techniques that are customary in a nation's businesses are conducive to success in particular industries. Also, particular industries may attract the most talented managers in the nation. In addition, strong competition can force competitors to excel, thus making them stronger in world markets.

These factors can indicate the potential for developing a nucleus of companies that are globally competitive. Basically, the reason companies can develop a highly competitive nucleus is that tough market environments can create world-class competitors only if the competitors are also endowed with the resources they need to compete. If home markets are uncompetitive, firms will not be sufficiently motivated to produce a superior product. On the other hand, if home markets are highly competitive but the factors of production, support industries, and human talent are not available, firms will likewise be incapable of producing globally competitive products. When these two conditions are met, however, an environment is created that both motivates and rewards excellence.

The logical conclusion from Porter's analysis would seem to be to locate subsidiaries in the nations with the strongest home bases in particular industries. However, he argues that this rarely happens. First, it is difficult in some cases for an "outsider," a foreign firm, to become an "insider." Second, Porter suggests that it is unlikely that the foreign subsidiary in the nation with the natural advantages will be able to influence the parent company "long distance."

Porter does, however, suggest that firms should take advantage of their own nation's natural advantages. He also recommends that some of the principles that apply to the competitive advantages of nations can be applied in any company that wants to become more competitive in the world economy. Specifically, organizations can seek out the toughest, most discriminating buyers, choose from the best suppliers in the world, seek to excel against the most outstanding global competitors, form alliances with outstanding foreign competitors, and stay abreast of all research findings and innovations that are relevant to their core businesses.

THE CHALLENGE OF THE FUTURE

Without question, the greatest managerial challenges lie ahead. It is hard to predict with precision the kind of business environment the next generation of managers will face; however, judging from the recent past, it will probably be associated with increasing global complexity and interconnectedness. Advancements in technology are allowing critical business information to be available around the world instantaneously. Decision makers can communicate with each other from any place at any time. The World Wide Web allows open access to markets throughout the world. These technological advancements are making time zones, national boundaries, and the physical location of management increasingly unimportant. Furthermore, improvements in transportation and communications, coupled with increasing standards of both education and living in most nations of the world, are making the physical location of business facilities less important than in the past. Around the world, people are exposed to the same music, news, fashions, and movies—which is working to blend national cultures. Finally, as customers become more educated and improve their standard of living around the world, they will become more demanding of manufacturers.[32]

Several of our examples have illustrated a pattern. The same technologies that are allowing improved education and communications—inexpensive computers, wireless communications, and Internet access—are also making it easier for new entrepreneurial start-ups to enter and destabilize established industries. Traditional brick and mortar (BAM) book stores have lost substantial revenue to Amazon.com, BAM music retailers are losing to Napster-like entrants and will eventually lose even more to record companies who bypass retailers altogether, and computer distributors like Inacom and MicroAge are in bankruptcy because computer manufacturers are bypassing them and going straight to the market. A customer from anywhere in the world who wants to buy a computer can go to Buy.com and comparison shop with the ease of a mouse click. On the Internet, company size, age, and nationality are usually unimportant.

So what does the future hold—lower entry barriers in many industries, faster imitation, collapsing product life cycles, a global retail marketplace, a highly educated, increasingly mobile global labor market. Managers will face challenges in several areas—retaining valuable employees, creating and preserving competitive advantage, holding back new entrants, serving increasingly demanding customers, and choosing and timing technology investments at a time when change is so rapid.

The challenges that managers will face are extraordinary—but never dull. It is a very exciting time to be in business. We hope the tools, theories, and techniques found in this book can help you become an effective leader for this new century.

KEY POINTS SUMMARY

Some of the key points found in the chapter are as follows:

1. Global expansion and awareness are rapidly increasing in all industrialized countries.
2. Organizations evolve through four stages of international development: the domestic stage, the international stage, the multinational stage, and the global stage.

3. With regard to an international product/market approach, a multidomestic strategy entails custom tailoring products and services around individual market needs, whereas a global strategy means production and marketing of one product design throughout the world.
4. Among the most common global expansion tactics are licensing, franchising, exporting, joint ventures,

and greenfield ventures. In general, moving down the list of alternatives entails greater cost and greater financial risk but also greater profit potential and greater control.

5. Organizations that are involved in multiple global markets have many advantages available to them in pursuing their business-level strategies. However, international business also entails higher risk.

6. Significant changes in the global environment have created great opportunities for organizations that are willing to take a risk and wait patiently for returns. Currently, great opportunities exist in the countries from the old Soviet Union, Latin America, and all over Asia. Changes in Europe such as falling trade barriers have made it increasingly important for companies to be involved there also.

7. Many characteristics must be evaluated when considering a foreign country for investment. Many of

them fall within the general areas of the remote environment, including the social environment, the economy, the political/legal environment, and the state of technology. Other characteristics are related to specific industries and markets.

8. Some nations seem to produce many highly successful companies in particular industries. Four variables that seem to explain this phenomenon are factor conditions; demand conditions; related and supporting industries; and firm strategy, structure, and rivalry.

9. The greatest managerial challenges lie ahead. The tools, theories, and techniques found in this book can help you be an effective leader in the 21st Century.

END NOTES

1 C.A. Bartlett and S. Ghoshal, "Going Global: Lessons from Late Movers," *Harvard Business Review* (March/April 2000): 132–145.

2 Bartlett and Ghoshal, "Going Global: Lessons from Late Movers."

3 N.J. Adler, *International Dimensions of Organizational Behavior*, 2nd ed. (Boston: PWS-Kent, 1991); R.L. Daft, *Organization Theory and Design*, 4th ed. (St. Paul: West Publishing, 1992): 228–229; T.T. Herbert, "Strategy and Multinational Organizational Structure: An Interorganizational Relationships Perspective," *Academy of Management Review* 9 (1984): 259–271.

4 D.W. Grigsby, "Hasbro, Inc.," in M.J. Stahl and D.W. Grigsby, *Strategic Management for Decision Making* (Boston: PWS-Kent Publishing, 1992): 725–738.

5 "Nike Net Surged 21% In Quarter to Record; Stock Rises by $6.375," *The Wall Street Journal* (July 9, 1992): B4.

6 J. Sheth and G. Eshghi, *Global Strategic Management Perspectives* (Cincinnati: South-Western College Publishing, 1989): 13.

7 C.A. Bartlett and S. Ghoshal, "Global Strategic Management: Impact on the New Frontiers of Strategy Research," *Strategic Management Journal* 12 (1991): 5–16.

8 S. Tully, "The Hunt for the Global Manager," *Fortune* (May 21, 1990): 140–144; J. Main, "How 21 Men Got Global in 35 Days," *Fortune* (November 6, 1989): 71.

9 K. Ohmae, "Managing in a Borderless World," *Harvard Business Review* (May/June 1989): 152–161.

10 Adapted from R. Jacob, "Trust the Locals, Win Worldwide," *Fortune* (May 4, 1992): 76.

11 T. Levitt, "The Globalization of Markets," *Harvard Business Review* (May/June 1983): 92.

12 S.P. Douglas and Y. Wind, "The Myth of Globalization," *Columbia Journal of World Business* (Winter 1987): 19–29.

13 M.A. Hitt, R.D. Ireland, and R.E. Hoskisson, *Strategic Management: Competitiveness and Globalization* (Minneapolis: West Publishing Company, 1995).

14 This discussion of tactics for global expansion was based, in part, on C.W.L. Hill, P. Hwang, and W.C. Kim, "An Eclectic Theory of the Choice of International Entry Mode," *Strategic Management Journal* 11 (1990): 117–128; C.W.L. Hill and G.R. Jones, *Strategic Management: An Integrated Approach* (Boston: Houghton Mifflin, 1992): 254–259.

15 "Court Dismisses Rivals' Bid to Stop Sale of Beer Brand," *The Wall Street Journal* (July 14, 1992): B9.

16 Some of the options contained in this list were based on information found in M.L. Fagan, "A Guide to Global Sourcing," *Journal of Business Strategy* (March/April 1991): 21–25; Sheth and Eshghi, *Global Strategic Management Perspectives*; and Stahl and Grigsby, *Strategic Management for Decision Making*: 205–206.

17 Some of the options contained in this list were based on information found in Sheth and Eshghi, *Global Strategic Management Perspectives* and Stahl and Grigsby, *Strategic Management for Decision Making*: 205–206.

18 P. Nulty, "The Black Gold Rush in Russia," *Fortune* (June 15, 1992): 126.

19 K. Pope, "A Steelmaker Built Up By Buying Cheap Mills Finally Meets Its Match," *The Wall Street Journal* (May 2, 1996): A1, A10.

20 N. Banerjee, "Russia's Many Regions Work to Attract Funds From Foreign Investors," *The Wall Street Journal* (April 30, 1996): A1, A13; S. Liesman, "Some Russian Officials are Moving to Reverse Business Privatization," *The Wall Street Journal* (March 20, 1996): A1, A6; C. Rosett, "Communists Mount Comeback in Russia, and Mean Business," *The Wall Street Journal* (March 27, 1996): A1, A4.

21 T. Kamm and J. Friedland, "Spanish Firms Discover Latin America Business As New World of Profit," *The Wall Street Journal* (May 23, 1996): A1, A9.

22 G. Smith, "A Vote For Change?" *Business Week* (July 3, 2000): 56–58.

23 L. Kraar, "Asia 2000," *Fortune* (October 5, 1992): 111.

24 J. Barnathan, "A Pirate Under Every Rock," *Business Week* (June 17, 1996): 50–51; L. Kraar, "The Risks are Rising in China," *Fortune* (March 6, 1995): 179–180; K. Schoenberger, "Motorola Bets Big On China," *Fortune* (May 27, 1996): 116–124; K. Schoenberger, "Arco's Surprisingly Good Fortune in China," *Fortune* (February 5, 1996): 32.

25 K. Chen, "Anti-U.S. Sentiment Surges in China, Putting a Further Strain on Relations," *The Wall Street Journal* (March 15, 1996): A11.

26 P. Steidlmeier, "China's Most-Favored-Nation Status: Attempts to Reform China and the Prospects for U.S. Business," *Business and the Contemporary World* 4 (1992): 68–80.

27 B. Schlender, "China Really is On the Move," *Fortune* (October 5, 1992): 114–122.

28 L. Kraar, "A New China Without Borders," *Fortune* (October 5, 1992): 124–128.

29 J. Labate, "The World Economy in Charts," *Fortune* (July 27, 1992): 62.

30 S. Tully, "Europe 1992: More Unity Than You Think," *Fortune* (August 24, 1992): 136–142.

31 M.E. Porter, *The Competitive Advantage of Nations* (New York: The Free Press, 1990).

32 C. St. John, A. Cannon, and R. Pouder, "Change Drivers in the New Millennium: Implications for Manufacturing Strategy Research," *Journal of Operations Management* (in press).

Preparing a Strategic Analysis

Structuring an Environmental Analysis
Industry Analysis
External Stakeholders and the Broad
  Environment
Strategic Issues Facing the Industry

Structuring an Organizational Analysis
Evaluation of the Internal Environment
Identification of Resources and Capabilities
Performance Evaluation
Sources of Competitive Advantage

Developing a Strategic Plan
Strategic Direction and Major Strategies
Evaluation of Opportunities and
  Recommendations
Implementation and Control

A Note to Students

Strategic management is an iterative, ongoing process designed to position a firm for competitive advantage in its ever-changing environment. To manage an organization strategically, a manager must understand and appreciate the desires of key organizational stakeholders, the industry environment, and the firm's position relative to its stakeholders and industry. This knowledge allows a manager to set goals and direct the organization's resources in a way that corrects weaknesses, overcomes threats, takes advantage of strengths and opportunities, and, ultimately, satisfies stakeholders. This book contains a foundation for understanding these strategic management processes.

With case analysis, you can practice some of the techniques of strategic management. Case analysis, to some extent, mirrors the processes managers use to make real strategic decisions. The main advantages managers have over students who analyze cases are that they have more information and more experience. For example, managers have ongoing relationships with internal and external stakeholders, from whom information can be gathered. They may also have a business intelligence system and staff to help them make decisions. In addition, managers usually have substantial experience in the industry and company. Nevertheless, managers must still make decisions without full information. Like students, they never have all of the facts or the time and resources to gather them. In case analysis, you must sort accurate, relevant information from that which is inaccurate or irrelevant.

The authors of cases have attempted to capture as much information as possible. They typically conducted extensive interviews with managers and employees and gathered information from public sources such as annual reports and business magazines. Many cases include a detailed description of the industry and competitors as well as an extensive profile of one organization. You can supplement this information through your own library research, *if* your instructor thinks this is appropriate.

Case analysis typically begins with a brief introduction of the company. The introduction, which sets the stage for the rest of the case, should include a brief description of the defining characteristics of the firm, including some of its outstanding qualities, past successes, failures, and products or services. The industries in which the firm is involved are also identified.

The next section of a case analysis can be either an environmental analysis or an internal analysis. Opportunities are defined as conditions in the broad and task *environments* that allow a firm to take advantage of *organizational* strengths, overcome *organizational* weaknesses, or neutralize *environmental* threats. Consequently, both environmental and organizational analyses are required before all of the organization's opportunities can be identified. We have chosen to treat environmental analysis first because it establishes the context in which firm strategies and resources can be understood. However, reversing the order of analysis would not be incorrect and is even preferred by some strategic management scholars.

Environmental analysis is an examination of the external environment, including external stakeholders, the competition, and the broad environment. Systematic external analysis will help you draw conclusions about the potential for growth and profit in the industry and determine keys to survival and success in the industry.

An organizational analysis, which follows the external analysis, is designed to evaluate the organization's strategic direction, business- and corporate-level strategies, resources, capabilities, and relationships with internal and external stakeholders, and then determine the strengths, weaknesses, vulnerabilities, and sources of competitive advantage exhibited by the firm. These determinations must be made against a background of knowledge about the external environment so that the full range of opportunities and threats can also be identified.

STRUCTURING AN ENVIRONMENTAL ANALYSIS

An analysis of the external environment includes an industry analysis and an examination of key external stakeholders and the broad environment. Findings are then summarized, with an emphasis on identifying industry growth and profit potential and the keys to survival and success in the industry. Some organizations are involved in more than one industry. Consequently, a separate industry analysis is done for each of the industries in which a firm is involved.

Industry Analysis

Environmental analysis should begin with an industry analysis. The first step in industry analysis is to provide a basic description of the industry and the competitive forces that dominate it. Porter's Five Forces are evaluated, along with other relevant issues:

1. What is the product or service? What function does it serve? What are the channels of distribution?

2. What is the industry size in units and dollars? How fast is it growing? Are products differentiated? Are there high exit barriers? Are there high fixed costs? These are some of the forces that determine the strength of competition among existing competitors.

3. Who are the major competitors? What are their market shares? In other words, is the industry consolidated or fragmented?

4. Who are the major customers of the industry? Are they powerful? What gives them power?

5. Who are the major suppliers to the industry? Are they powerful? What gives them power?

6. Do significant entry barriers exist? What are they? Are they effective in protecting existing competitors, thus enhancing profits?

7. Are there any close substitutes for industry products and services? Do they provide pressure on prices charged in this industry?

8. What are the basic strategies of competitors? How successful are they?

9. To what extent is the industry global? Are there any apparent advantages to being involved in more than one nation?

10. Is the industry regulated? What influence do regulations have on industry competitiveness?

External Stakeholders and the Broad Environment

A complete environmental analysis also includes an assessment of external stakeholders and the broad environment. The identity and power of competitors, suppliers, and customers was already established during the industry analysis. At this stage of the analysis, other important stakeholders should also be identified and their influence on the industry determined (see Chapter 2). If any of the external stakeholders pose a threat or opportunity, this also should be identified. One of the outcomes of this part of the analysis should be the establishment of priorities for each external stakeholder group. High-priority stakeholders will receive greater attention during the development of the strategic plan.

The broad environment should also be evaluated. Four of the most important factors are current social forces, global economic forces, global political forces, and technological innovations. Remember that each of these forces is evaluated only as they relate to the industry in question. Forces in the broad environment may also pose threats or provide opportunities.

After describing the industry as it exists now, it is important to capture the underlying dynamics that will create industry change and require new strategic approaches. One useful way to accomplish this is to group factors that influence the industry into two categories: those that create and influence industry demand and those that create and influence industry cost structures and profit potential. The findings from this part of the analysis will help you decide whether the industry is "attractive" (growing and profitable) and worthy of further investment (i.e., time, money, resources). It will also help you identify areas in which the firm may be able to excel in an effort to create a competitive advantage.

Factors that Influence Demand. There are many industry factors and stakeholder actions that create and influence demand for products and services. Some of the factors are part of the broad environment of the firm, such as the state of the economy. Other factors are part of the task environment, most of which are related to the actions of two key stakeholder groups: customers and competitors. If the underlying factors that create demand are changing, then it is likely that demand patterns will change. For example, demand for washing machines is a function of household formations and replacements. To predict future demand, you would study the numbers of people in the household-forming age bracket, durability of washers, and economic conditions.

Some of the industry factors and stakeholder actions that create and influence demand and growth prospects in an industry include:

1. The function(s) served by the product.
2. The stage of the product life cycle (i.e., degree of market penetration already experienced).
3. Economic trends, including income levels and economic cycles (i.e., recession, boom).
4. Demographic trends (part of social trend analysis) such as population and age.
5. Other societal/cultural trends, including fads and commonly held values and beliefs.
6. Political trends, which may include protectionist legislation such as trade barriers.
7. Technological trends, including new applications, new markets, and cost savings that make prices more competitive.
8. Programs developed by firms in the industry, such as new product introductions, new marketing programs, new distribution channels, and new functions served.
9. Strong brand recognition, domestically or worldwide.
10. Pricing actions that stimulate demand.

After analyzing the factors that create and influence demand, you should be able to draw some conclusions about industry growth prospects for the industry and firm. Since you can never be certain about the timetable and ultimate outcome of a trend that, by definition, is changing over time, one technique that may be useful is to develop alternative demand scenarios. For example, if the health of the economy is a major driver of a product's demand, you could consider the upside and downside of an economic recovery using the following type of format: "If the economy recovers within six months, then industry demand for the product could be the highest in five years. If the recovery does not materialize, then demand might linger at last year's levels."

Factors that Influence Cost Structures. After determining growth prospects for the industry, you will want to determine the cost structure and profit potential of the industry. As with demand, there are various factors and stakeholder actions that create and influence cost/profit structures in an industry. Among these factors are the following:

1. *Stage of the product life cycle.* In the early stages of the life cycle, firms have large investments in product development, distribution channel development, new plant and equipment, and workforce training. In the latter stages, investments are more incremental.
2. *Capital intensity.* Large investments in fixed costs such as plants and equipment make firms very sensitive to fluctuations in demand—high

levels of capacity utilization are needed to cover or "spread" fixed costs. Industries that have a lower relative fixed cost investment but higher variable costs are able to control their costs more readily in turbulent demand periods.

3. *Economies of scale.* Larger-sized facilities can achieve lower costs per unit than smaller facilities in some instances because of lower per-foot construction costs, more efficient use of equipment, and more efficient use of indirect labor and management. If a facility is so large that additional equipment and management are needed, economies of scale may be lost.

4. *Learning/experience effects.* With repetition and an environment that encourages and rewards learning, employees can become more productive over time.

5. *The power of customers, suppliers, competitive rivalry, substitutes, and entry barriers.* Powerful customers, suppliers, competitive rivalry, substitutes, or low entry barriers can erode profit potential. The forces, which are part of Porter's Five Forces Model, were discussed in detail in Chapter 2.

6. *The influence of other stakeholders.* These may include powerful foreign governments, joint venture partners, powerful unions, strong creditors, etc.

7. *Technological changes that provide opportunities to reduce costs.* Technological innovations can allow a firm to invest in new equipment, new products, and new processes or to alter the balance of investments between fixed and variable costs.

After systematically profiling the factors and stakeholder actions that influence cost structures and profits, you should be able to draw conclusions about industry profit potential. After the basic environmental analysis is complete, the next step is to perform a more detailed examination of the major strategic issues facing the industry.

Strategic Issues Facing the Industry

A thorough environmental analysis provides the information needed to identify factors and forces that are important to the industry in which your organization is involved and, therefore, your organization. These factors and forces may be categorized as follows:

1. *Driving forces in the industry,* which are trends that are so significant that they are creating fundamental industry change, such as the opening up of Eastern Europe or networked computer communications. Of course, each industry will have its own unique set of driving forces.

2. *Threats,* defined as noteworthy trends or changes that threaten growth prospects, profit potential, and traditional ways of doing business.

3. *Opportunities,* which are important trends, changes, or ideas that provide new opportunities for growth or profits.

4. *Requirements for survival,* identified as resources and capabilities that all firms must possess to survive in the industry. An example in the pharmaceutical industry is "product purity." These factors do not command a premium price. They are necessary, but not sufficient to be successful.

5. *Key success factors,* which are factors firms typically should possess if they desire to be successful in the industry. An example in the pharmaceutical

industry is the ability to create products with new therapeutic qualities. This ability may lead to high performance.

Having completed an analysis of the external environment, you are ready to conduct a more specific analysis of the internal organization.

STRUCTURING AN ORGANIZATIONAL ANALYSIS

Understanding industry trends, growth prospects, profit potential, and key strategic issues can help you critique an organization's strategies and evaluate its strengths and weaknesses. For example, what might qualify as strength in one industry may be an ordinary characteristic or a weakness in another industry. A good organizational analysis should begin with a general evaluation of the internal organization.

Evaluation of the Internal Environment

The following questions are useful in assessing the internal organization:

1. What is the company's strategic direction, including its vision, business definition, enterprise strategy (i.e., which stakeholder groups does it appear to give priority), long-term goals, and attitude toward global expansion? If some of these factors are contained in a formal mission statement, share it.
2. How has the strategic direction changed over time? In what way? Has the evolution been consistent with the organization's capabilities and planned strategies?
3. Who are the principal internal stakeholders? In particular, who are the key managers and what are their backgrounds? What are their strengths and weaknesses? Are they authoritarian or participative in their management style? Is this appropriate for the situation? What seems to drive their actions?
4. Who owns the organization? Is it a publicly traded company with a board of directors? If there is a board and you know who is on it, is the composition of the board appropriate? Is there an individual or group with a controlling interest? Is there evidence of agency problems? How active are the owners and what do they value?
5. What are the operating characteristics of the company, including its size in sales, assets, and employees, its age, and its geographical locations (including international operations)?
6. Are employees highly trained? If a union is present, how are relations with the union?
7. How would you describe the organization's culture? Is it a high-performing culture? Is it supportive of the firm's strategies?

Most instructors also require a financial analysis to identify financial strengths and weaknesses, evaluate performance, and identify financial resources available for strategy implementation. A financial analysis should include a comparison of ratios and financial figures with major competitors or the industry in which the organization competes (cross-sectional) as well as an analysis of trends in these ratios over several years (longitudinal). Some commonly used financial ratios are specified in Chapter 3.

When analyzed superficially, ratios can be more misleading than informative. For example, in comparing return-on-assets for two firms in the same industry, the one with the higher ratio could have superior earnings or devalued assets from too little investment. Two firms can differ in return-on-equity because of different debt-equity financing policies rather than from true performance reasons. When accurately interpreted and considered in the larger organization context, the analysis may also uncover strengths, weaknesses, or symptoms of larger organizational problems.

Identification of Resources and Capabilities

The foregoing analysis of the internal environment provides an excellent starting point for identifying key resources and capabilities. For example, outstanding resources and capabilities may result from (1) superior management, (2) well-trained employees, (3) an excellent board of directors, (4) a high-performance culture, (5) superior financial resources, or (6) the appropriate level and type of international involvement. However, these potential sources of competitive advantage barely scratch the organizational surface.

You should also evaluate the organization's primary value chain activities to identify resources and capabilities. These activities include its (7) inbound logistics, (8) operations, (9) outbound logistics, (10) marketing and sales, and (11) service, as well as the support activities of (12) procurement, (13) technology development, (14) human resource management, and (15) administration. Chapter 3 provided a description of how to use the value chain.

In addition, an organization may have (16) an excellent reputation, (17) a strong brand name, (18) patents and secrets, (19) excellent locations, or (20) strong or valuable ties (i.e., alliances, joint ventures, contracts, cooperation) with one or more external stakeholders. All of these potential resources and capabilities (and many others) are discussed in this book. They form a starting point that you can use to help identify the potential sources of competitive advantage. Each company will have its own unique list.

Performance Evaluation

The next step in internal analysis is to describe and critique the organization's past strategies. In critiquing strategies, you will need to describe them in detail, discuss whether they have been successful, and then *evaluate whether they fit with the industry environment and the resources and capabilities of the organization.*

1. What is the company's *pattern* of past strategies (corporate, business, functional, international)?
2. How successful has the company been in the past with its chosen strategies? How successful is the company now?
3. For each strategy, what explains success or failure? (Use your environmental and organizational analyses to support your answer.)

Many instructors require their students to evaluate the success of an organization on the basis of both qualitative and quantitative (financial) measures. The financial measures were developed during your financial analysis, so you only need to make reference to them here. Some common qualitative measures include product or service quality, productivity, responsiveness to industry change, innovation, reputation, and other measures that indicate key stakeholder satisfaction (i.e., employees, customers, managers, regulatory bodies, society).

Sources of Competitive Advantage

You are now ready to consolidate your internal and external analyses into lists of strengths and weaknesses, as well as expand and revise your lists of opportunities and threats. In Chapter 1, strengths were defined as firm resources and capabilities that can lead to a competitive advantage. Weaknesses, on the other hand, were described as resources and capabilities that the firm does not possess, resulting in a competitive disadvantage. Consequently, each of the resources and capabilities identified during the organizational analysis should be measured against the factors identified in the environmental analysis. The next paragraph describes how this is to be done.

Resources and capabilities become strengths if they have the potential to lead to a competitive advantage. This happens when (1) they are valuable, which means that they allow the firm to exploit opportunities and/or neutralize threats arising from the external environment, and (2) they are unique, meaning that only a few firms possess the resource or capability. Using these criteria, a list of strengths should be assembled. If strength is also hard to imitate, then it can lead to a *sustainable* competitive advantage; consequently, these types of strengths should be highlighted. Finally, if a resource or capability could have broad application to many business areas, it is a core competence or capability.

Weaknesses also should be listed. These are resources and capabilities the firm does not possess that, according to your environmental analysis, lead to a competitive disadvantage.

Opportunities are conditions in the external environment that allow a firm to take advantage of organizational strengths, overcome organizational weaknesses, or neutralize environmental threats. Consequently, now that the organizational analysis is complete, you should re-evaluate your list of opportunities to determine whether they really apply to your organization. You also should evaluate threats to make sure they are applicable to your firm. Threats are conditions in the broad and task environments that may stand in the way of organizational competitiveness or the achievement of stakeholder satisfaction.

At this point, you also may want to add to your list of opportunities some of the potential linkages and alliances that the firm could develop with external stakeholders. For example, if your company is strong in production but weak in foreign marketing, you may see an opportunity to enter a new foreign market through a joint venture with a strong marketing company. Another example may involve neutralizing a threat of new government regulation by forming an alliance with competitors to influence the regulating body.

DEVELOPING A STRATEGIC PLAN

Your environmental and organizational analyses helped you to (1) draw conclusions about the growth prospects and profit potential in the industry and any trends that are critical to the firm, (2) evaluate the past strategies and strategic direction of the firm, and (3) develop a list of strengths, weaknesses, opportunities, and threats. The next step is to make recommendations concerning the strategies the firm may want to pursue in the future. If the firm is not a stellar performer, this should be an easy task. However, even firms that have been highly successful in the past should consider taking advantage of opportunities and should respond to threats. History has taught us that firms that are unwilling to progress eventually decline.

Strategic Direction and Major Strategies

You should probably begin your strategic recommendations by focusing on the strategic direction and major strategies of the firm. Based on your earlier analyses, you may want to consider adjustments to the mission of the firm, including its vision, business definition, or enterprise strategy. Of course, the business definition also helps identify the growth orientation of the business. Are the growth plans taking advantage of industry opportunities? If the industry is becoming mature, should horizontal integration be pursued rather than market penetration alone?

If you determined earlier that the business strategy is not as successful as it should be, what adjustments should be made? Could the company have more success by focusing on one segment of the market? Or if the company were pursuing a focus strategy, would broadening the target market be appropriate? If the company were pursuing cost leadership, would a differentiation strategy work better? If differentiation doesn't seem to be working very well, would a cost leadership strategy be better? Or, would a best cost strategy be the most appropriate?

Finally, you should examine the corporate strategy (concentration, vertical integration, related or unrelated diversification). Is your corporate strategy still appropriate, given your environmental analysis? Is your dominant industry stagnant? Is it over-regulated? Is competition hurting profitability? Should you consider investing in other industries? If so, what are their defining characteristics? What core competencies and capabilities could be applied elsewhere? What opportunities could be explored that relate to the corporate strategy?

It is possible that you may want to leave the strategic direction and major strategies alone, especially if the organization has enjoyed recent success. Regardless of whether you altered the direction and strategies, at this point you have now established what you think they should be. The direction and corporate- and business-level strategies provide guidance for fine-tuning an organization's strategies. Each of the recommendations you make from this point on should be consistent with the strategic direction and major strategies of the organization. At this point, it is time to explore strategic opportunities further.

Evaluation of Opportunities and Recommendations

Using the strategic direction and corporate- and business-level strategies as guides, strategic opportunities should be evaluated further. These alternatives were generated during earlier analyses. They include the following:

1. *Opportunities that allow a firm to take advantage of organizational strengths.* These opportunities may involve alternatives such as better promotion of current products and services, new products or services, new applications for existing products and services within existing markets, exploring new domestic or foreign markets, diversifying into areas in which

strengths can be applied, creation of joint ventures with companies with complementary strengths. These are only a few examples.

2. *Opportunities for the firm to overcome organizational weaknesses.* Do any of the organizational weaknesses relate to an area that you described in your industry analysis as essential for survival? Do any of the weaknesses relate to key success factors? Firms can overcome their weaknesses through strategies such as learning from joint venture partners, creating new alliances with organizations that are strong where the organization is weak, or fixing problems internally through R&D, better controls, efficiency programs, IT, TAM, etc. Again, these are only a few examples.

3. *Opportunities for the firm to neutralize environmental threats.* These often involve creation of strategic alliances to offset the influence of a powerful stakeholder such as a government regulator, a strong union, a powerful competitor, or an influential special interest group. The firm may form an alliance *with* the powerful stakeholder or with other stakeholders in an effort to balance the power. Firms may also form alliances to help cope with threats emerging from the broad environment.

Evaluation of opportunities means much more than simply accepting them on the basis of earlier environmental and organizational analyses. They also should be evaluated based on factors such as the following:

1. *Cost/benefits analysis.* Do the financial benefits of pursuing the opportunity appear to outweigh the financial costs?
2. *Ethical analysis.* Is pursuit of this strategy consistent with the enterprise strategy of the organization? Could there be negative effects on the reputation of the organization?
3. *Protection of other strengths.* Does pursuit of this opportunity in any way detract from or weaken other strengths? For example, could it damage a brand name? Could it weaken a strong financial position?
4. *Implementation ability.* Will implementation of this strategy be easy or difficult? In other words, does the strategy "fit" the capabilities, structure, systems, processes, and culture of the organization?
5. *Stakeholder analysis.* How will this strategy affect key stakeholders? Which ones are likely to support it? Are they high priority? Which ones are likely to oppose it? Are they high priority? What are the strategic ramifications of their support or opposition?
6. *Future position.* Will the strategy continue to be viable as the industry and the broad environment undergo their expected changes? Will it provide a foundation for survival or competitive success?

The result of this analysis should be a recommendation or recommendations that the organization should pursue. Many evaluation tools can facilitate the evaluation process, such as a pay-off matrix that provides an evaluation of several alternatives based on a standard set of criteria (see Appendix Exhibit 1). However, the tools should never act as substitutes for in-depth analysis of the alternatives themselves. In other words, even if a numeric score-keeping system is used, the numbers should be explained based on detailed strategic analysis.

You may not be required by your instructor to conduct a formal analysis of alternatives based on a standard set of criteria; however, you should still make recommendations concerning changes the organization should make to remain or

Appendix Exhibit 1   *A Pay-off Matrix Approach to Evaluating Opportunities*

	Criterion 1	Criterion 2	Criterion 3	Total
Opportunity 1	−2	1	2	1
Opportunity 2	2	1	−1	2
Opportunity 3	1	2	1	4

Note: In this matrix, −2 means that the opportunity is very weak based on the criterion, −1 means weak, 0 means neutral, 1 means strong, and 2 means very strong.

become competitive and satisfy its stakeholders. Through this entire process, remember that many companies identify areas of strength that are no longer capable of giving the company a competitive edge. What was a key to success yesterday may be a requirement for survival today.

Implementation and Control

Recommendations should always be accompanied by an implementation plan and basic controls. The following are major questions that should be addressed during this section of a case analysis. Items 7 and 8 relate specifically to control.

1. How do the recommendations specifically address concerns that were identified during the analysis?
2. What will be the roles and responsibilities of key internal *and* external stakeholders in carrying out the recommendations and how are they expected to respond? What actions should be taken to smooth out the transition period or avoid stakeholder discontent?
3. Does the organization have the resources (funds, people, skills) to carry out the recommendations? If not, how should the organization proceed in developing or acquiring those resources?
4. Does the organization have the appropriate systems, structures, and processes to carry out the recommendations? If not, how should the organization proceed in creating the appropriate systems, structures, and processes?
5. What is the appropriate time horizon for implementing recommendations? What should the organization and its managers do immediately, in one month, in six months, in a year, etc.?
6. What are the roadblocks the organization could encounter while implementing the recommendations (i.e., financing, skilled labor shortages)? How can the organization overcome these roadblocks?
7. What are the desired outcomes or changes the organization should expect once the recommendations have been implemented? How will the organization know if the recommendations have been successful? In other words, what are the objectives associated with your recommendations?

8. What were some of the major assumptions you made with regard to the external environment? Which of these factors, if different from expected, would require an adjustment to your recommendations?

Following the implementation section, you may want to update your audience (your instructor or other students) concerning actions the firm has taken since the case was written. If a case update is required, it should center on actions that pertain to the focus of your case analysis. If you do an update, remember that what the organization did, even if it appears to have been successful, may not have been the optimal solution.

A NOTE TO STUDENTS

If you are reading this appendix early in the course, you will have the rest of the semester or quarter to practice the case analysis process and study the chapter readings. If you are reading this appendix later in the course, we encourage you to go back to earlier chapters and refresh your memory concerning the concepts that were covered. Just as this course integrates material you learned during your years of business study, the case analysis process integrates material from all sections of the strategic management course.

The material in this appendix represents the way we teach case analysis. Since there is not a standard method for analyzing cases, your instructor may teach a method of case analysis that differs from our approach. Also, cases can be treated in many different formats, including class discussions (complete with discussion questions to be answered before coming to class), written papers, formal presentations, and class debates. After reading this appendix, check with your instructor for specific instructions and requirements.